To J[...] you will [...] some of th[...]

HEAR ME TALKING TO YA
TALES FROM A FAIR DINKUM JAZZMAN

hope you enjoy

Bob Sedergreen

M

MELBOURNE BOOKS

Published by Melbourne Books
www.melbournebooks.com.au

The National Library of Australia Cataloguing-in-Publication entry:
Sedergreen, Bob.
Hear Me Talking To Ya : Tales From A Fair Dinkum Jazzman.

ISBN 9781877096976 (pbk.).

1. Sedergreen, Bob. 2. Jazz musicians - Australia -
Biography. 3. Jazz music - Australia. I. Title.

781.650994

Cover photo: Courtesy of City of Stonnington

Printed in Australia by Shannon Books.

To my family

*To the two girls in my life, Rae and Tammy — your unselfish,
soft, warm, and generous hearts never stopped helping me, and
so many others pursue our goals, artistic or otherwise.*

*To my sons, Mal and Steve — your outstanding talent and brilliance
as musicians, composers and as fine human beings have bought joy
and inspiration into my life. Remember... it's knowing that counts.*

*To my daughters-in-law, Christine and Ria for their support and
love of music and my two wonderful grandchildren,
Sebastien and Maya.*

FOREWORD

My purpose in writing this book is not to write an autobiography even though it is autobiographical, nor to write an accurate history of Jazz in Melbourne even though dates and times and places are mentioned. Neither is it my purpose to try and define the meaning of the word Jazz, the very nature of this abstract art form makes it impossible to do so.

What I have attempted here is to set in motion a series of revelations devoid of mystique, romanticism and pathways to personal glory. I have written a series of adventures; musical adventures without fixed outcomes. Each encounter reaping its own particular reward.

I'm hoping the reader is happy to share these experiences with me. The joys of discovering Jazz at a time when Jazz was king; the inner glow that comes from the encouragement and help of peers and mentors; the thrill of being accepted and acknowledged as a recognised performer; an integral figure of Jazz in Australia.

The challenge of 'making it' with some of the world's best known Jazz players, both at home and overseas; the power of the creative urge propelling me towards my finest achievements.

Finally, the ability to inspire and pass information on to others and to have them in turn inspire you. Like the music itself, it's spontaneous, honest and in the moment - Enjoy!

Bob Sedergreen

ACKNOWLEDGEMENTS

I would like to thank a group of special people who are not included in the following chapters, but have been important in my life and career...

People like drummer Barry 'Tippy' Buxton for a lifetime of friendship and melodic trio Jazz; pianist Geoff Sherman brother-in-law and Monk devotee; Vibist and entrepreneur John Williams for spreading the joys of Jazz to the Mornington Peninsula; Michael Caesar dedicated Canberra music teacher for inventing 'Jazzabout,' a festival for young musicians, and for appointing me as Patron; Gabrielle O'Shannassy Educator at the Lismore Conservatorium and Artistic Director of the North Coast Jazz Festival, Bangalow, NSW for being the first to document my work on DVD; Adrian Jackson and the Wangaratta Jazz Festival for the privilege of running the Jazz workshops for the last ten years; The RMIT for appointing me Adjunct Professor, with special thanks to Professor John Powers and David Forrest; The Victorian Arts Centre for the Ken Myers Award for contribution to The Arts in Victoria.

Master wine maker David Traeger of Nagambie for his Jazz, food and wine afternoons; as well as Carmel Taylor at St Huberts. To Warren Townsend and the Basin Jazz Festival for including me every year.

To my incredible soul brother, 'Howling Wind' aka Andy Richardson of Apollo Bay, and his talented family for introducing me to 'Magnetic Heaven.'

The ABC, especially Jim McLeod of Jazztrack fame as well as Gillian McLeod, Derek Guille and Jeremy Lee and Annie Dutton (ABC TV).

To radio station 3PBS for their ongoing contribution to blues and Jazz especially Gerry Koster, Steve Robertson and Len Davis; singers Christine Sullivan, Linda Cable; the Aspeling sisters Trude and Anastasia; and Melbourne's famous Glaswegian 'godmother' Ruby Carter.

Hammond Combo Duo, Paul Williamson and Tim Neal; Janine Pero and Scott Evans trombonist husband and wife; Janine for choosing me to educate her students at Ringwood Secondary College; trumpeter and gardener supreme Sandro Donati; bassist Ivan Rosa for helping me with my workshops; Virtuoso drummer Virgil Donati who replaced David Jones in the Brian Brown Quartet and recorded with me; drummers Marshall Clark for his unwavering support; and Carlos Ferreira not only for his fanatical drumming approach but also for helping me with my website — *bobsedergreen.com*.

The City of Stonnington, for appointing me as musical director of 'Jazz in the Gardens' series as well as initiating the Stonnington Youth Jazz Initiative; The City of Kingston, for appointing me coordinator of their ongoing Jazz series.

Dr. Tony Gould who despite receiving minimal coverage in my book remains my partner in our precious head to head piano concert series and for including me in 'Groves.'

The many instrumentalists and vocalists who undertook my Join a Jazz Band/ Join A Jazz Vocal courses at Deakin University; M.L.C. and Dizzy's Jazz Bar - The smoothest stage manager ever - Dorian Jones.

Finally, many thanks to the loyal supporters who consistently keep turning up at a variety of venues, people such as Helen and Bruce Wells who have attended more Jazz gigs in New York and Melbourne than any one I know.

CONTENTS

PART THREE — DIZZY TIMES

PART FOUR — ON THE BOIL

PART FIVE — FAITH REAFFIRMED

PART ONE

SEEING IS BELIEVING

MUM & DAD

I T WAS MARCH 1903, the turn of a new century, a time of great optimism and invention.

No such luck for Seamus (James, Jim) Sedergreen, who was born in the borough of Bow within the loud pealing of Bow bells. A child of a mixed marriage, his mother Mary, an Irish Catholic, and father Henry, Swedish Reform church. They were amazingly poor. This was a time of child labour and dad had to forgo schooling in order to work alongside his own father.

They worked for the famous British Pharmaceutical manufacturer, *Bryant and May*. It was the job of the Sedergreen boys to cart bucket loads of toxic chemicals to the well-head, where the ugly concoction was turned into match-stick heads.

There were no safety regulations, no masks, no air conditioning and no ventilation. They worked slavishly long hours for pitiful pay. Recreation times were therefore spent in what dad called, 'skylarking.' This form of Cockney fun probably included vandalism, robbery, bouts of heavy drinking, joke and story-telling and checking the odd petticoat or two. It wouldn't be hard for dad to draw the conclusion that his future, along with other boys in the district, was not only far from bright, but the nick (prison) was where he was heading in a hurry.

Perhaps the only way to secure a brighter future was to escape, so he set off to his mother's hometown of Enniskellen, in County Tyrone, Northern Ireland. Once there, he lied about his age and was enlisted in the hometown's famous regiment, the *Enniskellen Dragoons*.

"Before you mount a horse, you must first learn to be a stable-hand" said the Warrant Officer.

"That means at least eighteen months of living with them, feeding them, sleeping with them, cleaning up after them, shit and all. Because as a Dragoon, your very life will depend on your horse."

Dad did this, and soon commenced tours of duty to the near and far reaches of the empire: Burma, India, Sardinia, Malta, Gibraltar and the like.

Lean, tall and athletic, the blond, blue-eyed London lad became a popular figure and was soon promoted. Promotion meant privileges and dad became obsessed with it, reaching the highest rank one could achieve in the regiment, Warrant Officer First Class. You may have heard of the phrase an 'Officer and a Gentleman,' and so it was the British class system that prevented dad or any other commoner from higher promotion (or so he thought), until one of his mates tipped him off about joining a new organisation, His Majesty's New Colonial Police Force, which promoted men on their examination and policing skills.

Posted to Palestine, he commenced work as a constable, working his way up the ladder to inspector, thereby fulfilling his dream of holding a rank equivalent to major in the Dragoons. There was talk of further promotion to superintendent, but soon he would have to make the supreme sacrifice and give up everything he'd worked so hard to achieve, for the love of a woman — my mother.

"Nooh boy" (my mother still called me boy),

"Sit down and have your breakfast and I will tell you how your father and I got hooked up."

Breakfast consisted of a very large bowl of heaped cereal to create a mountain on which rested half a punnet of cut up strawberries. The first attempt at using a spoon created a landslide, spilling cereal over the plate. For mum, food was never a meal, it was a statement of lifestyle.

"You see boy, I had two shops in Allenby Street in downtown Tel Aviv. It was a fashion capital of the world. Do you know what this means boy?"

Not wanting to disappoint her obvious sense of achievement, I nodded.

"You see, to be a successful milliner, I will give you one word. It means everything and that word is 'reputation.' A milliner (especially a French milliner) must not only make good hats and be able to sell them but also give and take advice. Her morals should be without question, as should those of her staff. So naturally, I was surprised when a police van pulled up in front of the shop.

What could they want? What will people think? Am I a criminal? Has one of my girls slept with somebody? Maybe they will go away soon. Not wanting to be seen in the street, I sent one of my best girls out to ask if they wouldn't mind moving the van. She returned to the shop saying to me, they only want to see the milliner. After a while, I could not stand it any longer and went out to the van. When I looked inside, I saw the driver wearing the stripes of a sergeant and next to him was a young English officer with two crowns on his epaulets, and boy, was he handsome!

I knew the driver, so I asked him: "Why don't you guys shift this van?" He answered smiling at me saying: "The officer has instructed me that this van will stay outside your shop until further notice unless you agree to go out on a date with him tonight." "What? Me date a man I don't know? An Englishman? It's out of the question!" "Well until you change your mind, the van stays put." "So what else could I do boy, but give in?"

Mum was a consummate storyteller who never got sick of telling the same story over and over again to whoever was prepared to listen. Her stories were always about the bravery of women overcoming prejudice.

Of course, her favourite role model was herself.

Born Leah Erlichman, six years after dad, on a small farm, somewhere between Lublin and the Russian border, she did not really enjoy the rural lifestyle with its simplicity — milking cows was definitely not for mum. Although mum and dad were like chalk and cheese, they both saw escape as the only solution to what would have been a very hard and ordinary future.

Somehow she convinced her father that their family would be better served if she went to Paris to study millinery. Parisians are not noted for their tolerance of foreigners, but sheer will and determination saw mum patrol the streets of Paris, visiting every milliner until one gave in. An excellent apprentice, she learned the skills of colour, shape, texture and chic. This was about the time of Lord Balfours' declaration. advocating a national home for the Jewish people. Encouraged by this and passionate about Theodor Hertzl's concept of Zionism, she became a pioneer in Palestine.

Back at headquarters, the word had got around that Jim Sedergreen had eloped up north and married a local girl. It was an unwritten rule that any officers who set the wrong sort of example by not taking English wives would be punished and so dad was transferred from his cushy desk job to a job as an assistant prison governor in the notorious Acre Prison.

It was a prison full of civil criminals as well as political prisoners, like members of the Irgun and Stern Gang, fanatical Zionists. Dad was now on their hit list. He was also given the unpleasant task of supervising the hanging of criminals sentenced to death. So my first four years of childhood were spent in prison, and I was called the 'little officer' as I kept following dad around like a puppy.

My memories of this time are vague but I remember spending many hours in a large kennel with dad's police dogs, Bill and Sue, and also crawling away to a nearby house and being found in the lap of an Arabic clarinet player and his band.

In 1947, His Majesty's Government sent the P&O steam ship *Ortranto* to evacuate all British families, as the British Mandate was coming to an end and Palestine would finally become Israel.

Mum, my sisters Joyce and Millie and I settled in London and Dad followed in 1948. It was here dad's career went into decline as mum's accelerated. She became milliner to the cream of London's society including Lady Christopher Russell and the Mountbattens. This afforded us a luxurious lifestyle, and in those days a piano was a status symbol. Soon, one was purchased and placed prominently in our lounge room.

Mum ensured I had the best teacher that money could buy. And so I was confronted each week by a hard-faced Austrian lady, armed with a heavy metal silver-coated bar which would come down with great force on the back of my hand just below the knuckles every time I made a mistake. Of course the fear of making mistakes led to making more mistakes. I can still feel the sharp pain in that area of my hand. Naturally I began to dislike her and the classical music she stood for. However, this was a time of rationing in the UK and mum, dad and my sisters would pool their rations to bribe me with a plentiful supply of sweets provided that I become a 'performing seal' and entertain their adult guests with musical items. I was even entered in a pianoforte competition at London's famous Albert Hall. The certificate was not so complimentary on my technical ability, but somehow I had come third in the country in the under-nine section.

My recollections of London are little cameo memories of thick pea soup fogs with men walking in front of buses with large torches guiding them through. I remember white Christmases, going to the football with dad and watching his beloved Spurs play Arsenal (traditional Cockney rivals) and swinging on a hammock with my first girlfriend, Pauline, the dentist's daughter.

The other memory is the price of fruit. You see, I'm a fruit fly but a single peach cost two shillings and sixpence, then a veritable fortune. But relief came in an unexpected canister labelled *Golden Circle Tropical Fruit Jam.* I would drool at drawings on the label of pineapple, passion fruit, paw paw and mango. I was addicted to this jam and I began to wonder about its country of origin, Australia. To make matters worse, Australia House in London had commissioned a series of advertisements exhorting Poms to come to sunny Australia. There were palm trees, pretty girls in swimsuits, surf, sun and the said pineapple in that advert.

However, the straw that really broke the camels back, were the letters from my sister Joyce in Melbourne, glowing with reports of warmth, wonderful people and the opportunities of a lifetime.

They say that only women nag, but you should have seen dad and I continually conduct our 'let's go to Australia campaign'. We were oblivious to the fact that mum was happy to be kicking severe butt as London's top milliner, which afforded us an affluent lifestyle. Dad and I never cared too much for money, and in an instant everything was sold (at a loss) and we boarded the famous Flying Scotsman for Glasgow. Here we embarked upon the *SS Cameronia*, a shoddy, black, coal-fired steamship on its last voyage before being scrapped. As we steamed across the boundless oceans, I found it easier to play indoor and outdoor games with the passengers rather than play the piano — their broad Scottish accents a source of much amusement.

The ship finally docked in Fremantle on a day as hot as Hades. We disembarked into a town that looked like the Hollywood set for

Dodge City with its dusty unmade streets and its old wooden pubs. Everybody on board named it the Wild West.

We arrived in Melbourne on a cloudy day in November '51, disembarking on Princes Pier. Joyce and her husband Henry showed us to our one bedroom flat in Armadale.

You've heard of the expression 'whingeing poms', well no wonder! This must have been a new universe for my parents. The palm trees, tropical fruit and vast expanses of rambling sandy, surf beaches were nowhere to be seen.

Too busy to notice, I was enrolled into the Cubs and a brief stint at Armadale State School.

Mum and dad worked hard in menial jobs and we shifted to Malvern as tenants with an Irish couple.

My 'performing seal days' weren't quite over yet as dad would make me busk, *Galway Bay*, the only tune I could now play on the piano. I was rewarded with a banana bread and butter sandwich, a new taste delight. How very Irish! I became so hooked on banana sandwiches that I could still turn out a heart-felt rendition of *Galway Bay* to this day.

We finally settled in a solid brick home, right on Whitehorse Road just down hill from the famous White Horse.

Mum loved Box Hill; its Methodist founders had ensured that it and the surrounding areas were free from the evils of alcohol.

Mum and dad were as opposite as any couple on earth. He was tall, she was short, he was blue-eyed, she dark-eyed. He was lean and straight, she short and curvy. He was fond of alcohol and she was a wowser.

This was a time before television, so everyone listened to the radio. Like most homes, we had two radios and they were to have a huge effect on my future.

One Sunday morning, dad had tuned into 3AW to hear a programme by local pianist Roy Sparks, who ran the *Easy School of Piano Playing*. Sparks played piano somewhat like Charlie Kunz, Carmen Caballero and Winifred Atwell. Much to my horror, dad thought this style of playing was brilliant.

"It's a shame if you don't go," he said.

"And if you do I'll double your pocket money."

It was an offer he knew I couldn't refuse.

As I made my way up in the old, dark, pulley-operated lift in Allan's music shop in Collins Street, I stepped out into Roy's teaching room. Sitting at the keys of a brown baby grand, Roy looked more like a cowboy than a piano teacher, with his flashing red hair and loud cravat.

"Come in junior. Have you been downstairs to the sheet music section?"

I had, and I triumphantly waved the three music sheets I was about to learn: 'I still see Elisa,' 'From the time we say Goodbye to the time we say Cheerio' and 'The Naughty Lady of Shady Lane.' All three were unexciting pieces and as boring as bat shit.

"Oh and one other thing junior, play everything in octaves and tremolos just like this."

I could not believe that anyone would want to play piano like that. But Roy was a successful motivator.

"And by the way junior, we're having a chord competition where I play a series of chords, and you with all my other fifteen students, must guess what they are. The winner gets a gold medal and five quid cash."

While me and fourteen other kids older than myself stood around the piano, Roy played a series of chords, each one more difficult to guess.

And yes, you guessed it, I won the medal and five quid, a veritable fortune.

I heard Roy and the other students debating over the hours I must have spent at the piano in order to win the competition. But this was not so.

Left alone in the house one Sunday afternoon I could not resist the temptation to fiddle with the Pye mantel radio. As I tuned in to 3UZ, I heard a large radio voice saying, "Hi kids, Stan the Man (Rofe) here, happy to be spinning some platters for you. This one's by Little Richard."

To this day, I can remember that scream that penetrated my soul. It was primitive, it was uninhibited, it was joyous, and it was a release of tension and promised sensual and sexual pleasure. Subconsciously I knew that Little Richard must be African because if any person in Box Hill screamed like that they would have been arrested, locked up and put away. Following the scream was another source of pleasure, a raunchy tenor sax solo, dripping with blues licks, hard-edged and horny.

Yes I had tuned into Stan the Man, Melbourne's famous Rock'n Roll DJ, who would introduce me to Chuck Berry, Fats Domino, Freddie Bell and the Bellboys and Bill Haley and the Comets. Stan also managed to convince me that I was a teenager and that Rock'n Roll was new, exciting and meant for teenagers. The famous film *Jazz on a Summers Day* documents the fact that Pops (Louis Armstrong), Monk, Mahalia Jackson, George Shearing and Chuck Berry were all happening at the same time.

Just a short walk from home in Box Hill was Teo's Music shop. Its window display was very much like a European delicatessen where sausages hang in the window, but instead of sausages hung six shiny brass instruments, the biggest of all being a Lafleur trombone. I would pass Teo's Music shop on my way home each night and would gaze at the trombone as though it was some sort of magic wand.

Just a short bike ride down the road in North Box Hill lived my sister Joyce, and my brother-in-law Henry. This was a time of the Hi Fi revolution. Being a gifted engineer, Henry had built a superb sound system with a big fifteen-inch speaker, for the bass tones, a seven-inch mid range speaker, for the middle tones and a tweeter, a small speaker enhancing treble. Add to this, a belt driven turntable and a diamond needle. With the new long-playing vinyl and micro-groove discs, the sound it produced was so real that one could imagine an orchestra playing in the living room. It's arguable that these warm analogue sounds will never be surpassed by today's digital technology.

Henry was passionate about Jazz, but preferred white band leaders like New Orleans trumpeter Jack (Papa) Laine and British trombonist Chris Barber. I immediately fell in love with Chris Barber's band and their album *Barber in Berlin*. I played it repeatedly for hours, absorbing every nuance that sprang from Monty Sunshine's clarinet, while at the same time nagging mum and dad endlessly about acquiring Teo's trombone.

So persistent was I, that they finally relented.

You see, mum and dad did not really approve of Jazz. After all, it was played by 'niggers' (Australian kids happily chewed on Nigger Boy licorice with a picture of a Nigger Boy proudly displayed on the packet) — 'niggers' who stuck pins in their arms (they were obviously referring to Charlie Parker). Also, they still considered musicians, especially Jazz musicians, to be at the lower levels of society's spectrum. They had an image of a lazy, good-for-nothing being paid for hanging round places of ill-repute and pick up joints; places where sex, drugs and alcohol ran freely.

Like so many other children, I would rebel against the previous generation's values and the harder mum and dad pushed me away from Jazz, the more I would pursue it.

SEEING IS BELIEVING

WHEN I WAS nine-years old, my brother-in-law Henry, sensing my aptitude for music and particularly Jazz, (he remembered I had tuned into the BBC Jazz Club when he was dating my sister Joyce), decided to take me to the Australian Jazz Convention, which in 1952, was held in the Railways Institute Hall near Sydney's Central Station.

I glanced at the programme and couldn't help wondering why the bands had funny names like *The Polites, Coyle Jelly Rollers, Neville Stribblings Gum Nut Stompers, Frank Couglan* and *His Port Jackson Sharks* and *The Melbourne New Orleans Jazz Band* (how could a New Orleans band be from Melbourne?)

Henry gave me complete freedom to attend whichever concerts I wanted. As a young boy who loved boats and the harbour, I chose the *Jazz and A Jug* segment that took off by ferry from Circular Quay. I could not help but notice how wild and unruly the musicians were, especially a young trombone player Dave Rankin, who for some reason, delighted in smuggling on board the largest flagon of sherry by hiding it under a towel.

Pretty soon the cruise had left and the ferry slowly steamed towards Vaucluse, but so hard-drinking were the bands and the clientele that the ferry was forced to dock at Wooloomaloo to empty its passengers. Everybody headed for the nearest pub to replenish supplies of grog before commencing the journey home.

As if by magic, the ferry had suddenly become mine, docked in the shimmering harbour. I wandered towards the stern of the lower deck where I encountered an old, brown, upright piano. It had seen better days but I just couldn't resist playing one of the few songs I knew really well, 'You Are my Sunshine' in the key of F.

So engrossed was I in what I was doing, I failed to notice the group of musicians who had surrounded me and were watching my private concert.

"Gee that sounds great son" said the curly-haired Graeme Bennett, sitting at a drum kit next to me, as one by one the members of both bands teamed up and joined in. Some of the stars included Graham Anstey and John Costello from the Cootamundra Jazz Band, as well trumpeter Frank Turville.

To me the music was full of energy, raucous rips, squeals and wild counterpoint improvisations around the melody. The fact that musicians far older than me were happy to share the music and to accept me as an equal filled my heart with joy.

We kept on jamming with the same song for at least twenty-five minutes or more until the ferry arrived home. For me, this was twenty-five minutes of heaven, and for all their wild and larrikin behavior these musicians had shown me love and respect, resulting in my determination to pursue Jazz whenever I could find it.

Some four years later, dad took me to see Louis Armstrong at the Palais in St Kilda. What a thrill! The band opened with 'When It's Sleepy Time Down South,' which I thought was a slight dig at being in the Southern Hemisphere, followed by the scream of his gravelly voice, with its "Good evening everybody." A scream that somehow transmitted a warm and friendly invitation to enjoy. What's more, I could not get over each note that pierced the air from the bell of Satchmo's trumpet. They were big, bright, round, juicy and all heart-felt. How he could put so much into each note was beyond my comprehension.

Every member of the band was showcased. The incredible Creole clarinet sounds of Edmond Hall, the snarling trombone of Trummy Young; everybody in the band was given a feature and allowed to star, including Arville Shaw's bass, shining on 'How High The Moon.' There could be no doubt that they were slick, polished and delivered the spirit of Jazz like no one else on planet earth. What's more, in the middle of the show, Louis stopped to tell a barrage of gags in a twelve-minute comedy cameo spot, which had us all howling in laughter.

That was the other thing about Jazz, not only was the music

exciting, energetic and entertaining, but Jazz musicians like Louis were fun to be with.

Everyone left the concert in high spirits; singing or whistling their favourite tune, mine being 'The Tin Roof Blues.'

SCHOOL DAYS

MUM AND DAD decided that my education was to be their number one priority, and so I was transferred from the quiet oblivion of Armadale State School to Haileybury College, a Presbyterian school for boys, located in the beachside suburb of Brighton. Their justification for sending me there was that British Prime Minister Clement Atlee had been educated at the sister school of the same name in Britain.

I remember the junior housemaster telling dad that my solid English schooling would mean that I would enter at a grade five level, rather than grade four. His decision was based on the assumption that students who were educated in England would somehow be more advanced than Aussie kids of the same age. Of course this incompetence meant that I would never understand the basic of science and mathematics.

Politicians, soldiers and sections of academia waxed lyrical about the nation's pride in being of British lineage; the truth of the matter was that people who had settled in this country, be they Scottish, Irish, German, or even of English extraction, had a deep inbuilt dislike of the Poms.

My first learning experience would involve dealing with this problem. In just six months my cultured English accent vanished. I remember coming into class, looking up at the blackboard, and reading the transcription written in large capital letters.

"The only good Pommy is a dead one!"

"How do you like that Seders?" sniggered one of the larger boys, and before I could find time to answer, he had issued me an invitation to prove myself,

"See you at lunchtime, behind the bicycle shed."

It did not take a genius to figure out that Pommy-needling, and Pommy-bashing were considered great fun, not just by my classmates, but also by their parents and teachers, as well as the community in general. I made a mental note to outwardly rid myself of all English affectations, but at the same time realised there must be something special about being a Pom, otherwise one would not be singled out for such attention.

For the next few months the warfare on my British citizenship continued. One of the stronger pupils would unashamedly interject in the middle of a lesson with the following question:

"What's better than a double-decker busload of one hundred and fifty Pommies falling off the Sydney Harbor Bridge? What do you reckon cheddar?"

There was much joy and mirth by both teacher and pupils at my inability to answer.

After a few seconds of silence, came the answer.

"A bus load of one hundred and sixty Poms of course."

Howls of laughter would follow an invitation to another fight featuring myself and the gladiatorial joke teller.

Unlike my father who had been trained by His Majesty's Government in the art of killing, I had no idea how to hurt the other guy, and for me it seemed wrong to inform dad about my trivial problems. So I learnt to cop it sweet and accept the physical punishment handed out, until the time came when I would be recognized as a fair dinkum Aussie.

So rather than learning the syllabus, self-defense became my number one priority. I was hopeless at boxing, so I began to wrestle with my opponents, the headlock being my favorite hold.

I enjoyed clamping my arms around opponents' necks and using my considerable advantage in weight, twisting their heads towards the sun, forcing them to fall off balance and land on their backsides, or the back of their skulls.

This was the only fighting skill I employed, but constant repetition ensured I would acquire the necessary skills to perfect this hold, resulting in a new development — only the toughest bullies would now confront me.

This would now buy me time in my quest to be fully accepted. I was determined to become one of the mob.

There were only three ways of achieving at Haileybury: one was to be a sporting hero, the other involved being academically gifted, and the last method was sucking your way up the ladder; the pupils called it arse-licking.

I was determined to try the sporting hero approach, and as it happened some of my mates were sporting captains. It took two years for me to pluck up the courage to ask for a place in the team, and then I was a fully out-fitted cricketer, ready to do battle against our arch enemy Scotch College. "You're fifth drop Cheddar,"exclaimed Gus Gardiner beloved captain of the under 13s, as he walked out to open our innings. Neither Gus, Russ, Dennis nor Bill had made reasonable totals; here was my chance to achieve instant glory.

"Go on, you can do it, give them something to think about," were the remarks I heard as I strode out to the crease.

My decision to attack the first ball was rewarded with the exhilaration as the jarring contact between bat and ball resulted in the ball speeding towards the offside boundary, forcing my teammates to evacuate their bench.

"Four" declared the umpire.

Flushed with success, I was determined to repeat the performance. However before the next delivery, the Scotch College captain, having glanced in my direction with a look suggesting nothing but contempt for my batting ability, told his bowler in a voice loud enough to be heard,

"This fellow is nothing more than a blind swipe."

The second ball was contacted by my bat, but unfortunately too close to the top. I was out, caught behind, my cricket career ending as abruptly as my first innings.

Zombie Andrew was reputed to actually enjoy inflicting injury and pain on those unfortunates who had been foolish enough to arouse his temper. He was nicknamed Zobba and those he chose to fight always finished up having to visit the doctor. He was one dude I knew who had to be avoided, however John Playfoot, a wicked and masterful trouble-maker had bought a large Shanghai (catapult) to school. During lunch hour he loaded it with a sharp yonnie (stone), and at close range, fired it into a prominent portion of Zombie's arse. Aroused by the pain, Zombie let out sounds as wild as any animal, as he slowly turned around to confront the responsible person. In the meantime the cunning Playfoot managed to sprint past me, planting the weapon in my hands, and without being noticed, disappeared into the larger background of the crowded oval. So good was his timing that Andrew could only conclude that I was the offending culprit. Voices were heard shouting,

"Fight! Fight! Fight!"

Summoning all and sundry to watch what promised to be a nasty confrontation between two large combatants, Zombie his fists at the ready, began to close in. I knew that if the fight involved boxing, I would suffer the humiliation of everybody realising just how easily I could be beaten.

"Box, you coward," snarled Zombie.

"I want to wrestle," said I, "How about we toss a coin?"

To my surprise, he agreed, but seconds later I had lost the toss.

"C'mon" said Zombie "I reckon you're just a chicken."

And then the pain and humiliation as his accurate jab loosened some front teeth and drew blood for all to see. By this time some eight hundred boys were milling around the oval jubilantly as Zombie moved in for the kill. Fortunately for me, the male staff room overlooked the oval and the slender form of science teacher Doogle Macleish ran out only to be enveloped in a melee of students whose job it was to stop him entering the imaginary ring. One by one the other teachers came out to help but were also jostled and pushed around. Fortunately for me, one of them managed to penetrate the giant circle and escort Zombie away, leaving me bloody, and battered.

Naturally these incidents were the gossip of both staff and students in what was considered a polite and highly disciplined Presbyterian environment. Even though I'd lost the fight I'd suddenly become notorious, a fair dinkum school character.

My bid for notoriety was to lead to my undoing, for I had succeeded in exposing a weakness in the school's system of discipline. Teachers were able to punish offending boys with one hour's detention after school. Two such detentions led to a two-hour spell on Saturday morning. The problem was that I had been given so many detentions, that I was booked in for every Saturday for the rest of the year, and with the school year only half completed, this meant the only way I could now be punished was to receive six of the best, a caning by the headmaster Mr. 'Donkey' Bradshaw, or alternately face the leather strap from the vice-principal Jock McGregor. Being caned or strapped was a routine occurrence for me, consequently the headmaster and his deputy were more familiar with me on a personal and social level than most of the other pupils, and would speak with me more often than some of the teachers. So it was no surprise when I was asked to visit the headmaster's office.

"Sit down Seder," he said,

"I have something distressing to tell you. Unfortunately you have been unable to conform to our standards of discipline; therefore forcing us to discontinue your education here. As of now you are expelled from this school."

Going home meant facing the local bodgies who would be waiting for me to emerge from the subway.

"Here comes the kid with the purple cap."

Nobody in Box Hill except the pastor at St Andrews church wore purple.

Happy Days, the long-running television series, documented an imaginary bodgie called The Fonz. Believe me, he was a cream puff compared to Dennis, the nasty leader of the Box Hill bikie gang. Dennis would get right into my face and surrounded by his toughest hoods, would playfully rearrange my tie before pushing me around. This humiliation was trivial pursuit compared to the emotional battering I received from mum and dad when they found out I'd been expelled.

Such is the chic of French culture that some French women dress and make up to kill even if they are only posting a letter. Imagine the exotic figure my mother made when walking up the school drive.

"Is that your mum Seder?" asked one of the boys.

"Yes" I answered sheepishly fully expecting to be the victim of a bout of wog-bashing, which fortunately didn't develop.

Mum was on a heroic mission to accomplish the impossible, my reinstatement at the school. I knew for a fact that not only would she charm the headmaster but outline her struggle of long years of hard work just to send me to this posh private school. Pretty soon I was sitting in the headmaster's study next to mum.

"You see Mrs. Sedergreen, I'd love to help you but Bob wouldn't last two minutes without incurring some sort of punishment" he said looking at me with the knowing smile a headmaster shares with one of his naughtiest boys. Then mum did one of her favourite things; she made a pronouncement.

"He will *have* to Mr. Bradshaw."

"So be it Mrs. Sedergreen, but one mistake and he's out and that's it."

"What about me?" I thought.

I would be at the mercy of every prefect, and made to undertake nasty fatigues (supervised cleaning up of the school). All the teachers would delight in exacting revenge, and my results, so far a disastrous failure, would have to improve. All this for a long period of two and a half years. How could this be accomplished? There was only one answer; through humility.

Humility came in the shape of a shortish, beady-eyed school chaplain, the Reverend Frank Elmore.

Possessing a voice of calm, he epitomised so many Christian virtues.

This did not work for most of the students who were forced to cop a double dose at church and school; others were simply bored by it and some were suspicious and called it bible-bashing. Not me. I was the perfect target, enthralled by the revolutionary concepts of the teachings. The first thing that burned a lasting impression was a verse of the hymn exhorting one to 'pour contempt on all one's pride.' This, together with 'turning the other cheek', 'loving one another as I love you', 'being a good Samaritan', 'walking the extra mile' and the blessings from the 'sermon on the mount' were attributes that inspired me.

Perhaps the reason for this was the religious vacuum at home. For their own reasons, mum and dad had made religion a taboo in our house. This meant no attendance at church or synagogue, no prayers, no sacraments, or any symbols of religion were to be found at home. As a result, I had neither been barmitzvahed nor confirmed. Frank Elmore had so influenced my spirituality that to everyone's shock I topped scripture class. Nobody could believe it as I headed up to receive my prize. And so, a new, more humble and charitable school career began.

As a reward for my reformed personality, I was to learn trombone from Norm D'Arth, reputedly one of the best brass teachers in the country. As I sat in the tiny music room practicing my Kid Ory rips, Norm walked in and said contemptuously,

"Play like that Seder and you'll finish up in the circus."

Not only did I not like what he had to say but was totally unprepared for what followed.

He took the mouthpiece from my instrument, handed it to me and then proceeded to lock the case, keeping the key in a drawer and placing the case in a locker, which he then locked.

"Don't bother coming back," he said "until you can play 'God Save The Queen' on your mouthpiece. Now leave!"

I was too young and too angry to realise that a brilliant music lesson had just taken place.

Like all kids I was in love with the golden brass instrument and not the crappy mouthpiece. Without knowing it, Norm had let me discover that the mouthpiece was the most important part. Wanting to get my horn back I learnt to play 'God Save The Queen' and quite a few other pieces.

I was hopeless at art, but art Teacher Ian Bow who inspired so many Victorian artists, including bassist David Tolley, realised that even though I could not paint or draw I had potential, offering to pass me as long as I gave demonstrations at the grand piano.

Tolley's brother ran the school's Jazz club. I remember walking into the room where they were playing a 78 of Dave Brubeck. Like so many people I would meet later in life, I had become obsessed with traditional Jazz and nothing else.

"This is crap" I pronounced, symbolically smashing the record into many pieces.

It was 1960 when our music teacher, Laurie McLennan, came up to me and said, "I need you to be in charge of the speech night orchestra and it better be good because the Moderator General of the Presbyterian Church will be our guest of honour."

"What do you want us to play?" I asked.

"Just some good old fashioned numbers like Paul Robeson singing 'I've Got A Robe,' 'Swing Low Sweet Chariot,' 'Go Down Moses' and stuff like that."

Paul Robeson might have been black but he had nothing to do with Jazz and I was determined to rectify this come speech night. So I began to recruit a motley collection of young lads that I could assert my authority over.

"Hey kid," I yelled at trumpeter Brett Iggeludon.

"You'll never be anything if you play with your cheeks puffed out like that. And you son, what's your name?"

"Allan Browne" replied the perplexed long-haired drummer.

"Get that kit set up and be quick about it."

I didn't know then that I was talking to two seminal figures in the history of Australian Jazz. Anyway, it turned out that the Moderator General was not impressed with our performance, calling it a racket. But as I walked up to receive my prize for completing Form 6, a rousing cheer broke out from both the students and parents. I had indeed become a much-discussed character and a part of the school's folklore.

JAMMING AT THE WILSONS

T HE POETRY OF Lord Byron, Shelley and Wordsworth was the spark that created a lifelong friendship between Stephen Wilson and me.

"I don't know about Bishop Hatto, but you look like you should be called Bishop Fatto," said Wilson laughing cheekily.

"Well mate, with your black hair, broad shoulders and stocky build you wouldn't look out of place in bishop's robes either" I replied.

From then on we referred to each other as 'bishop' or 'bish' if time was short. Steve would go over the top if he got enthusiastic about anything, be it golf, girls, trumpet, bass, poetry, a business idea or an artistic concept. His enthusiasm was so overwhelming one could not help being swept along and convinced of his words and deeds. Steve has not changed to this day, as those lucky enough to know him at Sydney's Balmain Art School or hip enough to witness his paintings or photographs of the gold diggings around Sofala, NSW will tell you.

I had heard rumours that even though I was just sixteen and studying at school, I was being head-hunted to join the local Rock band. The school had two guitarists, Gary 'Mouse' Mennie only played rhythm and Noel Miller played lead. The sax player 'Daisy' Davis, chopped meat in the local butcher shop and Doug Campbell, the drummer, worked at a printers. We would rehearse at Noel's house overlooking the bay at Hampton. We knew there were thousands of kids who wanted to dance to the back beat. As Chuck Berry sang, 'It's got be Rock 'n Roll music if you want to dance with me.'

One night we checked out the band at The Sandringham Life Saving Club. A long, narrow, wooden hall, right on the beach, with a boat ramp almost tipping into the bay. To us, this band were oldies, dressed in their black and white suits and ties (clarinet, piano and drums), playing a corny brand of dance music. Someone finally plucked up courage to ask the boss to give us a chance. This was a time when people were open to change and new ideas.

"Sure lads, I'll give you a go. Turn up next Saturday."

From the very first notes of our covers of Chuck Berry, Little Richard, Bill Haley and the like, young kids (we were called teenagers) flooded into the hall in droves, keen to jive to the beat. My job was to stand up at the piano playing heavy duty eight to the bar, and making sure I waggled my legs like Jerry (Lee Lewis.)

At the end of the night someone handed me three quid, in those days a fortune and a quarter of what my father earned weekly working as a storeman. Sometimes I think musicians are so dumb because fifty years later we're still working for an equivalent of that or less.

This gig led to other dances at halls and churches in the area, enabling me to buy all the things young school boys dreamt of: *Playboy* magazines, Kent cigarettes, suede shoes, fluorescent green and orange socks and a coon skin streamer for my future car aerial.

Middle Brighton boasted two picture theatres, *The Dendy*, which still exists to this day, and *The Prince George*, just across Church Street from the station. This was turned into a Jazz Club called *Basin Street*. Being now a fully-fledged Rock'n'Roll musician, I couldn't resist calling in, hoping for a sit-in. The problem was that the band played soft, smooth, sophisticated songs, none of which I knew. Before I had time to make an exit, the alto player invited me over for a blow.

My blues-based, boogie-style piano was totally out of place and I felt ashamed and inadequate as this was a brand of Jazz I could not play. Wanting to know more, I asked the alto player:

"Where do you get this style from? Who do you listen to?"

Like so many other musicians I would learn to respect, George Jury spoke in a soft voice and said,

"Art Pepper! Who else is there?"

Immediately he could see that I had no clue and suggested that he teach me this new modern Jazz language. So every Friday at about five, I would call in to see George and his wife Maureen who lived just around the corner.

George's patience was astounding. He would play each note of each chord and let me learn it by ear. It was also a time when the Pope decreed that all Catholics eat fish on Friday and Maureen's baked tuna casseroles were unforgettable. Slowly but surely I began to understand the modern Jazz language.

Max and Marge Wilson's house stood on the corner of Royal Avenue and Lefevre Street, Sandringham. Max owned and operated a button factory called *Maxart Buttons* which generated enough income for them to live the Australian dream. He owned his house and had a big yard, a motor boat parked out front to go fishing with his mates and an open house policy where friends come in for a drink. He also always had on hand tons of snacks, especially salada biscuits that were coated generously with tasty cheese, tomato, pickled onions or gherkins.

I began to feel like I had traversed the world a few times over thanks to Victorian railways. My commuting involved a fifteen-minute bus journey to Middle Brighton Station, a thirty-minute train journey to Richmond where I would change trains for another thirty-minute ride to Box Hill and another bus ride home. While normal kids would be home at about 4.30pm, I'd be lucky to be home at 6.30pm, just in time for dinner with mum and dad and the prospect of commencing homework and study at about quarter to eight.

So I found it easier to spend each weekend at the Wilsons.

"Just call me Aunty Marge and him Uncle Max," said Steve's mum smiling at me.

"And Bob, we want you to feel at home here" she said with genuine warmth.

How could I not feel at home? Steve had a collection of records to die for, including Les McCann, Bobby Timmins, Paul Horn and Errol Garner. We'd just lie about listening to these on Friday nights. On Saturday afternoons Max would return from fishing with his mates, all inebriated. They would gather around a new upright grand player piano. Max would stick in a piano roll, which was a scroll of thick paper punched with square holes where air from a bellows inside the piano would depress the keys. The bellows operated by pedals like a church organ. Max had piano rolls of Scott Joplin and other Ragtime favourites and would go into his act to perform the piece. There would be roars of laughter from the gathering including Steve and his brother, Paul, who we called Nipper. After a while would come the dreaded sing-along.

"Oh, come on Seder how about getting on the piano and giving us a song. How about 'Little Sir Echo?' " Max demanded.

Being surrounded by a group of beery-breathed blokes, each one determined to have his way and sing the song of his choice may have been their idea of fun but for me it was a form of torture, which as a guest, I had to endure. So I was grateful when it was suggested we invite some of the local musicians for a jam session. There was Bb Bailey, a clarinetist only capable of playing in B flat, and Warwick Johnson, a larger-than-life, heavy-weight left-handed drummer. Steve would play the bass and after a while, the hospitality of the Wilsons grew. I remember my teacher, George Jury, an alto player, admiring uncle Max's brand new Valiant and being amazed by his generosity in offering him the keys,

"Take it for a spin." Max said,

"And go as long as you like."

This sort of generosity as well as free grog and food saw the jam session grow into a full house, taking up all Saturday afternoon and attracting an ever-growing network of musicians. No one moved on Sunday mornings; they were either at church or more likely sleeping off the excesses of Saturday.

OPUS '61

EVERYTIME I MENTION that I'm writing a book I am constantly reminded not to forget to include how vibrant Melbourne's Jazz scene used to be. Readers today may find the following unbelievable. Today's musicians would drool at the mouth for so many opportunities to listen and play.

So here is a typical Jazz crawl, like a pub-crawl, sometimes without even a drop of alcohol. The most dangerous things sold at some clubs were tomato soup, toasted raisin bread, coffee and Welsh rarebit. Let's start in Malvern with *The Green Man*, a coffee lounge (in High Street just near the Town Hall), and the Jazz Art Gallery near the tram depot. (I played there with Barry Duggan).

In Kings Arcade, Armadale was *Hernandos*. In South Yarra, *The Fat Black Pussy Cat* where Barry Mckim and Chuck Yeates once played. Across the road was *The Embers*, the home of Frank Smith. *The Embers* became part of Melbourne jazz folk lore in the sixties due to the visit of the dynamic trio of pianist, Oscar Petersen, bassist, Ray Brown and drummer Ed Thigpen, whose concerts there left every musician spellbound. People still rave about the night Oscar Petersen played at Embers.

Opposite Wesley College, Melbourne, a grey stone building called Ormond Hall stands. It is still a venue today (and you can still get a drink there). It was called *Opus 61*. This was the venue I would always gravitate to. As you entered the hall you could see 400 under-25s dancing to the high-energy Jazz played by the house band, *The Driftwood Jazz Band*. The young dark haired-pianist, John Adams, had a warm and beckoning smile and played fluent lines and harmonies (definitely not New Orleans). The bass player Graeme McClean had a plywood bass painted green with chalk marks on the fret board to ensure the best possible intonation, while the drummer Peter Barker swung.

Adjacent to the dance floor was a smaller hall with a side bar that had naughty alcoholic drinks, served under the counter in lily white plastic cups: brandy and coke, neat scotch, gin or vodka, with prices triple those charged in a hotel. The protocol at the time demanded all the girls (sheilas) sit demurely on chairs waiting for a guy to ask for a dance. Perhaps the alcohol was to help us guys pluck up the courage.

Across the tramline in St Kilda Road was *Club 431* and not far away *Club Keyboard*, both Jazz dance venues in competition with Opus. Not far away in Albert Park, the *Allan Eaton Big Band* played at a popular club called *Powerhouse*. Within a one square mile triangle on a Saturday night, some one thousand young eager bodies were pulsing to the beat of Jazz.

Not far away in St Silas church, traditional Jazz buffs were moving to the sounds of *The Melbourne New Orleans Jazz Band*, with its star clarinetist Nick Polites. Frank Traynor's *Jazz Preachers* ruled the roost at *The Beaumaris Hotel* further down the Bay. As one came back into town one could call into *The Hampton Hotel* to hear Trevor Firth's band play prior to watching a floorshow, a mix of Modern, Jazz and Cabaret.

In Acland Street St Kilda, where McDonalds stands today, was *Jazz Centre 44*, home of the famous *Brian Brown Quintet*.

In the city, underneath the *Capitol Theatre* in Swanston Street in a basement, was the *Purple Eye*. I remember the house band of Martin Lesware on tenor sax and Ray Rayburn on trombone had a Jazz Crusaders type sound. Then of course there was *The Little Reata* in Little Collins Street, where I remember hearing Keith Hounslow's *Jazz Hounds*.

Around the corner was the *Downbeat Club*, in a lane off Russell Street next to a large music store, *Bob Clemens*. This was one of my favourite haunts because of the talent that played there. At street level, The Salvation Army was in full force: men and women in navy and maroon uniforms that contrasted with their golden and silver brass instruments and tambourines and who ministered to the crowd with megaphones about the evils of drink, prostitution and such like. It was ironic because as soon as you cleared their ranks you would climb up the wooden stairs that lead to the entrance of the Club where musicians would be playing Jazz, reputedly the devils' music.

Then there were the dances. Firstly in Greville Street, Prahran, in what must have been an old cinema was the dancehall *Leggetts*, where an excellent big band led by reedman, Ron Trigg, played exclusively for dancing. In Burwood Road, Hawthorn was the Manresa Hall, another big dance. Heidleberg Town Hall as well as Moonee Ponds ran big band dances on Saturday night. At the same time many churches ran dance socials where the predominant music played was a sort of Jazz.

There were many more venues but I can't remember where or when, but as Pops sang to Bing in the movie High Society,

"Jazz is king, Jazz is the thing that folks dig most!"

It was a time when no one could foresee that in a few years, pop groups led by *The Beatles* and then *The Rolling Stones* and those that followed them would almost wipe out Melbourne's thriving Jazz scene.

Did I mention girls? How unromantic of me! This was a time when modesty was still prevalent, where any sort of physical contact was dynamite, where kissing or making-out was heavy duty. After all, it could lead to sex or even more scary, engagement and marriage. The guys who frequented Jazz dances did so in hope of attracting the girls hanging around there because when the jiving and jitter bugging numbers were over, the band might play something slow and here was a chance to hold a woman close.

I remember a friend, Ross, who had installed spring-loaded lay back seats in his car and had spent all night dancing with a girl at *Opus*, then offering to drive her home to Dandenong. When they got to a suitable spot Ross applied the spring-back loaded seats, scaring and frightening the poor young lady who ended up running down the highway and pulling up a car. Ross managed to escape before the police arrived. Not everyone was like Ross; it was surprising how often many young married couples said they'd met at a Jazz dance. The other method was to invite a young lady out for a cultural experience, i.e. a Jazz club, making sure you sat close together in the dimly-lit environment and hoping that the music at some stage of the night would ignite that passionate first kiss. It was surprising how many couples could be caught making-out in the dim light of a Jazz club. This all happened before The Beatles and the sexual revolution of the sixties. Sex like Jazz, was something that had to be discovered.

Talking about the Beatles, when the Driftwood band left the stage at Opus, *The Max Reid Trio* (consisting of piano, bass and drums) would come on, with long hair and tight straight suits, looking like a forerunner to the Beatles. They played a modern brand of Jazz for the kids, making Opus a total musical package.

Of course the pianist in the Driftwood band, John Adams, insisted I sit in every time I visited. It was good to play on the stage with a high energy band of horn players like Derrick Harris, Barry Veith (who ran the dance) and clarinetist Terry Cairns

This was a time when musicians were held in some regard and were rewarded with all the grog they wished to drink. Beer flowed through the hall on a regular basis. One of the saddest sights was clarinetist Terry Cairns, whose instrument continually dripped like a leaking tap. The droplets of beer would build up in a bucket suitably placed directly underneath the bell.

It was also satisfying to play on an elevated stage to large numbers of one's own appreciative peer group.

THE FRED BRADSHAW YEARS

ANOTHER SIGNIFICANT DEVELOPMENT in my musical life was to unfold on the night of my 19th birthday.

I was playing at a church dance in Ashburton, more importantly, I had been asked to do the gig by an alto sax player I really admired, Frank Leonard. He was a short and stocky guy who I met at the jam sessions held at Stephen Wilson's house.

Frank always chose to play a number called *Move*, well titled due to the fact that to execute the melody took a fair amount of dexterity. Frank was also the unofficial president of the *Cannonball Adderley Fan Club*, possessing more albums of this artist than anyone else I knew in Melbourne. He was happy to play you any selections from his collection. He was attempting to play his alto in that spirit, so naturally I enjoyed working with him. On the night, I happened to mention that it was my birthday.

"Why aren't you celebrating?" asked Frank.

Unable to explain my lack of social development, I came up with the answer that our family did not put much stock in such occasions.

"I know what we can do to celebrate your birthday," said Frank cheerfully.

"We will go to a jazz club, I know just the place, we'll ask for a sit in and then you and I will carve up the house band," a mean smile breaking out on his face at the thought of such fun.

I was excited at the prospect of what promised to be sheer adventure.

The name of the club was *Hernando's*, located in a large shop in the King's Arcade in High Street Armadale. There was a bouncer waiting at the front door. Frank was convincing the bouncer that he and I were two interstate musicians who had come to check the joint out. This was so we would avoid paying the cover charge.

We were ushered into a dimly lit room, most globes covered with lampshades. One either sat on the few wooden chairs or benches provided, or on the large cushions covering the floor. One end of the shop was a counter where one could buy staple jazz club food like spaghetti, coffee and a selection of cinnamon or raisin toasts, as well as warm soup and melted cheese sandwiches. At the other end was a small stage on which the house band was playing. The first thing that caught my attention was the sound of their music, it was jazz, it was swinging, but it was surprisingly cool, with the saxophone intonation being very much in tune with a round melodic tone I had not heard before.

In fact my ears and eyes seemed drawn to the tall blonde dude playing his horn effortlessly. This tall silent saxophonist looked like he had broken his nose in a fight. Instead of the usual hard edged sound associated with jazz, this guy produced pleasant sounds and improvising in the most melodic way, often constructing long and lilting phrases that flooded from the saxophone like a gentle ripple that rides the river. As soon as their set had finished Frank was at them organising a sit in for us.

"This is where we get to play," said Frank gleefully.

"What would you like to play?" asked tall sax man.

"How about 'What is this thing called love,'" said Frank trying not to give away the fact that we had destroyed the tune virtually just two hours ago at the church gig.

Frank counted in the tempo making sure it would suit our present standards of dexterity, the head was played in unison, and Frank not waiting for anybody cut in with a masterful solo, intense, energetic, boppy, each note clearly defining in detail the harmonic progression of the piece. The tall dude must have nothing left to play I thought, but he followed Frank, eyes closed, seemingly unaware of our intentions. Unlike Frank who had put so much physical and mental effort into his work, this guy seemed to be making music effortlessly, his fluidity and dynamic control of the bebop language sounded loose and pliable, creating the impression that Frank possessed a certain stiffness in his projection. I was next and played the best solo I could on an old upright piano that should have been condemned to the scrap heap years before. Strangely enough the drummer insisted on lifting the velocity of his attack, playing stacks of accents, perhaps meant to inspire, perhaps with the intention of keeping things on the move. The bassist was producing the normal dull thud, a sure sign of loss of enthusiasm. Unhappy with the way things were progressing Frank decided now was the time to take on the stranger.

"Swap phrases" I heard Frank call, and with that, he and stranger began trading alternate eight bar phrases. Frank first followed by the stranger, his eyes still closed as if unaware that this was a serious challenge.

At this stage Frank decided to make it obvious, playing the fastest and most obtuse runs he could muster, and it was then the stranger's eyes opened and he started to smile, playing replicas of what had gone before, with ever so slight variations, whereupon Frank's assurance seemed to fade, his sound seeming to crack and despite continuing on, it was time to play melody again, thereby ending the jam session and ending the gig.

Nobody said anything about what had happened. Frank packed up his alto and made a quick exit. I sat there dumbfounded, but before I could collect my wits the stranger came over and said,

"Hi! I'm Fred Bradshaw and I really dig the way that you play." This was more than I wanted to hear.

"Do you realise we were trying to carve you?" I asked.

"I'm not into that. I can't stand musicians who knock others, it's a waste of time. I don't know what goes on when I start playing, I get so involved maybe because I'm only here for the music and to enjoy what can happen when the right people come together."

Fred's whole approach and manner was so humble, I fell in love with every word he spoke and every note that had spilled out of his horn. Here was the soul brother I had been searching for, someone I knew possessed the musicianship that would win my respect and admiration.

The gig finished around 4 a.m. and Fred invited me to his house in nearby Caulfield. Apologising for having no coffee in the place, he proceeded to make us two warm glasses of Turban chicory, a coffee substitute.

"Won't your wife be mad at us?"

"She understands," said Fred smiling at me as though I had asked a ludicrous question. To add to my bewilderment he asked,

"What would like to hear?" pointing at the stereogram.

"Well my favourite style seems to always come back to blues," I confessed.

Fred produced a glossy two album boxed set, *Dave Brubeck at Carnegie Hall*.

"Surely you're not going to play this now? You will probably wake your wife, if not the whole neighborhood."

"It won't be too loud," said Fred convincingly

"You'll just love what they do to St Louis Blues."

I enjoyed listening to the track and was quick to observe Fred's ability to point out the musical skills and nuances that each musician contributed as the music unfolded.

By the time the track finished, he had convinced me that Brubeck and Desmond were musical gurus worth following, white guys, musical giants, whose music was capturing the new up-and-coming college jazz audience.

Having met Fred, my first project was to find him an alternate job to being a bus driver. *Grenda's Bus Lines* took Fred to outposts like Dandenong and beyond and he also had to work night shift.

My first job was at *Lamson Paragon Ltd* where I worked as a Trainee Purchasing Officer. I managed to line Fred up a job there as a printing estimator. We could work together by day talking music. Pretty soon we struck a regular gig, at a wedding factory called *Kenilworth* in Chapel Street South Yarra (later to become The Salt night club).

Kenilworth was a mock Tudor two-storey mansion. This was at a time when getting married was a very regular event. I remember mum and dad taking me to see the first cinemascope film at the Hoyts Broadway picture theatre in Camberwell, *Seven Brides For Seven Brothers*, a movie where everyone ends up getting married. It was the thing to do. So Kenilworth House was a virtual gold mine for the owner, Fred McConachie. It had a little red carpet out the front and downstairs was all set up with bridal tables, chandeliers, candles and other decorations. Fred didn't like hiring musicians for too long so he could get away with paying them less. He organised an accordionist and violinist to traverse the tables downstairs, playing requests, toasts and formalities. We were the dance band, the *Fred Bradshaw Quartet*, Ron Hayden on drums and

Alan Liversidge on bass. Fred McConachie would ring our homes when the bride and groom were about to finish their speeches saying: "Get here as fast as you can."

Just like the fire brigade we'd have to climb into our cars, speeding all the way to Kenilworth because we had to arrive in time to be sitting at our instruments as the bride and groom walked upstairs. We were there just for the dancing. We played in a little alcove next to a bar where more drinking could go on.

The piano I had to play was a little Ronisch upright, something that should have decorated a flat rather than be a regular workhorse for bands. You would have thought it was alive like some pet dog or cat, as he was ready to kill anyone who would so much as mark it and of course placed its back onto the thickest velvet curtains one could imagine, creating a natural muffler. Six nights a week of playing on that little piano without any amplification and matching the sounds of Ronnie's propulsive drums and Alan's amplified bass led to me obtaining an incredible technical facility. I had to play loud and hard just to get a sound.

In later years, people like Nat Adderley and McCoy Tyner and Sydney pianist Serge Ermol would claim I was the loudest piano player they had ever met (They never said I was the best). To this day I believe my volume is due to this experience at Kenilworth.

NUMBER ONE

I N THE SIXTIES, a mother's worst nightmare would be that her child turns out to be gay or lesbian.

Mum was getting very anxious. One night I heard her conversing with dad saying, "Oh god, I hope he doesn't turn out to be one of those."

The reason for her concern was that all my friends were either schoolmates, local lads from Box Hill or Jazz musicians — and all blokes. Whilst the Brighton brigade had access to dancing classes with St Leonard and Firbank girls, (that's how Allan and Sally Browne met) I had spent most of my spare time on Victorian railways, hardly the place to pick up a date. All my non-musical mates had elder sisters who seemed to prefer drooling over posters of Elvis Presley in their bedrooms rather than paying attention to me. Besides, I was more at ease in the company of blokes, be it while motorbike riding, shooting, or acting out dares like diving off the high perch at the *Surrey Dive*, into the bottomless canyon of water. (*The Surrey Dive* was a large and very deep quarry filled by water from an underground river.)

The other thing that was plaguing mum was the fact that I was totally ignorant of Jewish customs, culture and lifestyle. So mum arranged visits to homes of families with appealing young daughters of my age. Yes, girls for me were not only a new area, but totally mystifying. Mum was as subtle as a sledge-hammer about her motives and expectations, which left me feeling even more awkward, as I would have preferred to find things out for myself. Perhaps a more subtle approach was needed. Then my folks hit on a brain wave. The Trower family lived across town, their son was not only my age but like myself, his father was a British police officer and had served with my dad in Palestine and like dad, had also taken a Jewish wife. Ronnie was a member of a youth group and it was suggested to him that perhaps he could introduce me to the right sort of girl.

Young, dark-haired and handsome, he said: "Let's take a spin in my Renault. I'm going to pick up my girlfriend so why don't you sit in the back and check the engine out?"

Ron's Renault was the tiniest car I had ever seen. Glad to be free of parents, I gratefully hopped in the back. Our first stop was a house in Kew where two gorgeous and shapely blue-eyed blondes appeared.

"It's fairly cramped, why don't you sit next to Bob?"

I felt like a king, smelling the sweet perfumed softness of these princesses on either side of me. Pretty soon we all started to giggle and laugh, and I was euphoric at being so close to the girls. The other thought that entered my mind was how far away these pretty young things were from the nasty stereotyping of Europeans, and in particular Jewish people. The next stop was Carlton where Ronnie's girlfriend Tova appeared, a stunning young brunette.

We arrived at our destination, strangely enough across the road from the Jazz dance Opus 61. But soon my companions had dispersed into their social groups engaging in friendly yet superficial conversation. Bored, I strolled out to the front of the building onto St. Kilda Road to have a quiet cigarette. There I saw a tram approaching; it had come from West Coburg but it might as well have come from Yugoslavia, the Northern suburbs being a world apart to those of us who had grown up in the Eastern and Southern suburbs. The sole passenger leaving that tram was a young lady. She had dark wavy hair and blue eyes and was sort of skinny. As she passed me, she struck up a conversation.

"Have you been to a meeting here before?" she enquired.

"Oh no, this is my first one" I replied.

"You must be either brave or foolish to travel on your own at night" I remarked.

"Not really" she replied.

She escorted me back into the building, re-introducing me to all the people I'd met plus a whole lot of other people. I found her bright blue eyes and friendly manner totally exhilarating. But could she be bothered with things that I loved? As a first step, I turned the conversation onto a subject every self-respecting girl would hate. You guessed it, twin carburettors. I asked her whether she preferred Weber or Armstrong and how you adjusted them. This young girl was undeterred by the thrust of the conversation and seemed to know about cars and their various workings.

I couldn't tell her how impressed I was.

OK, I thought, let's switch the conversation to another one of my favourite topics that girls at that time didn't handle too well — sport. Girls detested gambling but this girl knew more about horse racing and trotting than I did. My male ego began taking a serious dive and in desperation I turned to football, only to find out we supported the same team — Carlton. After all, Rae was Carlton-born and bred, and her football knowledge about the game, team and their positions on the ladder actually surpassed mine. This really blew my mind.

For the first time I had met a girl I could be myself with and I was determined to see her again.

Every subsequent visit to Rae's place in Pascoe Vale South was a total shock to my system. I had never seen foods of this nature or taken part in blessings spoken in Aramaic and unlike my family, which delighted in our separate existences, this mob did everything together. But with each visit, I gained greater insight into the girl I was becoming very fond of.

I admired her unbelievable zest for life and hard work, a work ethic that one might encounter in Melbourne's northern suburbs and certainly one not shared by myself. Her eagerness to participate in any activity, be it going to a movie, a Jazz club, a lecture or even a long drive. Her bubbliness was over-flowing and joyful. Rae's devotion to her family was an object lesson in humility. She gladly mowed the lawns, drove her family anywhere they wanted to go, collected her dad's TAB tickets and willingly helped her mum every time she called out to her, which was often.

One night I called in to find her hard at work at her desk in the tiny back veranda alongside her Astor play gram. The music emanating was the hard bop of Miles Davis. Fascinated, she showed me the cover *Miles at Carnegie Hall '61* a green dragon emblazoned on an orange cover.

"Wow that's really advanced," I exclaimed, tuning into a Wynton Kelly solo.

"Do you really listen to this stuff?"

"Oh, yes" Rae replied triumphantly, her eyes meeting mine.

"I play this every time, it helps me with my work."

What she didn't tell me was the family were members of the World Record Club and had been sent a package of Jazz albums by mistake, not bothering to return them.

But the icing on the cake was on my nineteenth birthday. She could not conceal her delight in surprising me with the greatest gift I could have possibly been given at that time, a copy of Oscar Peterson's album, *My Fair Lady*. It wasn't so much the gift but the element of surprise, because you see, many months earlier in an off-hand sort of way, she had asked me the following question:

"If you were giving someone a gift for their birthday what would it be?"

"Why, a copy of the album Oscar Peterson Plays *My Fair Lady* of course."

An answer I gave and promptly forgot. That was it! My whole life would consist of defining moments I would instantly recognise and this was one of them. I would pursue her until she became my number one.

PART TWO

LESSONS FROM THE MUSIC SCHOOL OF LIFE

LESSONS FROM
THE MUSIC SCHOOL OF LIFE

NOW THAT I was a married man and on a weekly wage from my day job, it would be most beneficial to earn a little extra money from music.

In those days, a good source of work was the Musicians' Union. One would ring them and ask to be placed on the availability list for the following weekend. The only requirement was that you had to be a paid up member of the Union. Details such as age, standard of musicianship and style of music played were not deemed relevant. In fact the Union made no check on the character of their clients — anybody was welcome to request a band. This situation ensured that musicians who rang the union for work became victims of circumstance, forced into posing as a band rather than a bunch of individuals thrown together by the Union. I quickly found out that we musicians had to fulfil both the expectations of the client and the guests attending the function.

The Union had phoned in my instructions as follows:

Location: Legionniare's Hall, adjacent to the side of the North Melbourne Town Hall. Starts at 8.30pm, finishes 11.30pm. Wear a dinner suit and black bow tie. That was it.

In anticipation of a great night of music-making, I began to sing the Bobby Timmons Jazz classic 'Sack of Woe,' whilst accelerating my Hillman sedan through the suburbs in order to arrive at the gig early. To some musicians, arriving at a gig early was just as important as anything else that happened during the night. After all, Melbourne was a small town and one did not want a reputation for being unreliable.

Being a piano player all I had to do was park the car close to the gig and walk.

As I entered the hall, the familiar smell of draught beer flowing from a nine-gallon keg in the corner filled my nostrils. The hall was drab, the wooden floors and walls having seen better days some 40 years earlier. All its polished surfaces had lost their lustre, even the gold lettering on the dark polished wooden honour boards were beginning to wear off. It seemed the only bright thing in the place was a framed photo of the young Queen Elizabeth, which hung in a prominent position.

The organisers had used the standard procedure of hanging balloons to hide the dismal state of the hall. Nestled in the back corner were two trestle tables displaying the plates of food each lady had contributed. These tables were adorned with party pies, sausage rolls, bowls of tomato sauce, potato chips, Twisties, cracker biscuits with tasty cheese, asparagus rolls, an array of pavlovas, a few slices of ham, lamingtons, cream cakes, jam tarts and a chocolate cream cake. Standard fare for this type of function.

In between the items of supper stood a few bottles of lemonade, Coca-Cola, and orange or lemon squash, obviously there for the females, children, or men despicable enough to be wowsers!

My colleagues were setting up on stage, which unfortunately was mounted within easy reach of those on the dance floor, meaning the band would be at the mercy of all and sundry capable of dancing close to the music.

It's perhaps a shame that I can't remember my colleagues' names, having washed them out of my memory after the first song we played. But just for fun, let's call them Bill and Ben.

Bill, who sat behind the drum kit was approaching retirement. He played every beat on the bass drum in a slightly different place. He played rat-a-tat fills on the snare drum so jerky and unpredictably that the time could not be maintained. When he hit the cymbal to find beat one, he usually found himself in the middle of a bar of music. Bill showed no emotion when playing, so I could not tell if he was cleverly disguising his musical inabilities, or if he just did not know any better and perhaps even cared less.

As for Ben, as flat as his King saxophone with its white ebonite mouthpiece sounded, his violin (which he doubled on) was sharp enough to crack the toughest timber in the hall. Also a man soon to retire, he chose to play obscure tunes, music popular in the old-time dance halls at the turn of the century. Dances like the *Albert's*, the *Gay Gordon's*, the *Pride of Erin*, and the *Evening Three Step*. I was supposed to understand and follow this by ear, and even if I had been provided with, and was able to read the music, I'm sure what was being played had nothing to do with the original score.

Such a disaster was this band, so out of tune and time were we that the people, surprised and shocked by such an awful sound, desisted from their usual fun of taunting us with jibes like,

"Can youse play something we know? Can youse jazz it up a bit? Can youse play something fast, something we can dance to?"

We were so bad that we escaped this usual friendly mocking from the audience. There was nowhere to hide. When the first set finished I immediately ran out onto the dark stone steps of the town hall hoping to escape the embarrassment. Much to my surprise, Bill and Ben had found a shorter escape route, and were sitting on the steps enjoying a quiet cigarette.

After some six minutes of silence, I couldn't bear it any longer, and despite the fact that I was 40 years younger than them, I began abusing them, saying things like, "That was really shithouse gentleman! Surely you guys can play better than that. I mean, that's the worst playing I've ever heard! Look, I honestly don't think I could last another set."

At first some anger filled Bill's face, then he calmly turned to Ben and said to me, "Look kid, we're here to do a job. What do you want from us? What would you like us to play?"

"That's easy" I said, "Surely you guys have heard of Charlie Parker, or Oscar Peterson? Do you think we could play something of that nature?"

After a few minutes of silence, Ben said, "Look here son, it's going to be a long three hours for you. Bill and I have no idea who you're talking about," and then his tone hardened saying, "There is a bottle shop across the road. Why don't you run across and buy yourself a mid-size bottle of whisky, take a few swigs, then when you come back into the hall, pretend that I'm this Charlie Parker, and he is that other guy you mentioned. You'll find the gig will pass much quicker that way."

What absurd logic! I thought. But I knew I couldn't face another set, so I ran to the bottle shop, purchased a medium-sized bottle of Dewar's old malt whisky, and began gulping it down. I tried to pretend my colleagues were now Charlie Parker and Jimmy Cobb, but that only worked for two numbers.

However, Ben had been right, I felt less embarrassed, and the time between dances passed faster than before. The problem was that when the gig finished, I was too incoherent to thank Bill and Ben for their wisdom. Thankfully I never saw them again, but I had learnt what was to be my future philosophy: do your utmost to make others sound better than they are without telling them, and if you can't do that, then head for the bar.

FRANK SMITH MUSICAL GIANT

IN THE SIXTIES, there were many different classes of musicians. When one musician met another, they would ask: "Are you a pro?"

Pros could be found in symphony orchestras, underneath the pits of stages, in television bands and the like. If you weren't a pro you were considered to be in some sort of scene. The Melbourne pub scene was crawling with restaurants, bars and lounges with all types of bands.

The rest of us would have to answer, "I'm on the casual scene." We were considered lesser lights; music being our second income.

As described in the previous chapter, a source of extra income was the Musicians Union, an organisation that invited members who were not getting regular work to join an availability list. Most of the gigs organised by the Union were musical disasters, but on this night, as the list of personnel was read out, I heard the name Frank Smith on flute and reeds. Was this the legendary Frank Smith? That cool, hard alto sax player who sat next to Don Burrows and Charlie Munro in Australia's premier orchestra, the *Bob Gibson Orchestra*? Frank Smith who led his own group at Melbourne's most up-market nightclub, The Embers, and on a legendary night had shared the stage with the greatest trio in Jazz history: Oscar Peterson, Ray Brown, and Ed Thigpen,. Frank played above his usual ability that night, giving a performance remembered for many years by those who attended. Oscar let it be known that he regarded Frank Smith as one of the greatest musicians he had heard and tried in vain to persuade him to move to America where his talents would be better recognised and rewarded.

There was also a story circulating in certain pubs where musicians congregated, that when Oscar reached America, saxophonist Benny Carter was boarding the flight back to Australia. Apparently Oscar asked Benny for his itinerary, and is reputed to have said,

"This looks cool but don't go to Melbourne because there's a cat there called Frank Smith. Mess with him and he'll really take care of you."

I also remembered how important it was to support Australian Jazz, and had purchased the album *Old Gold*, an Australian Jazz assortment. This album was released by chocolate manufacturer MacRobertson, a firm that marketed high quality chocolates, and had decided to capitalize on the current popularity of Jazz. Frank Smith was prominently featured in various groups on this album. I just loved the way he executed his phrases: there was no wasting of notes; most ideas were expressed in lines that cut across the then normal custom of defining chord changes in a series of fast rolling connected triplet and quaver spills. Wow! "Is that the real Frank Smith?" I asked the Union secretary.

"No Bob, it's just someone with the same name we were thinking of sending out there in a dinner suit! Of course it's the real Frank Smith you idiot! And what's more, you and he have been asked to get there earlier than the others, to provide some quiet music for when they are dining."

The gig was at St. Kevin's, one of Melbourne's most fashionable boy's schools, a private college with its own assembly hall. On the stage in front of the over-hanging theatre curtains stood an old upright piano. I took up my position next to the piano, but where was Frank? It was then I heard a voice from behind the stage curtains saying,

"I don't know if I can face this, it's been a while since I've done one of these gigs and my dinner suit is full of moth holes."

" Come out here and let me see," I said. Frank emerged from behind the curtains and I was confronted by a large man of similar build to myself, perhaps slightly larger and broader across the shoulders. Being of Germanic background, it was no surprise that he had reddish hair and blue eyes; his dinner suit was moth eaten and his apperance unkempt.

"Here, let's swap jackets," said I, happy to be wearing the

jacket of this Jazz legend. Having combed his hair, Frank reached for his flute case and pulled out a flute totally devoid of lacquer. So black and ugly was this flute it looked like it had been buried in a Lithgow colliery.

"Well, aren't you going to give me a note to warm up on?" Frank enquired. I should have sounded the customary single note of A. Instead I heard a voice deep inside saying: he may be good, but make him earn it, let's find something special for Mr. Smith to warm up on. I then found myself trying to spontaneously invent ten nasty notes that would create the ugliest possible harmony. The element of surprise must catch Frank off-guard, and so, with unabashed pride I triumphantly produced this non-musical cluster on the piano.

Frank looked directly at me, the expression on his face communicating the fact that I had acted like a silly little boy, and with that he picked up his flute and commenced playing a series of lightning fast arpeggios repeated ad infinitum. What was even more distressing was as I listened to these repeating arpeggios, I looked down at the notes I had been playing, Frank was running up and down every note my fingers were on.

"I'm sorry Frank." I said in a tone that confirmed this was a genuine apology. He looked at me and said,

"What would you like to play?"

" Anything I'm told." I answered.

Frank smiled, "OK, 'Besame Mucho' in D Minor then" and the dinner music commenced.

The centre of Frank's daytime operations was a commercial recording studio. *Studio 31* located adjacent to the M.C.G was owned and operated by Frank, who had telephoned from these premises in a bid to convince me that I should take part in the production of music for an advertising jingle.

"Come on Frank" I argued, "you must be aware of the fact that I don't read music very well and you know I'm not part of the recording scene. There are so many other pianists you could ask who would be much better equipped for that sort of job."

"I know" said Frank, "but this will be easy, I'll write it in the key of C and make sure your part will be easy to read. It will give us an excuse to work together again."

Foolishly I agreed and turned up the next morning as Frank had instructed. He ushered me to an old upright piano, with my part already written out for me.

"Here have a go at this, and let me know when we're ready to record." So great was Frank's genius, he was able to discuss other business with his staff in the recording room and still have his hearing focused on what I was up to. Each time I made a mistake he would look around and say,

"Bob it's a G not an F Sharp," referring to one note in the five I had misjudged and then he would turn around and continue his conversation with his colleagues on a totally different subject. Unfortunately for me his quick mind corrected me immediately as I played each wrong note, causing my embarrassment to escalate as I began to notice the other musicians smirking at my discomfort. To make things worse, although bassist Ron Terry and drummer Ron Hayden may have been sympathetic to my cause, they could not be relied upon to keep such juicy gossip a secret.

Finally I had the notes under control, but Frank had written the piece in five/four time, with certain accents that did not fall naturally. This meant the accents would have to be read and played exactly as written. All the other musicians at the session did this with consummate ease, but I couldn't get my part right, and after ten recording takes, I couldn't stand the pressure any longer. I walked out of that studio, my head bowed in shame. I had wrecked the session and made an idiot of myself in front of colleagues. I had let down a person I admired, a non-wealthy man struggling to keep his business afloat. Because of me, this session would run at a loss. To make things worse, Frank followed me out of the studio, insisting that I accept payment. He wrote the cheque out for the full amount: thirty dollars being the award for a minimum call.

On the way home, my self-respect at an all time low, I cursed myself for once again being foolish enough to take on situations I was not equipped to handle. The very next morning, a phone call came from Frank Smith.

"Don't worry yourself about the session," he said, "it was my fault, I shouldn't have booked you." I could feel this was a genuine comment, which immediately released large amounts of tension, forcing tears I could not control.

"Thank you, I'm glad you said that," I blubbered. "I almost lost faith in myself."

"Well now for the good news," said Frank, "I've just won a contract for a Coca-Cola commercial and I want to hire you to play improvisation over the rhythm track I've put down. No reading and I want you to play what you do best; you never know, we may get some hooks I can mix into the track. By the way, it's urgent as the agency needs it for a campaign in Malaysia, so could you come in and do it today? I won't be there, but my engineer Gil Matthews will handle it. I've left a cheque for 90 dollars with him for you to collect, which means you can take all day if you wish."

"Your problem is that you're too generous" I replied, "but this is something I think I can handle, so I'll be in within the hour."

On the drive into Melbourne I found myself in deep thought about the genius of Frank Smith. Imagine having a drummer, what's more a Rock and Roll star who played with the famous Melbourne rock group, *Billy Thorpe and the Aztecs*, as a sound engineer. What an odd choice! Surely his hearing must be damaged by all those Rock gigs and he was not part of the Jazz world, so his artistic judgment could be questionable.

But then Jazz saxophonists like Graham Lyall and Bob Bertles had emerged from famous Rock bands like the *Thunderbirds* and *Johnny O'Keefe and the Deejays*.

I enjoyed the over-dubbing session and drove home feeling good about having made a contribution. Gil had told me there was no need for me to attend the mixing session, which he must complete before ten the next morning. Being a person not over-equipped with intuition, I don't know what prompted me to drive into the studio to check on the mixing session. All I know was that tapes were rolling, but not one scrap of piano could be heard. I rushed into the mixing booth shouting, "Gil there's no piano in the mix." Gil looking disappointed that I had turned up, said,

"Sit down, I might as well tell you the truth. There never was going to be any piano on this track. This was all Frank's idea.

He wanted to get you back into this studio. He wanted you to overcome your fears of this place so that you would feel natural about playing here the next time he called you."

On the slow drive home I tried to figure out what had motivated Frank to help a young up-and-coming musician like myself. Was it the satisfaction in helping a younger player develop their potential? Perhaps Jazz giants like him understood about giving; after all he gave his heart, soul, creative expression and total body energy every time he played.

In an attempt to pay him back I telephoned Frank and booked in for a music lesson. Frank lived in a rented flat in Elwood, along with his wife Barb and their tribe of red-headed kids. Frank escorted me to an old upright piano and sat on a rocking chair close by.

"All right" said Frank, "Play something easy, something you enjoy playing but give it your best shot."

I played a fast blues in G, remembering to quote as many Oscar Peterson licks as I knew.

"Well done," said Frank, "It's nice to hear that young guys are still interested in Oscar Peterson."

Frank's next question was put to me in a casual off-handed manner, "Do you read?"

"Sort of," I answered, trying to avoid the truth.

"Well here have a go at this."

Frank proceeded to unfold a piece of music called 'The Magpie,' a composition by Australian Jazz pianist Ted Nettlebeck. As Frank spread the sheet of music across the piano, a jolt of fear struck as I realised that this music would be impossible for me to play. It looked as though a few magpies had printed the score simply by walking across it. Quick as a flash, I grabbed the music and handed it back to Frank.

"I lied to you" I said.

Although Frank was smiling at me, I could feel the stony rebuke of someone who only recently had tried valiantly to improve me in this area. The next question Frank asked was so unexpected, I didn't know how to respond.

"Can you play an aborigine jumping from behind a bush, who runs forward and spears a kangaroo?"

Had the man lost his mind? I thought, time for a smart answer. "Anyone can play crap like that" said I, playing a mindless phrase for him on the piano.

"No, I mean like this."

Once again the black flute was brandished at me as Frank played a short phrase at speed. Angry because my lesson wasn't going well for me, I said,

"Anyone could have played that!"

"Try this" said Frank, then played each note for me. Two notes represented the Aborigine; these three were of him jumping from behind the bush and the last one was his spear striking the kangaroo. It now became obvious to me that each note had been chosen with careful deliberation and had been executed at various speed, attack and necessary effect to enable me to see the absolute logic of what he had improvised.

"Do you write anything?" was Frank's final question. Once again my answer must have angered him,

"I'm a player" I said proudly, "Let's leave the writing to those who want to make money from it."

"Well let's hear you play something," yelled Frank.

Frustration had replaced anything musical I might have played, so instead a short run commencing in the lower register and progressing up the piano was all I had left within me. I watched in disbelief as Frank put pen to blank manuscript and began notating something. Whatever it was, he seemed deeply involved and finished a few minutes after me.

"Here" he said, "take this home and learn to read it. Perhaps you'll recognise something of yourself when you play it."

" Is that what I just played?"

"You'll know when you read it," said Frank.

I became deeply aware that as an aspiring Jazz musician, I would have to learn to read music, be able to express my music in writing through the medium of composition and also develop some personal concepts relating to improvisation.

Frank was one of a few Jazz musicians who had a refreshingly positive attitude to the Jazz Rock genre. Like myself he loved the work of the then-emerging definitive recording groups like *Blood Sweat and Tears* and *Chicago*.

I remember him leaning against a wall, pulling out a packet of Marlboro cigarettes, three of which had been carefully emptied of tobacco and replaced with marijuana.

"I smoke these because I want to keep up with the younger generation. Do what they do. Think about what captures their imagination and of course tune in to what they are listening to. You see the music that we play and love might not be around much longer. Young kids don't want to listen to what they consider old music. They want something of their own and that's why I'm excited about hearing brass sections and young musicians improvising, especially on radio stations that would never play one note of Jazz. I know that these are the radio stations the next generation is listening to. Perhaps Jazz may live on and broaden its audience."

"You're not trying to tell me that jazz is dead?" I asked in horror.

"I hate to sound like a wise old owl, but anything that refuses to adapt and change with the times dies," said Frank finishing every last gasp his joint had to offer.

Another sport Frank and I enjoyed was arguing, especially about music. I would invite him home for dinner and then we would drive to the gig together. One night I decided to attack his mentor, Oscar Peterson.

"You know Frank" I said, "Oscar Peterson can be bloody boring and I mean I've got so many of his albums, but he plays the same licks on each one. It's like only the melodies change, so that he can show off his technical brilliance.

I don't think you would find an ounce of artistic temperament in his body, otherwise he would surely play different things on each album, sometimes perhaps playing something like Bill Evans, or Paul Bley, even Thelonious Monk?"

Frank's expression remained blank, ignoring my vitriolic point of view. However I hit a nerve with the comment, "or something honest from deep inside his soul," instead of all that show-off bullshit he plays every time.

"Bob, it's a pity to find out that you don't 1understand the business of music."

"I'm prepared to be enlightened, that is, if you can convince me."

And so began a parable that not only would win Frank the argument, but explain some basic truths that would be difficult for anyone else in Melbourne to comprehend.

"My story is about a young pianist, an artistic and innovative man, sort of like you Bob. Concerned that his talents may never receive a fair go in Australia, he saves enough money to travel to New York. He pounds the pavements of Manhattan trying to convince people of his talents. This is New York, the toughest city in the world; nobody wants to know about him, or his problems. Pretty soon he is wandering the streets. Having run out of money, hunger gnaws at him. Suddenly he hears the sound of music and laughter coming from a penthouse high above. He decides that this must be a party, and the only way to survive is to gatecrash that party. He is successful in his efforts and after helping himself to food and drink, becomes ecstatic at feeling normal again. He heads for the piano and plays what is in his mind, a pile of shit. Perhaps an angry reaction to his treatment so far in this city. Feeling very satisfied, he was about to leave the piano when a hand taps him on the shoulder. "I want you to know that I really enjoyed your performance," commented the well-dressed stranger.

"Do you think you could play like that again?"

"Why?" asked the young pianist

"My name is John Holmes, I'm the President of CBS records and if you can play like that, I'm prepared to sign you to a ten-year recording contract that will not only make you rich, but also famous."

In desperation the young man agrees. Pretty soon he is a household name in Jazz around the world, sort of like Oscar Peterson. Although he hates every bar of music he records, he knows how to resolve the problem and he must wait ten years until his contract expires.

At last the day arrives, he cancels his contract with CBS, rings the Manager of Carnegie Hall and books a date for a very special concert, a concert that features himself. Of course because of his profile, the concert is a sell-out. He walks up to the microphone and addresses his eager fans,

"Ladies and gentlemen, I want to thank you for being here at this special event. I know many of you have purchased my recordings, but unfortunately these don't represent the real *me*, but tonight you'll hear what to date I have not been able to offer. You'll hear my true artistry."

And with that, his head bent over the keyboard, he begins to play his thing.

At first it takes so much concentration, he breaks out in beads of sweat but then as he relaxes and lets go he begins enjoying himself and just before interval he allows himself the luxury of looking up at the audience to find Carnegie Hall totally empty."

I remained speechless and to this day, I could swear on a stack of bibles that such was the genius of Frank, that he had improvised this story as we drove along, in order that I appreciate its ramifications. The first being that Jazz greats like Oscar Peterson play consistently because they are expressing real and honest ideas spontaneously. The spirit of improvisation reveals the inner personality, which is normally a consistent identity. The next lesson from Frank's parable was that recording executives demand that artists display a consistency of style in order to maintain sales. It was axiomatic that artists retained loyal fans won over in previous recordings, whilst attempting to broaden their audience with a current release. Frank's story also warned young musicians like me who may be tempted to try their luck in New York that it could be a disastrous move, and if one was discovered it would be in unusual circumstances, and that success often meant huge personal sacrifice. Frank's story also raised the issue of artists' responsibility to their audience. I made a mental note that should I be lucky enough to get to Carnegie Hall, I would play with such excitement, imagination and honesty that not one member of the audience would want to leave.

I met Frank Smith in the twilight of his career, even then he was a gifted musician with the ability to play unbelievably inspiring improvisations. I kept imagining what it must have been like to play with him when he was young and fit. Frank was at a stage where he hated every note he played. It took a lot of effort to roll up to a gig and in the end I was the one who insisted that he continue playing. The only reason Frank agreed was due to the fact that I made sure we played low-profile, one-off gigs. This association only lasted for one year as Frank's health began to fail. I remember visiting him in St Andrews Hospital. It was here I met the composer of 'The Magpie,' pianist Ted Nettlebeck. Frank told us that upon his discharge from hospital he was taking up a position in the house band at Hobart's newest nightspot, The Wrest Point Casino.

"It's good money and an easy job," Frank explained. I never saw him again but a few months later the word got out that Frank had died on the job in Hobart. This was just a few months before I left the Fred Bradshaw Quartet and join the Ted Vining Trio.

At that time, one of the attractions of Jazz was that those who performed it had to be fresh and interesting each time they played. Age, reputation and past glory did not count. This was music of the moment. On stage Frank and I were equals who enjoyed matching musical skills, but off-stage it was Frank who was the Jazz icon. It was his knowledge, maturity and wisdom we shared, with the result that some of Frank's ideas were embedded in my subconscious, where they would continue to be an ongoing influence for the rest of my musical career.

FLOORSHOW NIGHTS — JAMMING AT THE TROIKA

J OE MARCHESANI WAS not a Jazz musician, but rather the
sort of player who worked in Melbourne's club scene.

It was therefore surprising when he rang me, begging that I
take over his gig at the Troika nightclub.

"That's impossible Joe; you know I don't read music. It's OK
for you, you can read fly shit going up a wall. I'm sorry but I
couldn't cut that sort of gig."

Rather than taking no for an answer, Joe's voice became more
desperate, "You've got to help me; I'm in big trouble and need to
disappear for a while."

It sounded like a line from a gangster movie, but I knew Joe
hung out with Melbourne's gangster element. You could see them
at the Carlton Football Club each Saturday. I remember trying
to gain access to a bar underneath the Alf Gardiner stand. As a
member I was entitled to move freely on the club's premises, but
on this day a young gentleman with that slick, well-dressed Mafia
look, stepped up to me, stuck something metallic in my ribs and
said in a broad Australian accent,

"Sorry mate this section's for Carltonians only."

This was the crowd that Marchesani was involved with and I
knew he was reputed to be a compulsive gambler who probably
owed them thousands.

"Don't worry Bob; it will be a piece of cake. We do the same
show with the same acts every night. The boss, Jordan Bakalov,
hates change. I've been playing the same songs every night for
eight months. I'll send you a tape and with your hearing you'll
have no trouble playing the show. Besides you can stick the music
up on the piano and pretend you're reading it.

Being a young father I know you could use the money. You'll be
fed each night and when you're not playing the show, play whatever

you want. In fact I've just booked Brian Jones on drums, who's very excited about playing with you and as you will be Musical Director, you can employ whichever bass player you want."

There are certain moments in one's life when driven by a fierce desire to achieve that foolish decisions are made. My decision to take on the job at the Troika was such a moment and it hastened my mid-life crisis.

I was on tenderhooks right from the start of my first evening at the Troika. I had employed my trusted friend Ray (Curly) Martin on bass and Brian Jones on drums. Brian had the best record cover knowledge of Jazz I have ever encountered. He had a photographic memory and could quote volumes of facts, as well as countless trivia gleaned from the back of the hundreds of 12inch LPs he possessed. Brian also kept up with the latest obscure Jazz artists like Denny Zeitlin and Lonnie Liston Smith, names that Ray and I had never heard of.

We were a Jazz trio, bonded by the fact that our favorite musicians made up the rhythm section of the Cannonball Adderley Quintet. Brian's favorite drummer was Louis Hayes; Ray's favorite bassist was Sam Jones and my favorite pianist, Joseph Zawinul.

After we had played three tunes, the club owner, Jordan Backalov, approached the bandstand saying,

"You are playing Jazz, this is a Russian Night club. For us Jazz is unsuitable."

Undeterred by this warning we played on.

Next came the floorshow, a buxom blonde vocalist, Irene Adrianne, sang songs obviously popular with Russian audiences, climaxing in the hit 'Kalinka' that was guaranteed to have the customers up on their feet, vodka glasses raised triumphantly.

There was a loud and spirited sing-along with a traditional accelerando at the end. The musical term 'accelerando'is obviously important in Russian music, as the next artist, balalaika player Paul Pavlov strummed his way through a programme of well-known Eastern European instrumentals.

Next came Gypsy violinist Frank Zorz, who played a medley of classical favorites, climaxing with a Hungarian Czardas, a gypsy folk dance. Following this, a small group of Cossack dancers, really fit dudes dressed in Georgian military outfits, hit the dance floor with such physical prowess as to leave the band, the audience and themselves breathless. And as if this wasn't enough, Jacki Varney, a beautiful young, model-like figure draped in silk and mink feathers, would do her contemporary dance.

Somehow using every inch of my ability to hear and follow, I had faked my way through the whole show; all that remained was to see if they had noticed I had not read their music. Jacki was first to come and collect her charts. She thanked me and said

"You probably know my father."

"No" I replied innocently.

"I'm Jack Varney's daughter; he's a famous guitarist and President of the Musicians' Union."

Even though I was a member of the Union, my profile was so low that there was little chance that Jack would know me. Irene collected her charts, smiled and said,

"Don't worry, Marchesani told me and besides you play my songs better than most floorshow pianists."

Pavlov and the Cossack just grunted as if to say, "You aren't Russian and you'll never know this music." The last person to approach me was violinist Frank Zorz; he spoke in soft tones,

"I just loved your Jazz playing" he said, "You know I listen to mostly Jazz people like Oscar Peterson, Charlie Parker, Miles Davis and Stephan Grappelli, of course."

I interrupted, "Have you heard of Stuff Smith?"

Frank smiled,"Yes' he replied, "He is one of the great black American innovators on violin."

"Frank, this is unfair; here you are a classical guy who knows more about Jazz than I do about classical."

"I find classical music involves having a good technique and reading skills" said Frank, "By the way do you read music?"

"I wish I could," I answered, feeling deflated at how easily Frank had detected my cover-up in this area.

"It's just a skill " said Frank gently, "Here, take my music home and learn to read some of the notes, and when you get them right, I'll let you know. By the way I'm not really a gypsy violinist, I'm just Hungarian. He laughed, "Let's retire to the bar and talk Jazz" and so began a lasting lifetime friendship.

So I had survived my first club gig at the Troika. I thought that soon I will have mastered the floor show, convinced Jordan of the need for Jazz and as time progressed, educated the chef Jim about serving the band steak instead of leftover beef stroganoff.

Although Jordan was Yugoslavian and therefore Jazz was foreign to his cultural upbringing, I managed to convince him that Jazz was indeed an important international language.

The famous Benny Goodman had taken a Jazz orchestra to Russia and I made sure Jordan saw the albums Goodman had recorded there. His interest intensified when I mentioned that because the club remained open until 4 am some of these famous people might visit us. Jordan even agreed to reserve a table should I let him know.

I did actually reserve a table when word got out that Jazz bassist Abraham Laborial was going to visit the club. I was excited because here was my chance to experience meeting face-to-face with my first Afro-American musician, a musician whose talent I was aware of, having heard him play on a Gary Burton album I listened to at home. I remember rushing to the front entrance, introducing myself to Laborial and drummer Harry Blazer and personally showing them to their table. I then called Jordan Backalov to their table. "Jordan, these guys are famous musicians from America, like what we have been talking about."

"Gentlemen, welcome to the Troika" said Jordan, "You are my personal guests."

Our Trio then proceeded to play a set of Jazz.

All this happened in the mid-seventies. Most of my life had been spent in Melbourne, so I was totally unaware there were cultural differences between Australian and American musicians.

For instance American musicians made a habit of dining out after gigs, then retiring to sleep with a stomach full of ribs, chowder, pork, bacon, beans and large helpings of fruit pie, topped with cream. Australians normally dined between six and eight pm. These differences would remain a source of wonder to me.

As we played our set I could sense Laborial was feeling our

groove, enjoying the energy and detecting our musical approach to be unmistakably Afro-American.

At the end of the set I walked towards his table and much to my surprise he rose from his chair, arms opening to engulf me. For a split second I thought this is was a dangerous position to be in.

I had heard rumours that black musicians secretly carried razors in their shoes. Will I feel his knife enter between my shoulder blades? But that didn't happen; instead I heard him say, "Oh man, that was really something!"

At the same time I experienced phenomenal warmth from him, warmth that said I respect you and I appreciate what you are doing. It was as if I had been blessed by the Pope.

This was the sort of love I had been seeking all my life. Perhaps if I treated local Jazz musicians I admired in this way, it could catch on in Australia!

That single incident at the Troika had a marvellous impact; it restored my self-confidence and reinforced many personal beliefs about how and why I should play Jazz.

By this time I had memorized the floorshow and was paying more attention to the behaviour of the customers.

One night a large, burly Russian fellow was sitting at a table opposite a young Asian woman. Her beauty was obvious to every man in the room. I found myself entranced, not just because she was young and beautiful, but also she sat opposite her man, her eyes only for this Russian, whose face and demeanor seemed to delight in ignoring her beauty and the signals of genuine love and devotion she consistently showed him.

It was in the middle of the set when I heard them raise their voices. They had started to argue in a strange language, then the unthinkable happened. He rose from his chair and spat a huge wad of saliva that landed bang in the middle of her beautiful young face. Enraged beyond imagination, I left the bandstand determined to punch his lights out, even though he was almost twice my size. Before I could lay a hand on him, six pairs of strong arms grabbed me and literally dragged me across the dance floor, so I kept repeating, "I'll kill that bastard, so help me I will!"

I remember finishing up in Jordan's office, Jordan thanking the five regular customers who had helped him drag me away.

They left us alone for what I thought would be my dismissal. Instead Jordan offered me some vodka and as I slowly gulped it down, he said "You're obviously not a man of the world. You are immature and foolish.

You are foolish because you tried to punch someone who I know would surely kill you. You are immature because a professional musician never leaves a bandstand and you are not a man of the world because you don't understand polygamy.

That man is a regular customer; he owns four plantations in Indonesia, that is his third wife. He follows Islamic custom that allows him to treat all his wives like baggage if he wants to. I suggest you go home and broaden your thinking and act like a man of the world."

A few weeks later I arrived at the Troika and was immediately summoned into Jordan's office.

"I made a hard decision last night" said Jordan. "I was sick of the same old floorshow; it had lost its magic, so I sacked them all, but don't worry the new acts are similar.

In fact they're waiting for you in the office; they want to show you your new music."

At last, for me the game was over. That evening everybody in the club became aware of how incompetent the band was. It was so obvious that I didn't bother trying to fake my way through their charts. I just played stuff I knew wouldn't match their act; they had to perform feeling the ridicule from our regular customers. Everyone was embarrassed.

Not wanting to risk any further humiliation I told Jordan the truth, accepted dismissal and the loss of a week's pay and drove home knowing I had allowed myself to be placed in a position where I betrayed one of my innermost principles, which was to be honest to all people at all times.

There were people now who could truthfully proclaim, "Sedergreen is a fraud."

I promised myself never to let that happen again.

PROSPECT HILL

F RED BRADSHAW, FRANK SMITH and a whole host of other musical chums had warned me: don't go anywhere near Ted Vining. He's a harsh and unsympathetic monster and will ruin the way you play.

"Not so" said my newly acquired, curly-haired, bass-playing friend Ray Martin, a kid from Colac who wanted to play what he called 'black toyme' like his idol Sam Jones.

"He's heart broken" he said, "he lost the pianist that played with him for so many years and he's tried almost everyone, to no avail. He's so down he might even give up playing."

And so I turned up at The Prospect Hill Hotel in Kew (now Dan Murphy's) on a Monday night, to play with the monster. Tom, the hotel's manager, showed me to a little upright piano. There was a contact mike from which a small lead was connected to the hotel's pathetic PA system— hardly sufficient to deal with a diabolically frenetic Jazz drummer. Sensing my discomfort Tom joked;

"You see we always want to give you musicians the best possible equipment to play on; we can't stand complaints."

I immediately took a liking to this dark, tall and crazy Englishman. Then Ted walked in. The first thing I noticed was a gold chain around his neck and the loose and flowing colourful top and cotton trousers, creased and sharp enough to slice toast.

"Let's play" he commanded.

I chose a piece that could not fail, 'You are my Sunshine' in the key of F. The groove Ted, Ray and I generated really swung and all of a sudden Ted exploded, saying words like,

"Yeah! Great! Boss! Gas kid!"

Other sounds of satisfaction emanated from the drum chair. To this guy, playing Jazz was as good as having sex, if not better, and the sounds he made exploded into a musical orgasm. No other musician has encouraged me this much, so openly. Suddenly my confidence began to soar and I began to take risks I had never taken before with the music. Even in the breaks, Ted would talk about how great it was that he'd found someone he could at last play with. Just before I left, he put his arm around my shoulder and said, 'Hey listen kid, do you know any Jazz tunes?"

"Fuck," I thought, we'd been playing Jazz all night. In my mind any tune could be turned into Jazz.

"Stuff like 'Round Midnight'. Have you got 'Cooking, Working and Relaxing'?"

"I'm not into that sort of stuff" I answered.

A few weeks later Ted added trumpeter, Keith Stirling to the band. The only time I ever understood Keith was when he asked me, "Do you have any Freddie Hubbard records?" I gladly lent him a couple. Keith and I were a mismatch musically and he would say the oddest things after each gig, like "music is the face of a drum." I spent many sleepless nights trying to fathom out this mystery. Next came, "Look son, imagine there are razor blades in certain cracks of the piano."

As he was older than me I tried my best to play softer, but it didn't work.

This must be an important gig I thought as one night a rather large man with broad shoulders and a ruddy complexion, armed with microphones and tape recorder, came to record the band. His name was Bill Thomson and he'd come all the way from Sale. What dedication I thought. Yes, the music we were making must be special! At the end of the night, Tom, the manager came up to me and said,

"I thought that was a truly shithouse performance under ideal conditions. Didn't you?"

We both howled with laughter and that remark became a tradition at the end of each gig.

Some years later trumpeter Keith Hounslow asked me to join his Jazz Hounds for the first concert by a new body, The Jazz Action Society. We composed a suite called 'A truly shithouse performance under ideal conditions'. No one objected to the music nor the title.

Ted replaced Keith with the saxophonist Graeme Lyall.

I couldn't believe it when Ted sacrificed Keith rather than me.

When I asked Ted the reason for this and what he said to Keith, he replied, "I just told him that the direction we were taking was too sad."

I remembered Graeme and Frank Smith practising together. Graeme had the firmest and most solid tone and could really burn technically. We played the grooviest version of the song 'The Shadow of your Smile', with Graeme exploring every possible extension of chords and melody at lightning speed, leaving every horn player in the audience wide-eyed.

"Good on you Graeme" I thought, "If you've got it, flaunt it"

Not so Ted, who called it showing off. I was crestfallen the night Ted dispensed with Graeme.

"Who are we going to get?" I asked incredulously.

"I'll get Boof" said Ted.

I didn't know who Boof was.

"But before I get Boof, I'll have to get Barry."

Barry Buckley was a bassist who had filled in with Freddie Bradshaw at Kenilworth. His notes were long and strong. I had never met Boof but I'd seen his shadow in the rear view mirror of my car when parked outside Rae's house in Pascoe Vale.

"Who's that?" I asked her.

"That's Brian Brown she said," he's in the Channel Nine band and lives in our street."

Strangely enough Boof turned out to be the same Brian Brown. Unlike Graeme's shiny tenor sax, Brian's looked old and worn.

Barry suggested we play a Freedom Rider.

"I haven't a clue," I muttered to Brian.

"Don't worry," said Brian softly, "just hang in there with us and only play if you feel comfortable."

What followed was a mystery and I was at a loss as to how I could contribute. Whatever I played was in the wrong place and at the wrong time. The other three walked off the stage elated. Sensing my disappointment, Brian said,

"Playing free is an adventure; you'll gravitate towards it

after a while."

This was a time when there had been no recording of modern Jazz in Melbourne for some years. Then along came Bill Hawtin of Jazz Note Records. At last The Trio would be in on an album. I was taken to an old wooden hall called The Viaduct Theatre. Perhaps the theatre should have been condemned but the piano certainly needed to be: it was pathetic. Undeterred we played a weird selection of tunes and of course Barry suggested a Freedom Rider. Unbeknownst to anybody, some carpenters were working outside the 'studio' door. In the middle of a quiet section, the sound of an electrical buzz saw split the air and penetrated the microphones. Strangely enough this added to the music, which we called 'Saw and Satisfied'.

Shortly after, Ted became Co-ordinator of Melbourne's Moomba Jazz Festival, sponsored by Sanyo and a host of other important organisations. It was committed to bringing out the best America had to offer. Lucky me! I was now part of Ted's Trio, a Trio that proved it was capable of playing along side anybody. And Ted made sure his Trio would open each concert. I couldn't believe the names that were mentioned: Count Basie, Oscar Petersen, Sarah Vaughan and Dizzy Gillespie … and soon I would be amongst them.

ALLAN LEE STORY

FOR ME, PLAYING jazz with someone like Ted Vining would be akin to a golfing enthusiast playing a round with Greg Norman.

As a teenager, I had spent many evenings at my favourite jazz haunt, the *Downbeat Club*, located in a laneway near the corner of Bourke and Russell Street. The house band consisted of: Allan Lee on vibes, Tony Gould on piano, John Grunden on bass, and of course, Ted on drums. To my mind, these guys were awesome jazz musicians. I remember the nights when visiting American tenor sax players from hard-driving rhythm and blues groups such as *The Goofers*, or *Freddie Bell and the Bellboys*, dropped in for an after-hours jam. These bands had been the major act featured at the famous *Tivoli* theatre just around the corner. I also remember the inner joy of knowing that pretty soon they would be unable to do anything else except play their arses off. It was fun watching visiting American internationals being caught off guard by the sheer power the quartet displayed. To see the look of surprise and delight on their faces as the Aussies stretched them to the limit of their ability. The intense energy and authority displayed by the quartet would challenge anyone sitting in with them. These were guys to be admired from a distance. As a schoolboy, I had watched Ted star on the Channel 7 show *Cool for Cats* whilst doing my homework, so for me it was a big deal when I was asked to join Allan's quartet.

Allan, or Alex as we called him, was an outrageous character with a bent sense of humour. He worked at *Thomas' Record Shop* underneath the *Southern Cross Hotel*. I remember walking into the store, browsing around and choosing a handful of albums that I was really keen on acquiring.

As I presented them to Allan, he would say with a stern

expression on his face, "Bobby, you can't be serious about buying this pile of nonsense! What you need is this..."

He would then triumphantly hold up a disc that he decided was too important for me to ignore. It would either be an artist that I'd never heard before, some obscure new talent like *Airto Moirera*, or someone he knew I liked like *Stanley Turrentine*, or his own favourite *Milt Jackson*. Alex would then proceed to confiscate the albums I had chosen, wrap up his selections, and I'd always end up walking away with a bunch of albums he had decided was right for me.

Allan was a persuasive salesman and his work environment often influenced his attitude to music. This was great because he did not fuss or worry about what style of jazz he'd play. He knew about the history and development of jazz, accepting it as Afro-American music that had originated in America, but with influences from Europe and Latin America. Caught up in the latest trends, he'd experiment with whistles, berimbau, congas, hand drums and various percussion instruments. Because he had access to the latest recordings at Thomas', he knew what directions jazz was taking, and recognised new developments. It was a fun band to be in due to the repertoire we played, which included elements of sambas, calypso, fusion, funk feels, John Lewis compositions and blues. Allan was open to input from band members and I remember introducing the Freddie Hubbard tune 'Little Sunflower' to him. He immediately fell in love with it, and as was his way, the band played it at the next gig. Alan and I shared the idea that it didn't matter what one played, as long as it was exciting and moved the audience in some way. Allan did not fancy himself to be a man with a mission; he just wanted to play straight jazz and have as much fun as possible.

Allan was a very bossy bandleader. During rehearsal he would stop the band and in a commanding tone yell at the unfortunate musician who had made a mistake with the lyrics: "No! It doesn't go like that, it goes like this!"

He would then proceed to play the passage on the vibraphone, expecting the offender to get it right during the next try, often laughing at his discomfort when he didn't. If the musician could not play the correct phrases after three repeats, a combination of frustration and impatience would force Allan to take his place at his instrument, leaving the note-wrong musician in a state of embarrassment. Allan was a bandleader who many might say lacked sensitivity, but I knew his tough exterior was nothing more than a shell protecting a soft and vulnerable soul that loved jazz with a blazing intensity.

I seemed to have a knack of being at the right place at the right time. Not long after joining Ted's Trio, we were asked to make an album and only months after joining Allan's band, Bill Hawtin of *Jazz Note Records* wanted to make an album with the current quartet: Ted, Allan, myself and my mate Ray Martin, whose bass lines closely resembled those of our favourite American bassist, Sam Jones.

On the morning of the recording session, Allan sent me on an unusual expedition to visit the homes of all of Melbourne's recognised vibes players. My mission was to pick up their set of bars. I was surprised to find out that the bars they hit can hang down just like a ladder hangs from a helicopter. Feeling like a bullion broker, the boot of my Valiant laden with gold bars, I arrived at the recording to find an anxious Allan. His frustration was increasing because he could not tell which set of bars would come up best in the studio. After two hours of this madness he decided to use his own original bars, leaving me the job of repacking and re-delivering them when the session finished.

About this time, the ABC broadcasted an extremely popular jazz programme. It was called *Music to Midnight*. Ian Neil presented the show, which had evolved from an earlier show called *Relax with Me* presented by Arch McCurdy. The ten to midnight slot was perfect for broadcasting a spectrum of jazz. As a regular listener of the show, it was relaxing and enjoyable to get into bed and appreciate the slick mix of jazz created before falling asleep round about midnight. Most of the band tuned in to the programme, and I'm sure Allan knew our album would get airplay. He had produced a selection of jazz that was easily marketable. He planned for our album to include: blues, a funky samba, two contemporary pop tunes, the modal piece 'Little Sunflower' which

I had introduced, and a minor mid-tempo groove – each track short enough to ensure airplay. Both Allan's and my solos were energetic and bubbly, while Ted and Ray provided solid time, with every note accessible to the listener.

Ian Neil picked up on this, and as a result, over a two-year period, played a track from our album almost every night. He often chose 'Little Sunflower' and the blues, both of which featured articulate piano solos. It was pleasurable to be relaxed in bed and hear Ian announce the track after it was aired: "That was the Allan Lee quartet from Melbourne with Ted Vining on drums, Ray Martin on bass and that marvellous pianist Bob Sedergreen."

Ian would say this every night. I loved him for saying this, because until now, no one had ever called me marvellous. Perhaps it was egotistical to enjoy hearing my music and my name on national radio, but at that stage of my life, I needed to feel good about myself, and the recognition that would enhance my profile.

I remember making it my business to call in at the ABC studios in Sydney so I could have the pleasure of meeting my favourite jazz radio presenter Ian Neil. Ian looked like a young prime ministerial type, with grey sideboards, friendly eyes and a ruddy complexion that suggested he probably enjoyed partying. The first thing I found out was that Ian's genuine knowledge about music was a result of possessing a photographic memory. I asked him all sorts of questions about the tracks he played on his programme. I wanted him to know that I was a real fan and a genuine listener, not just any artist featured on his programme. He was very supportive of my musical efforts. I think Ian was responsible for rocketing my profile nationally, because people would ring me and say, "Bob, I heard you on the radio the other night."

The telephone often rang with listeners from various parts of the Commonwealth letting me know I was on air. The album continued to receive regular airplay for two years. Ian seemed to be part of the audience at every important concert I played, and even though nothing was said, I felt he was the one who nurtured my career behind the scenes – a secret patron. At one stage, Ian was adviser to the Music Board of the Australia Council and used his influence to make sure any group I was part of would be recommended as most worthwhile.

Allan loved hanging out with perhaps the most mischievous jazzman in the Commonwealth, John Sangter. Sangter had given Allan the nickname 'Spotty'.

Both 'Spotty and Sango' were men tinged with a touch of madness, both irrepressible, both extremely childish and often found in a state of advanced intoxication. Both simply loved playing the vibes. They were two larrikins, each one responding to the most ridiculous challenges from the other, be it pie eating, jumping off a pier, or playing a trick on an unsuspecting stranger.

Allan's approach and reputation ensured he was one of the most talked about musicians at the time. Allan could either be very positive about what we were going to play and how we're going to play it, or he could be a drama king, who yelled at musicians and became hopping mad, even to the point of violence with musicians who were unable to carry out his orders.

We made the recording in 1973. At that time my day job was with the controversial newspaper *The Sunday Observer*. Nobody at work talked to me about jazz, not even my secretary, a pretty young lady named Liz. This was the age of disco dancing – jazz bands were yielding to DJs and go-go dancers. In fact *The Ted Vining Trio* had just landed a gig at a huge disco off Flinders Street. Imagine my surprise when my young and extremely attractive secretary arrived at the disco we were then playing at, arm in arm with Allan Lee.

"Who's that lady with Alex?" I asked Ted.

"That's Allen's fiancée Elizabeth, she's the daughter of Alex Doherty. Her dad is a fantastic saxophone player, who influenced most of today's young players."

The next day Elizabeth came round to my office and said with a smile, "I didn't know you played piano."

"That's okay," I said, wondering why would this young lady who had mentioned she admired Tony Gould, know anything about me? I was after all, the new kid on the block.

Soon after this, Allan and Liz were married. Rae and I were invited to the service at the Unitarian church in East Melbourne.

What a statement they made: the groom in a bright purple suit, and instead of the bridal march, Tony Gould played the Bobby Timmons jazz classic 'Moanin' on the pipe organ, swelling to a brilliant crescendo at the amen ending, and timed perfectly to allow the bride and groom to make a hasty exit into a waiting cab.

CONVERSATION WITH AN ART FARMER

I WAS STARING at the ceiling in my office at the Cook and Heathcote Printers in South Melbourne when the phone rang. It was Allan Lee speaking in excited tones:

"You won't believe this Bobby but there's a package of Jazz musicians just landed in town and guess who we're going to see this morning?... Jimmy Smith, I'm just dying to meet him, aren't you?"

Allan was in one of those moods when no one else could match his enthusiasm.

"Who else is there?" I asked.

"Well there's Dave Brubeck, Paul Desmond, Kenny Burrell and a whole host of others. It's a press conference. All we have to do is pretend we're reporters. C'mon Bobby this will be the chance of a lifetime to hang out with them."

The musicians were interned in a room full of gloom at The Old Melbourne Motor Inn. Maybe it was too early, maybe it was because of jetlag but these Jazz greats made it obvious they weren't in the mood to mingle. Kenny Burrell buried his face in The Age newspaper, Dave Brubeck and Paul Desmond kept up a continual confidential conversation. Jimmy Smith had that mean look on his face that translated into 'don't come close honky if you value your life.'

The vibes were not good and I realised the situation was hopeless so I adjourned to the bar, which despite the early hour had just opened. On the stool next to me perched a handsome, dark African American with beautiful black hair and soft enquiring eyes. He was not dressed conservatively like the others, preferring a casual shirt and denims. He too ordered a Scotch:

"Where are you from?" I asked.

"Vienna." He replied.

"What's the attraction in Vienna?" I enquired.

"I'm in love with the place," answered the stranger, "my lady is from there and in fact my child was born there."

"But it has to be difficult for you to adapt to a new culture and be surrounded by whites?"

'I know what you mean," said the stranger, "but I just love it. Take my mother in law for instance. Most guys hate their mother in laws, but I love mine"

"Really" I said (not wanting to tell him I felt the same way.)

"You see, she's Viennese and my baby's black. Now just imagine how I feel when I see that white woman kissing that baby's head and witness the love that's flowing between them."

"Gee, sounds like you're really converted, but let me ask you this."

Before I put the question to him I knew how much patriotic brainwashing Americans had been subjected to from childhood.

"Let's say that America declares war on Austria and you have to decide. Are you an American first or an Austrian?"

The stranger thought about it for a while before answering.

"I guess I'll always have to be an American somehow."

"And what do you do over there?" I enquired.

"I play trumpet and flugelhorn in a radio orchestra."

Before I could tell him I play piano, Allan Lee had broken away from the cordon of local reporters and was making a bee line for Jimmy Smith, his right arm stretched out preparing for a hand shake.

"Is he a friend of yours?" the stranger asked quietly.

"Why?" I responded.

"It's just that Jimmy holds a black belt in karate. Go and tell your friend to be cautious in his approach." It was too late, but Allan and Jimmy got on just fine and when they had finished their conversation, I asked Allan;

"Who's that guy sitting on his own at the bar?"

"That's Art Farmer of course" replied Allan

"Wow he's the nicest jazz musician I've ever met" I said.

"And he plays like it too" said Allan.

I returned to the bar and sitting next to Art said.

"I'm really sorry I didn't know who you were" and then I started gushing the usual stuff about how I admired him as one of the most melodic players ever. Art just smiled and said:

"I knew you weren't a journalist all along." But my over eagerness had turned him off and he moved away to join his colleagues at the press conference which was now underway.

MELBOURNE'S MOOMBA

M OOMBA IN THE seventies was a time of street parades. Children and parents would gather along Swanston Street to watch a passing parade of bands, entertainers, jugglers, clowns like Zig *and* Zag, horse-drawn floats depicting local retailers and organisations and dance troupes from exotic parts of the world. It was Melbourne's own Mardi Gras. The name Moomba derived from an Aboriginal word meaning 'Let's get together and have fun', which people did.

All along the river were stalls where the general public could enjoy themselves with circus acts, pony rides, shooting galleries, and other fairground rides and amusements. Moomba would culminate in a series of concerts including a Jazz concert at the Sydney Myer Music Bowl.

For me it was quite a thrill to be part of a public event, to feel the inner glow of seeing one's name on the official programme and participating in a dynamic musical event. I remember playing an original tune entitled 'Calypso De Moomba' written to capture the spirit of our carnival. The Ted Vining Trio would prove to be the ideal opening act, but unfortunately in 1973, the rain poured down, leaving only a few hundred souls at the concert.

The much flaunted Brian Brown Quartet was also to play at the festival. At that time the pianist in the group was Ian Mawson, whose music seemed to take the group in a different direction. Ian's time and phrasing were in a word 'out'! His musical approach somehow seemed inward and sad. Apparently this was the approach Brian Brown and David Tolley approved.

Brian Brown played tenor sax, soprano sax and flute. His mood was always to attack, to intone, to enchant, to thread his way through the band – you could always hear Brian up front. David Tolley often chose not to play bass lines, but rather a series of responses and improvisations. The sounds he produced were of a springing nature, incredibly plucked in the higher register and bowed in the lower one. He did not play time, yet he enjoyed the fact that his bass tone and technique were highly unconventional. Tolley had been heavily influenced by Ian Bow – the art teacher at Haileybury College and had developed an artistic approach to playing music. David liked dressing in sandals and Kaftans to look like a guru.

I remember they played 'Eleanor Rigby', a Beatles hit, their version of it was so overpowering in intensity and expression that it transfixed me. I could have never guessed that a few months later I would be a member of their group.

What I could not foresee was that Ted Vining would not tolerate music that was morbid and played in a fashion that suggested that the musicians were introverts. Wanting to change the band's direction, he issued the following ultimatum:

"If you want me to stay, you have to get the fat kid from Box Hill, Bob Sedergreen, he's always happy."

Apparently Brian and David Tolley said,

"But isn't he just a Blues player?"

Ted wrapped me up in glowing terms,

"The kid swings and knows how to lift a band. If you want me to stay, then get Sedergreen."

Ted would remain my mentor for life.

BILL BASIE'S BAND

IT WAS SATURDAY afternnon when the phone suddenly rang. It was Ted. He sounded as though a dozen arrows had pierced every part of his body.

"It's the piano" he moaned, "its a pile of shit and it's out of tune. What will I do? Basie will be here at five o'clock."

It was another case of Rae to the rescue. Having been briefed, she quickly started ringing every piano tuner in Melbourne and somehow managed to find a cat in South Yarra, who apparently used coloured disks to tune pianos. I rushed out into the hall — the look on the tuner's face indicated that he would not have enough time. As five o'clock approached the tuner managed to miraculously achieve a rough tuning. Wanting to change Ted's sombre state of depression, I said, "C'mon Ted, he's only going to do this..." as I imitated a slightly out of tune *Count Basie* ending.

As if by magic, Bill Basie suddenly appeared wearing a groovy waistcoat with a large and genuine gold fob watch in one of its pockets. His face shone with a bright happy radiance like the sun. "I've just been to the races with him," pointing at Sir Hilton Nicholas, (one of the heads of the V.R.C.) "...and we backed five winners!"

Bill Basie then proceeded to empty all his pockets, each bulging with bright new bank notes. He was also happy that Sir Hilton had introduced him to all the top jockeys and trainers and even showed us his race book suitably marked.

Seizing my chance I said, "Mr. Basie, what do you think of this piano they got for you to play?"

To my amazement, he chose to play his famous ending and much to everyone's relief smiled at us and said, "It looks as though Freddie (Green) is going to be busy tonight."

He spent the whole concert beaming at the audience whilst playing the piano only when he had to.

There was a great vibe in the band room afterwards and because I'd played the warm up, I was made to feel welcome. This translated into confidence as I bounced up to one of the horn players and said, "What makes a musician want to play in this band?"

Stunned by the stupidity of my question, he could only look at me in amazement as one of his brothers said, "We all play in this band for one reason and one reason alone, and that's the tempos. No one chooses tempos better than Bill Basie."

I made a mental note to improve in this area. Choosing the right tempo was important.

Then I was allowed a few minutes alone with Basie himself. I remembered that he was famous for keeping his bands working and together, and his bands always consisted of black musicians.

"Mr. Basie" I asked, "in the past, your bands have always been black but tonight you chose to feature a white drummer. Is it because you're in Australia?"

My innocent question had turned the bandleader's sunny radiant face into a cloudy grey.

"Well," said Bill seriously "it's like this: firstly this drummer is reliable, he turns up to each gig on time, dresses smartly and executes what is asked of him very well. He doesn't do drugs or stuff like that, and what's more he practices every day to improve himself. He's always first at rehearsals and is eager to get the parts right. Now... (and his voice softened even further) "if you can find me a black drummer who is ready to do exactly the same, then please send him to me and perhaps I'll have an all-black band again."

I made a hasty and appropriate exit.

OSCAR PETERSON & JOE PASS

ONE OF BRIAN Brown's greatest passions was that Jazz musicians should find their own voice. Brownie knew the extent of Oscar Perterson's influence on my piano playing. In a special moment he took me aside and said,

"Look in the mirror, do you look like Oscar Peterson?"

"No of course not," I mumbled.

"Can you tell me exactly what Oscar Peterson is thinking at this moment?"

"Of course not" I replied.

"And how bad would you feel if you were playing a gig and Oscar Peterson turned up, leaving you nothing to play?"

Fat chance of that happening I thought to myself. Only to discover some three years later that I would be playing the warm-up for Oscar Peterson and Joe Pass at Dallas Brooks Hall for the Melbourne Moomba Jazz Festival. Ted had to look for a full-size grand, as required by Oscar's contract. In the end they had to settle for a Steinway grand piano, which had to be dropped by crane and mounted onto the stage. As for me, I got to play the little brown baby grand that was dragged up from the basement of the Masonic Centre. It was the same battle- scarred piano Basie had played, but I would have no Freddie Green to help me out.

To get back stage I had to fight my way past people clamouring in queues for what looked to be a sell-out concert. Then Oscar walked in, dressed in a smart dark gabardine coat, suit and hat. As he hung his performing clothes in the wardrobe, the organiser walked up, and wanting to impress Oscar said, "Mr. Peterson, I've saved four seats at the front for the Canadian Consul."

"I don't care about that stuff any more," said Oscar, obviously in a mood to create space between him and any conversation that people might want to engage with him.

Joe Pass was pacing up and down the band room wanting to talk to somebody. He looked small and was partially bald with a Mexican appearance. He was dressed in a colourful check jacket and rope-like bow tie.

"Joe," I said, "I was looking at your amp, it's really tiny. Do you realise there's going to be hundreds listening to you tonight. Aren't you worried about not being heard?"

Joe chuckled as he answered, "It's a new thing, it's called a Cube Amp and that one on stage puts out a 120 watts. In fact I had it specially designed for myself. You see I've a little sports car at home and I like nothing better than driving it along the beach. I just pack it and the guitar in the back and take off north from Santa Barbara."

The Ted Vining Trio walked out and played a short, hot set to open the concert. As I looked up I noticed there wasn't a spare seat in the house, apart from the four reserved for the Canadian Consul. Just before Oscar and Joe were about to go on there was a persistent knocking on the steel security door at the back of the band room. A disturbed Oscar said, "Get the security guard."

The security guard opened the door and we saw two fair dinkum country lads with large straw brimmed hats and corks hanging down from strings. They must have been turned away at the door but in a desperate attempt to get in had tried their luck at our entrance.

"G'day mate" said one.

"Is this the Oscar Peterson, Joe Pass concert?"

Before the security guard and I could say,

"Piss off it's a sell-out!"

Joe interrupted saying,

"I'm interested in them. Ask them where they come from."

"Where are you guys from?" I asked.

"He's from Swan Hill and I'm from Lake Boga," said the other.

"How far would that be from here?" asked Joe.

Prone to exaggeration I replied,

"Probably a couple hundred miles"

"What?" said Joe, "You mean these guys have driven a couple hundred miles just to see the show?"

With that he grabbed them and sat them down in the two empty front row seats reserved for the Canadian Consul.

Imagine their surprise when Joe followed Oscar onto the stage.

"Jesus, its him. It's J... J... Joe Pass," stuttered his mate in disbelief.

I had made the mistake of letting my feelings for Joe's musical styles, which I thought relied too heavily on technical virtuosity, influence my judgment of the man. At the time I thought he was big-noting about his equipment and also playing god with me and the security guard. But in later years I found out that he had been to hell and back on drugs, done prison time and pioneered a finger- picking style as well as the development of small cube-like amps. He was also known for having a red car and for being compassionate.

Just before he died, he visited Melbourne, and just by coincidence I was playing solo piano at the Piano Bar when he walked through the Hyatt. To my amazement he remembered me and started strumming an air guitar as if he were accompanying Oscar, but smiling all the while at me. Before I had a chance to talk to him, he had turned away and disappeared into the afternoon.

CARLTON STREETS

I T WAS TIME for a change — the Prime Minister Gough
Whitlam and his Deputy Lance Barnard were single-handedly
running the country. I don't know how they had the time to think
of the Arts, but they managed to reward the band I'd just joined,
the *Brian Brown Quartet*, with an arts grant.

"What's it for?" I asked David Tolley, our bassist.

"Would you believe it's just to keep the band together?"

Just as the political landscape was changing, so was Melbourne's
musical landscape. A lot of our activities would be based in the
suburb of Carlton. After all, our bandleader Brian Brown had
grown up there. I would spend most Saturdays at Princes Park
Oval, cheering on the Blues, (Carlton being my favourite footy
team.) Rehearsals would be held at Tolley's place, a two-storey
house in Nicholson Street.

As I climbed the wooden staircase leading to the second floor, I
heard the familiar sounds of Stanley Turrentine's tenor sax ('Don't
Mess with Mr. T') playing on a speaker mounted at the top of the
staircase. What a groovy welcome, I thought.

But upon entering the back door I was over powered by the
smell of oriental spices. At the kitchen stove, leaning over a wok
was David's girlfriend, Dure Dara. Exotic and dark-skinned,
her magnetic personality and speech suggested she possessed a
mischievous sense of fun.

"We're cooking a special curry, would you like some?"

I found myself recoiling in genuine horror at such an invitation.

In those days, Australians knew only about beer, meat pies,
kangaroos and Holden cars. Box Hill was roast meat and potatoes
country. "I'm sorry, I just couldn't."

'That's OK" said Brian, leaning over the wok stirring the snow
peas and even Ted seemed excited at the new tastes that were being

prepared. There were no instruments visible in the house nor was there any sort of sheet music. The first part of the rehearsal was a discussion of the nature of the curry and its ingredients. In fact, food played an important part of bonding. Sometimes when Dure wasn't cooking we would go out to Jamaica House. Carlton was considered a place for wogs and foreigners but Monty the chef and owner, attracted a new breed of diners keen to taste the newest and hottest dishes. Brian loved ordering for the band, but Tolley took compassion on me and said,

"Bob will have barbequed bird (non-spicy fried chicken) and mango juice."

After discussing food, each member of the band would express his or her feelings on the direction the music should go. Tolley and Dure were obsessed with sound. Remember this was a time when electronics was a dirty word when it came to Jazz. Tolley had already canvassed most of the music shops in Melbourne, borrowing or purchasing effects, pedals, synthesizers and the like. One day I was shown into a room where this regalia was all laid out. I called it 'the Tolley Empire'. Dure also began collecting a series of bells, cow-bells, cymbals and various other implements that made sounds when shaken or hit.

"I'm not going to be a percussionist, I'm just going to make sounds," she triumphantly proclaimed.

Tolley and Brian had already purchased AKS synthesizers. To me, these looked like small Chinese checkerboards, complete with holes and pins. The type of sound it made depended on where you stuck the pin. Tolley preferred outrageous sounds whereas Brian created sounds that flew above or below the band's spectrum. Then they turned round to me, indicating in the words of Bob Dylan that 'the times, they are a-changing' and acoustic piano was no longer acceptable and I had better equip myself suitably.

The other subjects that were raised during rehearsals were themes for our soundscapes. Tolley talked about the fun he had at Melbourne's Luna Park. Not only did it bring back childhood memories, but he recalled joy and exhilaration when riding with the kids on the big dipper and danger when going through the ghost tunnel with all its scary apparitions. Pretty soon, the whole band started talking about how this could be the basis for a wonderful piece of music which we called *The Fair*. A lot of the music we finished up playing was in fact group composition, with everyone contributing ideas.

Brian, on the other hand, enjoyed bringing wine to the rehearsals. It was always rich, dark Shiraz from Baileys of Glenrowan. In those days, wine was either for 'wogs' or 'plonkos.' Real Jazz musicians were supposed to guzzle beer. Brian had written a piece named after his favourite bottle of red, labelled 'Shiraz', and we all agreed it was a revolutionary title that should be put in the bands repertoire. Brian had also mentioned reading a novel by Katherine Susannah Pritchard, an Australian book about the wanderings of a young Aboriginal girl in Western Australia. We all agreed to push the envelope of Jazz a bit further and to do something uniquely Australian by composing music to fit the story.

Ted would then describe some of the people in the advertising world, (he was a 'column inch' man at *Southdown Press*) and then talk about the sort of Jazz and energy that we, the band, should be producing.

"There are only three drummers in the world" he would say with a smile.

"There's Elvin, Philly Joe, Art Blakey and of course me."

We would all burst out laughing, having been suitably warned of Ted's intentions.

Then the attention would turn to me. There could be no doubt that I was so different from the rest of the band.

"Well, you know what I really like to do. I like cars and I love driving and I love nothing better than pushing my family into the car and taking off on a Sunday drive to places like Warburton, Healesville, Eildon, Wilson's Prom and the back beach at Rye."

The horror on their faces at such a square, un-hip, energy-wasting activity was obvious, but Tolley came to my rescue.

"Have you ever thought about how the sounds of a Sunday drive could be turned into a composition?"

"Are you serious? I'm not much of a composer."

"At least give it some thought" said Tolley, gently closing the rehearsal.

A rehearsal where not a note of music had been played, where no manuscripts existed— just great food, wine, background music and a pool table for us to release our competitive spirits. As I was from a good, drug-free background, I'd have to cut out early before Brian (now Brownie), Dure, now (Duke) and Tolley now (Tolls) would roll the largest joints possible and mellow out.

Our performance space was located in the Paris end of Collins Street, a little coffee lounge called The Outpost Inn where our thoughts and experiments turned into music every Sunday night. The music was loud, electronic, eclectic, powerful and above all unique, pioneering and paralleling the new music that was taking place worldwide, with groups like the Mahavishnu Orchestra, the ELO and Weather Report. And that's the kind of audience we attracted: young, long-haired, articulate, well-informed and lusting for musical energy. Even sportsmen like footballer Ron Barassi would come in, sit on the floor and play chess till the early hours.

I remember one night Roland Kirk's rhythm section, including the dark-haired pianist Hilton Ruiz, walked in, not believing what they were seeing or hearing. Firstly there was Tolley's bass attached to a string of pedals like a Cry Baby Wah, a Boss phaser and flanger and a host of effects finally leading to a Fender Valve Amp. Then there was Brian playing electrified flute and saxes amplified by a large powerful Yamaha Wedge. Add to this the synthesizers Tolley and Brian had programmed to automatically release myriads of musical colours to add to the maniacal cacophony of sound that Ted Vining was serving up on the drums. Oh yes, and add to this my electric piano. I had deliberately chosen the different sound of the Wurlitzer, having heard Don Hathaway play one on his *Live* album. On top of it stood a mini Korg synthesizer. At that time, the idea of having presets and numbers was unheard of. I would have to generate the sounds by knowing the shapes of various sound waves like a saw tooth wave or a square wave. I would also need to know the effect of various vibratos, registers and how to adjust the sound filters in order to obtain the sound wanted. As the oboe has always been one of my favourite instruments, I really enjoyed manufacturing my sounds and colours. Add to this the enchanting Dure Dara with a table full of bells, boxes, metallic objects and a host of other percussive implements. Her impeccable taste and sense of timing was a perfect addition to the quartet. It also meant that we had now become a Quintet.

Anyway getting back to Roland Kirk's guys, they looked at each other as though they had entered a mad house. This wasn't the sort of Jazz they played with America's leading pioneer Roland Kirk. This was also confirmed on our first visit to Sydney. We must have had quite a reputation because promoter Horst Liepolt programmed us to play alongside Sydney's finest Jazz group, *The Jazz Coop*: Roger Frampton, Howie Smith (who had come from the USA), Jack Thorncraft and drummer Phil Treloar. This was at the old Basement. The elite of Sydney's Jazz paparazzi and their finest musicians were there. I remember uncle Don Burrows and the ABC's Ian Neil, being very sociable. Nobody was prepared for the absolute contrast between the country's two finest bands, least of all the Sydneysiders, as we were treated like superstars. We even made the famous television rock show *GTK*. So big was the impression left on the Sydney psyche that many years later, our faces and the album *Carlton Streets* would be featured in Australia's most famous Jazz film *Beyond El Rocco*. The upsurge of all this was that Horst Liepolt, the most powerful figure in Australian Jazz, (a man who would later run a Jazz club, Sweet Basils in New York,) ensured we recorded for his *44* label.

Tolley – a recognised artist, sculptor, and photographer, designed a brilliant cover featuring a Melbourne tram in Carlton. Recorded on the album was some of the most revolutionary music made by Australian musicians. Unbeknown to me at the time, it would be this album, *Carlton Streets*, which would secure our trip to Scandinavia some four years later.

There was one final lesson for me to learn. Some years later, I decided to have a pool constructed in my home in Glen Waverley. The workmen were true-blue Aussies, none had heard a bar of Jazz before; their hands and faces hardened by the continual strain of hard and honest outdoor work. As they worked I would play *Carlton Streets* loudly on my stereo, especially the track 'Flight' that included the Jazzbird orchestra and featuring Melbourne's finest brass section. The track climaxed from wailing brass to a crescendo of a fan-jet, which was recorded at Melbourne Airport.

Just before the pool was completed the foreman asked if he and the guys could come in. Drying their work boots on the mat outside, they entered the lounge room.

"Ok we've got a favour to ask you mate"

"Oh, beer all around?" I said, heading for the fridge.

"Nah mate, we want to hear your music."

"Are you serious?" I asked. "I've made a few albums."

"You know the one we want," said the foreman sternly.

"Can you describe it?" I asked

"Yeh, it's the one with the jet engine at the end."

As I played the track for them, I could not help noticing how much these true-blue Aussie workmen were enjoying the music.

As they left, the foreman turned round to me and said, "I've got another favour to ask, mate. Can we hear it again?" And that happened another four times. This left an indelible impression – that high quality Jazz music could be appreciated by anybody with an open mind. Not just those who claim to love Jazz, but by many whose minds are open to any creativity.

DIZZY TIMES

PEOPLE WERE BEGINNING to notice the Moomba Jazz concerts, especially the work of Brian Brown and his Jazzbird Orchestra. Then the word got out that we were featuring in concert with the great Dizzy Gillespie.

Dizzy was someone you could not help but admire. Nat Adderley was my all-time favourite cornetist, but if you listened to Nat, you could hear that Dizzy was one of Nat's idols too. I just loved Dizzy's approach: his bebop, his Afro-Cuban leanings, his quirky humour, his bumble bee sound, and the way that his solos originated in the high register and slowly meandered down— one of the many reasons for the nickname Dizzy. I was most excited at the thought of seeing Dizzy and his band, as well as being part of the same concert.

Once when playing a gig in Adelaide, a young lady approached me with a most staggering comment. She said Brian Brown's music always sounded 'mediaeval' in some way to her. I wish I had followed that conversation up, because she had hit on something that I knew subconsciously.

Brian loved repetition and ostinato, the drama of minor keys, the way the notes stood close together, or in intervals of 4ths or 5ths. Harmonies were duplicated in octaves; it was indeed strong musical language and a strange thought entered my head. Perhaps because Brian had been an architect, it was as if he knew how to design durable music. His own sound and approach was strong, so that 'mediaeval' tag lasted with me for a long time. None of his music sounded like bebop, or traditional; not like Gospel, and not like Blues either, so I guess it sounded mediaeval.

Brian had to write out all the parts for the orchestra and transpose them himself, which was a lot of work for little reward. He had lined up his friend Keith Hounslow to play on a section, but this section was now ready for Dizzy. It was an open F minor blow for Dizzy in seven four time. We also had the pleasure of Don Burrows joining us on Alto flute. At this time, Don was Australia's best-known Jazzman. He was also from Sydney, which meant a totally contrasting approach to Brian's. Brian and I nicknamed him Uncle Don – the uncle of Australian Jazz. The band Brian chose consisted of the best professionals we could get, all were good readers of music, with young and strong lips on brass. We were ready for Dizzy, but we were not really ready for what often happens when a famous American international visits.

I would expect a visiting musician to be humble, happy to be in Australia and inquisitive about local customs and the music scene. I would also hope they would be enjoying themselves.

Unfortunately this was often not the case. On the night before our concert, I went to see Dizzy and his band. I was a familiar face at the Dallas Brooks Hall so none of the officials stopped me going wherever I fancied. In fact, I regarded the dressing room at the back of the hall as my own. I arrived there to find Dizzy leaning against the mirror, being brow beaten by his brash young guitarist, Rodney Jones. He was saying,

"Dizzy, should I play this one, or this one, or what about this one?" He was really giving Dizzy a hard time. I thought, If I was nineteen years old and playing with a great legend like Dizzy Gillespie, I'd sit there and be quiet. However Rodney did not stop, he was so young, so brash, and so full of himself. If this was the American way, then I wanted none of it. True-blue Australians hated skiting. Just as they were about to go on, Rodney's guitar input jack broke. He could not get a sound out of his guitar. The first person he approached was George Golla, the guitarist with Don Burrow's quartet, who was doing the backup for Dizzy.

"Poor fellow," muttered George.

"All I have is my 12-string instrument, and it's bloody hard to play." Then he saw my fender quadraverb valve amp, so he approached me really nicely, asking, "Can I use your amp?" Something new seemed to take over my personality, an attitude that would remain consistent for many years. You see, this was my first confrontation with a visiting international musician.

"Hey man," I said "I heard you say that you have played with Herbie Hancock and all these great things you have done and what a great player you are. You can have my amp, but I'm going to sit in the second row and if you don't play something to me that lets me know that you've played with Herbie Hancock, I'm going to know you're shit man!"

I thought that might stun him, but he just walked out smiling. I was amazed at how easily he handled George's guitar and in the middle of the concert he looked down at me and as we made eye contact, he ripped into a chromatic Herbie Hancock lick and I knew that yeah, I had heard that lick before on one of my Herbie Hancock albums.

After the concert he came and thanked me for the amp and asked me where he could get his guitar repaired. I told him I would pick him up next morning and take him to a music store in town.

Rodney was staying at the Hilton hotel opposite the MCG. As I drove up, I saw and heard Rodney giving a free concert to some birds and a few spectators in the park opposite the hotel. As we drove into the city, he seemed anxious because I had not locked the car. When he saw how quiet the traffic was, he relaxed.

"You're not in New York now," I said.

Upon entering Brash's music store, Rodney bounced up to the manager and said, "Hey man I've got a Guild guitar here and I'd like to get it fixed."

Remember, this was on a Saturday morning, and the shop would be closed in another half hour but this did not stop Rodney from hassling my friend with comments like,

"Why can't you fix it now?"

I wasn't used to this American hassle business, and then he turned round to me and said,

"Hey man, are the prices they're asking for these guitars right? Shit forget fixing it man, can I sell this guitar to you? Okay don't worry about it; I'll get it repaired in New Zealand."

Then he said to me, "Hey man, I didn't expect to find a place where instruments are this expensive, you people are being ripped off!"

I then realised that Rodney had made his first observation

about Australia and that he now wasn't in America anymore.

Perhaps what I had experienced with Rodney would be the norm, and that it may not be as easy as I'd imagined for Americans to adapt to our ways. Yes, the language was the same, but there were many differences, which could lead to much misunderstanding on both sides. For example, Dizzy's rehearsal for Brian's concert turned out to be an eruption of misunderstandings. Dizzy came in and did his crazy dance thing, dancing around the brass section and making funny faces at the players. Dizzy had done this all of his life; it was meant to be fun and to create a relaxed vibe. But we had never experienced this before and as I looked up at Brian, I could feel the steam rising out of his collar; he was really getting mad at Dizzy dancing around the band and checking out all the parts. Finally Brian pointed at a chair and said in harsh tone,

"Sit down Diz!"

Strangely enough Dizzy obeyed Brian's order and sat down.

The vibe had vanished. When he heard the section that he was to solo on, Dizzy said,

"That's in seven four measure, I don't want to count that. Have your drummer play on one for me, solid on the bass drum, I ain't counting nothing."

On the night of the concert, Dizzy came up to me and whispered in my ear, "Are we in C minor or F minor?"

He was gone as I answered,

"You can play in either C or F minor."

Dizzy was playing about two or three feet from where I sat, his solo dead in front of my electric piano.

I should have been in seventh heaven. There I was, listening to an authentic Dizzy muted trumpet solo, played strong rising above a loud rhythm section and even louder bunch of horns, but anger swelled inside of me. You see, Dizzy forever the clown, had taken my music, the largest chart on the bandstand and turned it upside down. His face and gestures indicating to the audience that we must all be in the Southern Hemisphere. The audience understood and responded in laughter.

Once again, I should have understood that Dizzy wanted

to relax the audience. But I was young, and this was my first international concert. Using the near perfect pitch the Lord gave me, I started to echo Dizzy's phrases, turning up in volume. Brian kept looking down at me signalling, "no, no, no, don't do that". He knew that this was non-international behaviour. Besides, I had played so decently behind Don Burrows and Keith Hounslow.

Later I would be sorry for imitating Dizzy's licks during the solo that evening. The night was actually recorded and it's a pity that it was never released. The concert was a personal milestone, my first international in Melbourne. Somehow I sensed there would be more and I would never have to go to America to play with these Greats; they would come here.

Although we received a polite response from the audience, they had gone crazy for Dizzy and his own band. Somewhere deep in the psyche of Australian audiences, someone planted the idea that Australian Jazz musicians were good, but could never be as exciting as American musicians. Dizzy was presented with a large bunch of yellow daffodils, which he held awkwardly and as he was leaving the hall he saw my wife Rae approaching and presented her with the flowers. She was thrilled to have the great Dizzy Gillespie give her flowers and at that critical moment when she bent over to receive them, he pinched her on the bottom, "Ooh!" she gasped as he smiled and walked away. Yes, we were totally unprepared for Dizzy, as he was unprepared for us.

PART THREE

DIZZY TIMES

BLOWING WITH THE
BLUES EXPRESS

O N THE PALM-LINED esplanade that runs between
St. Kilda and Port Melbourne, stood two very important
landmark hotels. There's the Beaconsfield in St Kilda, now part
of Australian sporting folklore due to the death of cricketer David
Hookes and Port Melbourne's Pink Vic, wherein the part-owner,
Peter Gaudion, had established his band, The Blues Express.

As I walked through the door, clarinetist Richard Miller handed
me a cocktail. "Here, have a deadly, Smedley."

It turned out that a deadly Smedley was a double serve of
vodka, slivovitz, (plum brandy), tequila, lemon juice and tonic
water slammed onto the counter. When imbibed, it warmed the
heart, numbed the brain and loosened the tongue.

"We're handing them out to everyone: band and customers, it's
a Gaudion marketing idea."

The first thing I noticed was everybody, with the exception
of the band's drummer, Allan Browne, was in various states of
advanced inebriation. The Vic was full of friendly drunks, me
included. The lifestyle at the time was free from booze buses,
breathalyzers and bloody idiots; there was much less traffic around
and those who drove home simply had to avoid the police by using
a network of back streets. It would be impossible to negotiate such
routes today.

After a successful stint at the Vic, the band transferred to The
Beaconsfield. People came to listen to the music; some had come to
dance and some had come for the happy ambience associated with
New Orleans. During the breaks, members of the band mingled
with the guests in bouts of drinking and merriment.

The band consisted of me, Peter Gaudion on trumpet and
vocals, Richard Miller on reeds, Allan Browne on drums, (both
had been members of the legendary Red Onions Jazz Band that

had toured the world in the sixties), trombonist Mal Wilkinson, and bassist Derek Capewell (who was already considered an international, having performed with the famous Johnny Dankworth and Cleo Lane).

Deep down I knew Gaudion wanted a show band capable of entertaining in the spirit of Pops (Louis Armstrong's All Stars). We both believed that all sorts of music could and should be turned into Jazz. The Blues Express was a band capable of pushing the envelope, of what could be played in traditional style and spirit. Peter's programme became a pot pourri of diversity. Songs included material such as Cannonball Adderley's 'The Sticks and Unit 7', Paul Simon's 'Late in the Evening', 'People Make The World Go Around' by Linda Creed and Tommy Bell, The Crusaders' 'Soul Shadows', Fats Domino's 'I'm Walking' and so on. I was astounded one night when Gaudion heard Keith Jarrett's 'Sombrero Sam', which I had originally performed with the Ted Vining Trio. He immediately incorporated it into the bands repertoire.

The most obtuse Jazz record I ever purchased was by the unknown Brooklyn saxophonist, Artie Kaplan. On it was a corny and commercial track called 'Music to my Soul', with lead male vocal and girl back-up singers. I couldn't believe how well Gaudion adapted this for the band. This open-minded attitude is something I have always considered special. In later life I would meet so many musicians whose music and minds were bound up as tightly as a book.

A lot of people found Gaudion a brash, drunken larrikin, easily capable of offending the gentler souls in the audience. Just like Dizzy Gillespie, he was forever the clown: jumping off tables, kissing womens feet, licking ears, lifting bodies and making fun of everyone, whether on or off the stand. Gaudion also believed in the larrikin approach adopted by most Aussie Traditional Jazz band leaders. A typical tune would start with an Allan Browne vocal, played with a Country Rock feel. Gaudion would then ask Allan to dress appropriately and Alan would appear at the drum kit in the uniform of a Texan cowboy. Allan would sing,

"I'm a long bent 'stralian, I wear a ten gallon hat."

Pointing at Allan; Richard, Peter and Mal would joyfully sing in chorus, with expressions of astonishment on their faces,

"He is the poofda in the ten gallon hat."

The band would repeat eight bars, then Allan would repeat also, climaxing with the whole band arriving at a break where Allan would coyly finish with,

"I've got a pussy in my flat."

The word 'pussy' was emphasised in such a way as to achieve maximum mirth from the audience and most members of the band.

The other gift Gaudion had was 'allocating features' to various band members. Mine was a rocking and raunchy trio version of 'Tobacco Road', (adapted from a version I had heard Lou Rawls sing). Gaudion knew that no other piano players in the State had the ability to deliver Blues, Rock and hard- driving Jazz grooves that generated this sort of excitement in the room. After each performance he would point at me and say, "Boss of the piano, ladies and gentleman." This became his standard introduction, that still continues today.

But my favourite feature was that of our clarinetist, Richard Miller. Peter knew that Richard admired the work of modernists like Roland Kirk, John Coltrane, Archie Shepp, Pharaoh Saunders and the like, and so Duke Ellington's popular 'Caravan' became the vehicle for an incredible range of sounds that emanated from the clarinet.

"More chook, more chook!" Gaudion would yell, supposedly encouraging Richard to greater extremes. Richard was even able to talk into his horn, creating a clarinet garble. The band would respond with sporadic bursts of rhythmic and nasty harmonic interjections. After a series of piercing high notes, Richard would become frustrated and start shaking his instrument, threatening to break it across his knee. He would then toss it up four feet into the air and catch it as neatly as any cricketer. Then in the darkest of moods he would walk away from the bandstand, circling the entire hotel until his anger dissipated and he would return for a 'Golden Wedding' type finale.

It is surprising how a spontaneous and creatively honest moment can be developed and perfected. A secret of musical development is repetition of repertoire. Frank Smith knew this, Brian Brown knew this, Louis Armstrong knew this and so did Brother Nat. Peter would make it his life's work to develop and repeat the repertoire that most affected the audience. The Blues Express would rival Australia's most popular group, Sydney's Galapagos Duck. Both bands had built up large followings and both were popular because of their ability to entertain. Of course certain sections of the Jazz world, which we used to call purists, would strongly disapprove. Purists believed the style of Jazz they played or followed, was so superior and special that they tended to be suspicious of Jazz musicians who wanted popularity. These musicians were branded as having 'sold out' or the derogatory term of 'commercial' was applied to them. Ted Vining admonished me one night with the following,

"You might as well go up there and juggle pizzas or perform magical stunts!"

PLAYING WITH THE SPOON

A S I PASSED the bar, I noticed Peter Gaudion in earnest conversation with a white American dude.

It was early in the morning and everyone: band, staff and a few remaining customers were all in advanced states of intoxication. I concentrated on Gaudion, who was saying, "It would have to be someone decent, a name that people know and it would help if he was black."

"What if I could get you Jimmy Witherspoon?" enquired the promoter.

"That might work" said Gaudion, his face showing no sign of his inner delight at such a prospect, "but he'd have to sing with my rhythm section."

What followed seemed to be an argument about the folly of condemning visiting American internationals to the embarrassment of performing with unknown locals. For Gaudion the price had to be right and for Noble he had to be sure the rhythm section was up to it. Unwittingly, in closing the deal Gaudion had pioneered the idea that Americans could visit Australia and what's more, be able to make magnificent music together with us locals. Nobody thanked him for it, but it would ensure a steady stream of high profile American Jazz musicians collaborating with their Australian counterparts. I had been in the right place at the right time.

Gaudion rang me and asked me to pick up Spoon, who insisted on a rehearsal with the pianist before rehearsing the rhythm section. Spoon was staying at the Diplomat Motel, a cheap and nasty part of St.Kilda. Obviously Peter Noble, the promoter had convinced Gaudion that Yanks loved staying there because it reminded them of home. Spoon and I drove to the Victoria Hotel in silence and on arrival were ushered into a small room equipped with just two chairs and an old player piano.

"Go-ahead, go-ahead, play something for me" insisted Spoon.

I realised that I was playing for someone who had heard the world's finest: Bird, Ben Webster, Art Pepper, Coleman Hawkins and Ray Brown. In fact Spoon had collaborated with more famous musicians than just about anybody.

So I ripped into the piano and played the fastest, hardest and the most energetic Blues I could muster. Rather than commenting on my effort, Spoon waited in silence and then ever so casually said, "You know my mother played the piano; she played it in church and there's one thing she told me that's stayed with me all my life."

'What's that? "I enquired.

"Well" drawled Spoon, "if you play one wrong note in this music, it's as obvious to the listener as a bell that doesn't sound right outside a Cathedral."

If what Spoon had just said was right, this was in direct conflict with the spirit of artistic freedom Jazz musicians bring into their playing when improvising. Most of my musical life had embraced the thought that there is no such thing as a wrong note, perhaps only a realisation that one could choose an unfortunate note or group of notes. My mind was racing. The truth was that most of my colleagues would only play the Blues as a warm up at the start of their sets or when they couldn't think of anything better to play. Many felt the Blues to be an inferior choice of material. It was considered cool, even witty to wait for a Blues to demonstrate one's weirdest sounds. I was quick to point this out to Spoon. Strangely enough he agreed with me, naming many famous American Jazz players guilty of the same mistake.

"What can we do about it?

'Well" said Spoon with a grin, "I've been sitting in my hotel room looking at the vast expanses of desert you people have here in Australia, so we could just charter a big plane and invite all those musicians who want to play bullshit rather than play the Blues on board the plane. The plane could then drop them gently into the vast expanses of desert you have here, where they would be able to hear in silence all those golden notes they wanna play and the rest of us would be left in peace. Aw Nah!" guffawed Spoon, enjoying the thought of what he had suggested.

"Now, just play me a simple 12 bar blues."

When I had finished, Spoon began pacing the floor.

"Tell me if I did something wrong?" I said innocently,

"Naw," said Spoon frustrated, "It's just certain things that I wanna hear and you ain't playing them yet!"

"What does he mean?" I thought to myself as I began a one-man workshop, playing the Blues in as many different styles as I could. Something good must have happened because a jubilant Spoon jumped up and said, "That's it! That's it! That's the second change."

"Oh!" I said, I thought that was optional in a Blues.

"That ain't optional, it's obligatory" Spoon replied, "it's like a big landmark, please play it on all my tunes. You see a lotta players, especially drummers, don't get to play Blues as slow as I sing them" and he began to count in the sort of tempo he had in mind, his big right arm descending followed by a strong verbal command "ONE!" Then silence.

"Where's two?" I enquired.

"It's coming" said Spoon, grinning at me like a Cheshire kitten, "take your time, take your time, never rush or force it from your body," said Spoon, still grinning.

After we had tried this slow 12/8 tempo a few times, Spoon explained that the slow tempo in fact gave him extra time to grab hold of a single lyric and squeeze it for all it was worth.

"Don't worry," said Spoon, "I've been singing these words all my life."

There were two more sounds I had to re-discover, the first was the church chord, which every musician in Australia called a diminished chord. When he heard me play it he would stop me and say, "Yeah! That's the church chord and see how it always seems to follow and add to the second change? Please always play that church chord in my songs when you feel right about it. And there's one more sound I ain't hearing, especially in the turnaround."

The only chord I hadn't tried so far was called an augmented. As soon as he heard it, Spoon excitedly announced, "That's it! That's the one I want you to play at the end of the turnaround, then everybody's got to know where we're at. That's great; we don't need to rehearse anymore. But two things before we leave, firstly people say my vocal range is that of a natural tenor, so a lot of the time we'll be in the key of A flat. The reason I'm telling you now is to give the band time to get familiar with that pitch. I don't want any of my musicians suffering pain. And one last thing, I want you to discuss the turnarounds you're gonna play on each of my tunes so the bass and the piano play the same lines. Ain't nothing worse than you both playing different turnarounds. I want it to sound tight not schizophrenic" laughed Spoon as we headed back to his motel.

On the drive back we talked about Spoon's personal philosophy and background. He told me about his childhood in Arkansas and how he had heard a conversation between a perfectly innocent white next-door neighbour and his wife.

"Blacks ain't nothing" said the neighbour, "in fact you gotta feel sorry for them; they can't read, they can't write, they can't even express themselves properly, they don't have any money, they don't own any property and how can they have any self respect?"

"I decided there and then" said Spoon, "this ain't gonna be my future. So when that predominantly white audience looks at me tonight, what are they going to see? The first thing they might pick up on is that I'm wearing no ordinary suit or shoes, but personally tailored and hand-made stuff they can't buy. Then check out these rings, solid 18 ct gold and silver, genuine Aztec ornaments you ain't going to find in no jewellery store here. And here around my neck, solid gold chain. As I walk up to the microphone, they might just get a whiff of the special expensive cologne I'm wearing, no cheap after shave for this dude. And when I sing, they are going to understand every word, every little nuance of what I'm expressing, they are gonna understand that they are dealing with the world's most articulate Blues singer. When I talk to them, I'll let them know that I live in a big home, with a twin garage and two limousines at my disposal. You see, I couldn't have anyone feeling sorry for old Spoon here. Should they ask me for my autograph, I'll pull out this Parker pen and write them a special note. Hell, I wouldn't want them to think I was ignorant" chuckled Spoon.

"Are there any other great musicians from Arkansas?" I interjected.

"Are you familiar with the work of trumpeter Harry Sweets Edison?"

"Sure" I replied, warm sound and careful choice of notes are his trademark."

"Well Sweets and I went through school together back in Arkansas and we work together as often as possible. In fact my next gig is in Paris with Sweets on horn. Naw, Arkansas wasn't big on producing Jazz players. All I know is I, Sweets and Red Holloway were the three major Jazz artists from that State."

Having dropped Spoon back at his motel, I began to understand the lyric Ray Charles sang in the blues 'What Did I Say? Tell your ma; tell your pa, going to send you back to Arkansas.'

On the way back to the gig Spoon insisted I pick him up. It was a great feeling sitting next to this Jazz/Blues legend who was treating me with as much respect as he would any other musician. His strength of character and self-belief were to leave a lasting impression on me.

"Can you tell me anything about Bird?" I enquired.

"Hell I can remember when Bird weren't anything but a raggedy-boned third alto player in Jay McShann's band. He was so out of it, the guys had to kick him in the arse every time it was time for him to solo. He'd wake up and then doze off again" Spoon laughed.

It was about that time we both looked out the window at a big blackboard Gaudion had placed outside the hotel. Under the words 'Jimmy Witherspoon' was 'Black Blues Singer'.

Witherspoon flew into a rage, "Whose idea was that? I hope it ain't Peters 'cos I don't need that and the world doesn't need that."

Spoon walked into the pub, giving Peter a piece of his mind and during the evening, made Peter his symbolic black slave.

"Fetch me up a double scotch" he demanded. Gaudion unaware of the significance of the symbolism, delighted at being made the centre of attention and acted his role out to perfection.

The gigs were most successful. Spoon even let me dress him in a Carlton beanie and scarf. At the end of the piece 'Sweet Lotus Blossom,' I reached inside the piano and randomly plucked out a chord. For me this was nothing new, after all I had done it at The Prospect Hill but I could not believe my ears when I heard him say, "Great pianist, another Monk, all of him."

Because Spoon was big, black and a famous American, the audience applauded approvingly. I couldn't wait to get at Spoon and after the gig.

"Hey man, what do you mean by equating me to Monk? Even Miles says Monk doesn't swing and some of my friends still think he's a phony!"

Spoon couldn't stand my negativity and said, "There are only three crazy piana players in this world. There's Stan Tracey in London, Monk and you. Let's never talk about it again!"

A certain magnetism had existed between Spoon and me right from the start and this now extended to my family.

"I don't want to speak to him; send his son over." Spoon said one night. Pretty soon Steve and Spoon were whispering in each other's ear. "Hey Steve, tell me what does your daddy say about me at home? You can tell old Spoonie here."

Steve innocently coughed up the fact that I kept complaining that everything was always in Ab.

"Does he now?" said Spoon, as he commenced the evening patter on the mike. Pointing at me he said, "I've just been speaking to his son, who tells me his Daddy's in pain because he does everything in Ab, Aww," yelled Spoon in mock sympathy, "Well tonight Bobby we're doing everything in Bb, because we'd hate you to be in any pain."

Everybody broke up laughing but I realised Spoon was giving me a subtle lesson.

There was a feeling of euphoria after the final gig at The Victoria and I could hardly believe my ears when I heard Spoon say to Gaudion, "Hey, Peter let's make a record."

Spoon turned around to me and said, "Don't pay attention to how I sing in the studio 'cos it's different from live. But when you hear the play back it'll sound fine."

Alan Browne, Derek Capewell and I had done the live gigs with Spoon but my heart went out to Peter, Mal (Wilkinson) and Richard (Miller) because this was their first exposure to a visiting international. The album simply entitled 'Spoon in Australia' has been re-released on CD and is still around to this day.

Sometime later I had a phone call from Ray and Adrian Jackson inviting me to a game of golf at Malvern. But golf was not on their minds; they were worried about their son and brother Martin Jackson.

"You see" said Ray, "he wants to be a Jazz promoter. He's really keen on it but how will he exist? He's talking about bringing out people the public has never heard of!"

I knew Martin was an unshakable character, after all, as my student he had insisted I find musicians for him to play with. I remember introducing him to one of my students, Jamie Fielding. I knew their tastes in Jazz leaned towards the so-called 'revolutionaries.' I then told the father,

"If you want your son to make money he should bring someone out like Jimmy Witherspoon. He sells out wherever he goes."

So he did, and Spoon and I were reunited.

The concept of Blues being grungy was epitomized at Sydney's legendary hotel in Rozelle, The Rose, Shamrock and Thistle known as the Three Weeds. It was a place for shadowy figures that flowed in and out of its dingy rooms which were laced with the smell of beer and marijuana. The joint was packed to the rafters, which leaked tiny droplets of water onto the band below. Many Blues luminaries lined the walls (even young Diesel was there.) On this night, the only mistake I made was to invite Sydney's most popular Blues guitarist, Dave Brewer for a sit-in. I thought this would be popular with the audience and also enhance the music.

The problem was Spoon insisted that Malcolm and I dress smartly, just like in America. Unfortunately Dave had dressed in the customary blue jeans and T shirt preferred by Australian Bluesmen.

"That guy ain't sittin' in with us." said Spoon.

"But he's one of the country's great Blues guitarists." I pleaded.

"Nah, he ain't no guitarist, he's a drug dealer. No self respecting guitarist is going to be dressed like that."

My dad had taught me that an Englishman's word was his deed. So I foolishly ignored Spoon and invited Dave up. The sit-in was greeted with loud cheers, but Spoon was so angry with me he was jumping up and down at the back of the stage yelling in his loudest voice, "It's just a cheap political stunt by our pianist, ladies and gentleman."

To cool him off I called him back up and our final number bought the house down. People were yelling and screaming for more. Flushed with success I rushed up to Spoon who had walked away from the stage. Pulling at his sleeve I said, "Spoon, Spoon, Spoon, they're yelling for more!"

I was greeted with a look of absolute disinterest.

"They'll get over it" he said, and to my surprise after a while they did.

I couldn't get to sleep, thinking about encores. It was true that people had paid money at the door and were hoping to get value for it. And on this night they surely did. It was also true that great musicians wanted to leave the stage washed out and devoid of all energy, having given everything during the performance. Why then did they (the audience) wait until the end to ask for more? I could not remember one occasion where I had been part of an encore that had been memorable or even remotely of a standard that was better than the main performance. I began to loathe encores and the musicians whose egos were such that they actually enjoyed basking in them. Because of this incident I remain one of the few musicians who try to talk his audience out of an encore.

In the documentary film, 'Skies Across America,' there is a special tender moment where Ornette Coleman and his son Deonaldo share a conversation that only fathers and sons working together in the same band might understand. Ornette reveals that he prefers playing with Deonaldo because not only is he a great drummer but as a son he understands what Ornette is about as well as his music. This was true of my son Malcolm, whose level of intensity and emotional expression on saxophone, not only matched but often surpassed mine. He'd listened and absorbed a huge variety of players, from the most obtuse to the most popular. The problem was that very few musicians, broadcasters and journalists understood that this was reality rather than nepotism. People preferred to worship at the altar of any stranger no matter where they were from rather than acknowledge Mal's musicianship. It was for this reason that I insisted he tour with Spoon, after all Spoon had worked with the world's best. It was on the 24th June 1989 that Spoon's favourite band arrived at Kiama, NSW. There was guitarist Dene Ford, drummer Mark Grunden and bassist Geoff Kluke. In the middle of Jimmy Reed's Blues 'Anyway You Want,' Spoon stopped the band dead in its tracks and declared to the audience,

"Ladies and gentlemen, I've sung this tune thousands of times but when I sang 'We're going up' our saxophone player didn't do the obvious and play a note that was going up, he played a note that was going down. And when I sang 'We're going down' he played up. That's a sure sign of creativeness and I know only two players in the whole history of the music that have done that; I'm making a prediction now that Mal Sedergreen will not only turn out to be one of Australia's greatest players but will make a great contribution to music in this country. "

The sad thing was, because we were in Kiama it was never reported.

Jimmy Witherspoon meant a lot to me and so I decided to write a Blues for him called 'Blues for Spoon,' which I recorded with Brian Brown with piano and pan pipe on Brian's album *Wildflowers*.

But the love affair between Spoon and me was soon to fade on our last tour together. The first publicity promotion was an appearance on the cult ABC television show 'The Big Gig.'

The band and I had turned up early. It was unlike Spoon not to be there. Television producers hate wasting time and I was asked,

"What's he going to sing?"

"He's going to sing 'Big Boss Man'" which I knew suited Spoon and suited this up-beat show. We rehearsed all the camera shots. Apparently Spoon had been asleep, arriving at the studio just in time to do the show.

"I ain't doing 'Big Boss Man' " he told the producer, "I'm doing 'Ain't Nobody's Business' and by the way, Bob, the key's changed to G."

What a pathetic choice, I thought.

"Listen Spoon," I said "if you won't listen to me at least have sympathy for our young bass player Dean Addison. It's his first time with us and he may not know that tune."

"Well he'll have to learn." Spoon said harshly.

Needless to say our television performance was lacklustre.

But the biggest disaster happened in Perth. Spoon was in fits of depression, having been diagnosed with cancer, of his throat, of all things. He just wanted to stay in his pajamas and sleep in the hotel room. The promoters, worried about the box office, wanted Spoon to appear on the ABC's Drive Time show. I did my best to cancel Spoon, telling the promoters he'd changed into a tyrannical monster, but they made me knock on his door and convince Spoon to do the interview. He agreed on one condition: "Just tell 'em I don't want any dumb questions."

I had a premonition of what might happen and so avoided going into town, but I turned the radio on. The presenter was a young and friendly female but as often the case, was clueless about Spoon, his history and his significance. The first question was, "How long have you sung the Blues?"

Spoon replied, "I told them, no dumb questions lady."

"And have you sung with anybody famous?"

She framed the question ever so politely.

"Hey lady, I told them, No dumb questions and I mean it."

I can't remember the third question but Spoon spat the dummy and said, "Lady I've been interviewed by a lot of people and I've been asked a lot of dumb questions, but you must be the dumbest interviewer I've ever had."

The ABC switchboard was jammed with hundreds of callers and the talkback segment was full of her fans wanting to know who that rude and offensive 'bastard' (or words to that effect) was. Only a few people turned up to the gig. But Spoon still insisted I go ahead and plug his CDs.

"Give him a message from the people of Perth," said the head of The Jazz Action society, "He sold two!"

It was after midnight and I was lying in bed in Adelaide when the phone rang. It was the promoter, Martin Jackson, wanting to discuss the final leg of Spoon's tour in Melbourne. He seemed oblivious and unsympathetic to the situation and unwilling to hear my complaints.

In a temper I said "You should try playing with the prick. I resign as your musical director." and hung up.

I arrived in Melbourne to find that Martin had taken every word I had said literally and booked a replacement band for the last gig; Dene Ford, Allan Browne, Tony Paye and Peter Jones who had never played together before. Malcolm and I were just dying to see the musical disaster that we knew would happen.

"Can you hide us somewhere?" we asked the venue owner of the Limerick Arms, Mike Hancock. Mike placed us out of harms away in an adjoining room, but we could still see and hear the show. Peter Jones had called for the charts. Spoon carried beautiful leather folders with his name embossed in gold on the front. Unfortunately, the charts were old, badly written and bourbon and beer-stained. Spoon had forgotten to tell them everything was now in G. So they were playing in the key of Ab and he was singing in G. It didn't quite gel. After two numbers, Spoon stopped the band and announced, "It's not my fault ladies and gentlemen; it's my musical director Bob Sedergreen, who has failed to turn up. He doesn't deserve to tour with me, he should be touring with Idi Amin."

From their point of view I had let them down. But on that tour, I had been through a personal and musical hell. If I was looking for forgiveness, it never came and little did I realise that in the future a hard penance would be exacted.

ON THE CUSP OF VIRGO

MY MEETING WITH the two Jazz greats, Dizzy Gillespie and Jimmy Witherspoon or Diz and Spoon as they preferred to be called, had made me aware that in order to become a better exponent of Black American music, one had to gain an appreciation of America, its geography, its lifestyle and the values that its inhabitants, especially African- Americans, held near and dear.

Perhaps that is why I began leaning towards the alto saxophonist Cannonball Adderley. Cannonball would rap in a most jocular manner about the nature of the music, the character of its composers and the hipness or otherwise of his audience. Joy and excitement were the hallmarks of an Adderley recording, especially the live performances.

So, as if by proxy, Cannonball became my instructor in what was hip, black and beautiful.

One of the band's big hits at the time was a song called 'Gemini', written by saxophonist Jimmy Heath of Philadelphia.

"It was simultaneously a chant and a waltz" proclaimed Cannonball.

What I did not pick up on was that Cannonball was making an astrological reference. That's right, in the 1970s astrology became a craze that permeated Hollywood, spreading like wildfire through Los Angeles and San Francisco, then across to New York. So big a fad had astrology become that people would ask for your sign rather your name as an opening to conversation.

I paid little attention to the song 'Virgo', written and recorded by none other than Miles Davis's sideman, Wayne Shorter. I was also oblivious to songs like 'Pisces on the Cusp', written and recorded by one of my favourite tenor players, David 'Fathead' Newman who had come up with Ray Charles. Even trumpeter Freddie Hubbard had written and recorded a song 'Arietus.' (aka

Aries) But the penny still did not drop.

More astounding was the fact that Cannonball had produced two albums for Capitol Records called *Soul Zodiac* that dealt with the twelve signs, both musically and rhetorically. I might have been the only musician who owned and enjoyed those two albums in Melbourne but who had not noticed the fact that astrology was considered a means of expression in Jazz.

One of the most controversial figures at the time was the pianist, composer and bandleader, Sun Ra, who when asked his birthday, would insist that he had entered the planet sometime in May but was born under Gemini. His band was called the Solar Arkestra, or intergalactic space Arkestra. They played tunes like 'Astro Black' and 'Saturn'. Sun Ra claimed to play inter-galactic music and his justification was the science of astronomy. Despite the many clues that had come my way I had not picked up on the significance of astrology. But astrology would soon become a personal discovery that would unlock the keys to my understanding of others and even more importantly, of myself.

It happened like this.

The word had come down the grapevine that Sydney promoter Horst Liepold had fallen for a visiting African-American singer, named Joyce Hurley and in her honour had organised a tour of NSW featuring all the musicians promoted under his banner. It was a conglomeration of the nation's finest musicians, all who had worked for Horst, including Australia's favourite Jazz band, The Galapagos Duck, as well as The Jazz Coop, the Mike Knock Quartet and the Brian Brown Quartet, with cameo appearances by pianist David Martin and trumpeter Keith Hounslow. Horst had decided to stage the gig at The Belmont hotel/Yacht Club in Newcastle NSW and when so many musicians were involved, sleep wasn't going to be an easy option.

It was early in the morning after the gig that celebrations subsided. I should have hit the pillow, but it wasn't that simple. I knew that most of the musicians would drive from Newcastle to Sydney so they could have lunch at the Malaya restaurant in George Street, a hang-out frequented by Sydney's Jazz players. People like Mike Nock, Serge Ermoll, Keith Stirling and old friends like John

Collins and Ray Martin. These lunches would be long affairs, with the finest oriental cuisine accompanying story-telling, jokes and discussion of personal preferences in the world of Australian and American Jazz. Of course the food was complemented by a never-ending flow of red wine. In this state of intoxication, the musicians would have to drive to Canberra and face up to a brand new audience, in a brand new club, *Clean Living Clives*. For the experienced fun-lovers in a band like Brian Brown and Ted Vining, this would make up the perfect day: driving, feasting, catching up with other Jazz players, talking, drinking and then repeating the process before performing. Who knew what might develop after? Though it would probably be more of the same.

I knew I wasn't up to this sort of a day, so I picked up the telephone and rang Aeropelican Airlines. I had noticed their advertisement in the hotel directory: they flew from Belmont to Sydney. The lady on the switch said, "Can I help you?"

"Yes" I said. "I'm sorry to ring this late, but I would like to book on your first flight to Sydney in the morning."

Having taken my name, she asked my address, to which I replied, "Room 169 at the Belmont Hotel."

"Funny I've just had a call from the Belmont, room 167 or something."

But I wasn't interested in coincidences. I rang the local Taxi company to make sure I would arrive at the airport in good time. The guy on the switchboard said he just had someone else from the Belmont book a cab. Just another coincidence I thought. Now I must ring for an early morning reminder call. As I did so, the girl at the hotel switch board said I was the second guy to ask for this service in a matter of minutes. Nothing registered because I merely thought there would be many wake up call requests.

The next morning, as I carted my keyboard and suitcase onto the pavement, the local taxi driver pulled up alongside shouting,

"Mr. Hounslow, Hounslow?"

"No," I said gruffly, and then much to my surprise, Keith appeared with his trumpets and baggage. I heard him tell the driver he was going to the airport. Within seconds another taxi appeared. "Mr. Sedergreen" he said, happy to have pronounced it correctly and pretty soon there were two cabs in convoy on their way to the airport, each carrying a member of Brian's band.

On arrival at the airport we both fussed and supervised the loading of our gear, reminding each other not to forget things. As the small aircraft climbed its way above the purple haze, I asked Keith what had prompted him to take this course of action.

"You see Bob, I can't stand wasting the day driving and getting involved in those long lunches at the Malaya. So I thought I'd fly direct to Canberra, get to the motel early, have a shower and a nap, and wake fit and ready for tonight's gig."

"Wow," I thought to myself, that's identical in every way to my plan; something strange is going on here.

The Zebra Motel in Narrabundah on the outskirts of Canberra was a budget motel. This did not surprise Keith or me. We were used to dealing with a mentality that feared Jazz musicians could party all morning, disturb the other guests, trash the rooms, and leave without paying for breakfast or other services. Keith and I entered our single rooms and emerged at the same time, both coughing and spluttering. Keith asked, "Is your room dusty?"

"Dusty!" I said," I think they've transported it from Alice Springs, especially my pillow. Someone must have dumped it in the Simpson Desert."

Keith suggested a solution and pretty soon we had both purchased brand-new Tontine pillows at the local shopping centre. We both walked back to the motel smug in the satisfaction of having clean pillows to sleep on, before retiring for our afternoon nap. We congratulated each other on our behaviour so far, reminding ourselves the others had probably reached the Malaya by now.

There is a wonderful moment when the mind is in full gear, when one's head seems to be spinning. For me, this often happens just before sleep. On this day, I was counting the number of identical actions that Keith Hounslow and I had taken in a 12 hour period. Too many to be coincidental. There must be an answer. Just before rolling over to sleep, I telephoned Keith and asked, "By the way Keith, when is your birthday?"

"The 19th of September," he replied.

At this time I knew nothing of astrology, my last thought was that mine is in August.

As I was glancing through some newspapers on the flight home, I happened to see the Astrology column and the dates for the sign Virgo. Surprise surprise, Virgos could have either August or September birthdays, so it followed that Keith and I must have the same star sign. Truly fascinated by this discovery I called in at *Readings Book Shop* in Glenferrie Road, Hawthorn, on my way home. Finding the astrology section, I noticed a small paperback, its cover varnished in grey and black, titled *Virgo*. I took it home and after tea, settled down in my favourite reading place, the toilet, and digested most of the information it had to offer.

The next day found me back at work at the Waverly Offset Publishing Group; I was responsible for purchasing and estimating. However my mind was 100 percent occupied with the thought that all Virgos I knew shared many common personality traits. But I had to prove it to myself.

In the typesetting department worked a compositor named Bevis Fenwick. Bevis was not a social butterfly; he kept very much to himself. He wore the most conservative clothes to work: dark grey trousers and check shirts in blue or grey. Rumour had it that he could turn nasty and criticise colleagues if they made even the minutest errors. The boss gave him the most critical makeup work, stuff like price lists and catalogues. This was perfect. I found myself walking up to Bevis, glancing into his gentle, yet clear eyes and asking,

"Hey Bevis, are you a Virgo?" It was as though I had shot him with a stun gun. His whole body coiled in disbelief as he answered, "How did you know that? Nobody at work knows that; that's something I wouldn't tell a soul."

"Sorry to startle you like that Bevis, I just guessed it."

From then on I was right into astrology, a passion I would share with many American musicians. For instance, take Basie's tenor man, Frank Foster, who proudly wore around his neck the sign of Libra, the scales, on a beautiful gold pendant.

"I see you're a Libran," I said wanting to start up a conversation with him.

"Oh yes man," Frank replied "but I'm not only just a Libran, I'm born on the cusp, the 23rd September, the same day and date as John Coltrane."

"Being on the cusp must be special," I said, relishing my own birth date, the 24th of August.

"It's not just Coltrane and me," said Frank, "Check this out: Ray Charles and Les McCann, we all share the same birthday."

Wanting to be genuine rather than cute, I said, "Wow, that's enormous!"

So many of my readers will want to echo the words of Miles Davis and say 'so what?' but to Frank and me, this was serious conversation.

ONAJE

THE TROUBLE WITH certain bands is that they only go in the direction the leader wants.

Allan Browne and Richard Miller were loyal members of the Blues Express, as well as foundation members of The Red Onions Jazz Band, purveyors of traditional New Orleans music.But Richard and Allan were keen to develop their own modern style.

Posters everywhere were reading 'Support Australian Jazz.' The Brian Brown Band had set the trend with free improvisation and original composition as being the key to an Australian approach. However the groove and swing of American jazz was not to be lost, (not just yet). So it was natural for them to approach me with a view to forming a new group, which was to be called Onaje.

Allan had named it after American pianist Onaje Allan Gumbs. This created an immediate problem. I was already a member of three groups: The Blues Express, The Ted Vining Trio and The Brian Brown Quartet. How does one split into four people, play four different styles of music and handle clashes of gig dates? Brian, Ted and Peter were already giving me heaps about this problem. But Allan and Richard were deadly serious and after all, Allan had played in my speech night band at Haileybury College.

"It's easy" said Allan "we'll just be the Blues Express without Peter. Don't worry, we'll use him as a guest from time to time."

Allan was certainly a unique figure, capable of producing drum sounds from early New Orleans figures Baby Dodds, to the modernistic stylings of drummers like Jimmy Cobb and Paul Motion. A natural comedian, he would spontaneously burst into side-splitting comedy routines. Allan is the only figure I have met in Australian Jazz brilliant enough to suddenly change the serious mood of music- making and have both audience and band in convulsions of laughter. Many people came just to enjoy his patter.

His humour was influenced by comedians from Lenny Bruce to Barry Humphries.

Allan would wait for the right moment and announce; "Ladies and gentlemen, tonight we're happy to present as part of the performance, an international floorshow. We're having samples of floors from many nations. There'll be floors from France, Spain, Portugal, Iceland, South America and much more, and they won't just be wooden floors, there'll be parquetry, linoleum tiles as well as vinyl."

Richard Miller remembers Allan convincing patrons that whilst touring London with The Onions he was granted an audience with the Queen who had insisted they play a washboard duet together.

"It was a magic moment," he used to say, "Until I got home to discover tiara scratches on my stomach."

It did everybody's heart good to know that Jazz could be fun and that Jazz musicians could be charismatic figures. This combination of fun and original music would lead to the band slowly developing a cult image, which was visualized on our albums *Onaje's Rage*, *Straight as a Brief Case* and *Waltz for Stella* which featured the talents of a brilliant new young bassist on the scene, Gary Costello, whose ability to solo at lightening tempos was freakish.

I was thrilled with the news that we were to back up Sam Rivers on his Australian tour. The band featured Sam on horns and piano, the bassist, Dave Holland and a happy young drummer, Steve Ellington. During the Brisbane gig, Steve would run into the room during Allan's solo yelling, "Go for it man! Go for it!"

This really disturbed Allan so we encouraged him to confront Steve.

"Why do you keep telling me to go for it? " enquired Allan. Steve came up with the amazing answer, "Those who go for it are doomed to ecstasy."

A single line that epitomised the spirit of Jazz.

So impressed were we that Allan wrote a poem called 'The Wasp' (which stood for White Anglo Saxon Protestant). The poem concluded with the line 'Remember Steve, who said those who go for it are doomed to ecstasy.'

As Allan read the poem the rest of the band would freely improvise. And in fact poetry and Jazz became popular with Onaje. We would even do sessions with beatnik poet Adrian Rawlings.

This was a time of the door deal. Imagine musicians forced to collect money for the landlord (operator of the venue) so that the landlord would have money to pay the band. Sometimes the band did not receive the full amount of the takings collected on their behalf. One thing was for certain, Onaje was a band destined to stay underground, seeking approval from purists. We would never be accused of being commercial or selling out.

Allan, who was determined to keep the band in a residency, decided to play on Monday nights, causing the least amount of financial strain on the venue and thus giving the owner/operators status as true purveyors of high quality under-dog Jazz. It was in this way we became favorites of SIMA (Sydney's Improviser Music Association) and we visited Sydney on their behalf regularly. This strengthened our cult image and finally would lead to international recognition, as we became part of the official programme of the world's greatest Jazz festival, the Montréal Jazz festival.

Our residencies included The Tankerville Arms, the Limerick Arms and Bennett's Lane (Allan can still be found playing there on Monday nights).

Onaje's contribution spanned at least a dozen or more years of highly original music, most of it penned by Richard Miller, who surprisingly enough, could turn out music from a personal and Australian point of view, but somehow still imbued it with the feel, groove and passion of the modern American genre.

Unfortunately, towards the end depression set in. It wasn't the music, or the relationships with Allan, Richard and bassists Gary Costello and Geoff Kluke, it was the public attendance (or lack thereof).

I used to ask myself if the band was so good, why weren't people coming to see us in droves? What was the use of being a communicator if there was no one to communicate to? To me a lack of audience meant a lack of acceptance. But no one else in the band was prepared to accept defeat and so I had to take it upon myself to tell Allan I could not continue. Perhaps it was I who was responsible for the breakup of Onaje.

Mum, Dad and me, Palestine, 1947

Rae and my engagement party,
East Malvern RSL, 1963

Brian Brown Quartet outside
Brownie's Jazz Club, Corner
Russell and Lt. Collins St. Melbourne,
circa 1977
Photo courtesy Victorian Jazz Archives

Phil Woods (Scorps) at the
Victoria Hotel, Albert Park, 1980

The Brian Brown
Quartet, 1976, Ted
Vining (drums)
Brian Brown (flute)
Barry Buckley (bass)
Photo courtesy Victorian Jazz Archives

Laying the Blues (scarf)
on the Spoon. 1980

Myself, Judy Jacques and
Sandro Donati.

Wrestling with Elvin Jones.
Montreal Jazz Festival 1994

Uncle Nat and The Button, Montsalvat 1990

Myself with Brother Nat and Cliff Foenander.
Montsalvat 1993. Photo: Norman Wodetski.

The Three Sedergreens: Myself, Mal and Steve

The Ted Vining Trio
Bennetts Lane, 2004

Six Of The Best,
Miettas, 1995
l-r, Gil Askey, Margie
Lou-Dyer, myself, Annette
Yates, Nina Ferro, Jackie
Gaudion, Beverley Hay,
Sonja Horbelt, Bridgette
Allen, Madame Pat Thomson

Jamming at home with Steve

Onaje, 1980
Allan Browne (drums) Richard Miller (tenor sax) myself (piano)
Gary Costello (bass)

Onaje Reunion, Gary Costello tribute, Bennetts Lane 2007
Myself (piano) Richard Miller (tenor sax) Allan Browne (drums)
Geoff Kluke (bass)

The Blues Brothers,
St Hubert's Winery, 2007
Mal Sedergreen (soprano sax)
myself, Dean Ford (guitar)

Rae and me at home, 2007

PHIL WOODS COMES TO TOWN

A S I WAS about to leave the Victoria Hotel, I spotted Peter Noble and Peter Gaudion, both obviously negotiating something important. I overheard Noble say, "I was thinking of bringing out Phil Woods."

"OK," replied Gaudion, "but only if he plays with my rhythm section."

"Well, he has his own quartet back home in the States. They've been together for some time now, and have released recordings that are getting rave reviews in the States. Phil might not want to tour without them."

"We would love to have him here," said Gaudion, "but it's no deal unless he plays with my rhythm section."

At that time, Phil Woods was one of the most important alto saxophone players in the world. I had spent many hours listening to his recordings with Benny Goodman in the USSR, with Oliver Nelson, Clark Terry, Michel Le Grand as well as his own European Rhythm Machine. His classic solo on Billy Joel's hit recording of 'Just The Way You' *Are* had given extra notoriety to this regular *Downbeat Poll* winner.

No wonder I felt a headache coming on at the mention of that name. As usual, I immersed myself listening to his latest recordings, reading magazine articles featuring him, even looking up his star sign in *Leonard Feather*. Phil was a Scorpio.

On the way to rehearsal, which would take place on the day before the concerts, all sorts of paranoid thoughts were going through my head, like how hard were the parts he would give us to read, would he abuse us if we couldn't get parts right, would he break into free-playing, or count us in at ridiculous break neck tempos? I didn't have long to wait; the door to the rehearsal room burst open to reveal a middle-aged white guy, dressed in a leather jacket and cap. I could easily imagine him flying a single engine aircraft or being the one-man captain of his own fishing vessel.

"You must be Scorps," I said.

And without hesitation he said, "You must be my band. Hey, do you guys know 'Secret Love,' in F?"

Before I had time to answer, we were playing it. Playing with Phil Woods is an uplifting experience, and we literally took off. However before the end of his first solo chorus, Phil jumped up excitedly saying, "That's it gentlemen, save the rest for tonight," and disappeared out of the room as quickly as he had entered. Surprised at the briefness of the rehearsal, I turned round to Derrick and Allan, (perhaps more cautious souls than I) saying, "Well that went alright didn't it?"

Derrick just shrugged his shoulders and Alan muttered, "We still don't know what to expect tomorrow night" as he packed up his drums.

When I arrived at the Vic, the room was packed to capacity due to the publicity and airplay Phil was getting internationally at that time. Musicians of all persuasions were in attendance: Jazz guys, Rock and Rollers, even many section heads from the Melbourne Symphony Orchestra. I walked up to a young bassist in the crowd – Lach Easton, and asked him, "What do you think they've come to hear?"

"Well Bob" he replied, " I suppose they've come to hear Phil Woods, but also to see if you guys can make it with him."

It was at that point I realised Australia was the toughest country when it comes to handing out recognition to its artists. I had not long ago returned from a most successful international tour of the world's major Jazz festivals in Scandinavia with the Brian Brown Quartet and had been publicly applauded as a great pianist by the legendary Blues singer Jimmy Witherspoon in this same room, but it didn't seem to matter.

Phil entered the room dressed in the same leather cap and jacket he had worn to rehearsal; an appropriate hush came over the audience as he found the microphone stand. He walked to the piano and quietly whispered in my ear 'Dolphin Street?'

"Yeah" I nodded, and before anybody realised it, Phil

commenced a solo saxophone improvisation of such dimension, range and intensity, with a logical build to the melody which he swung with amazing dexterity, that it stunned everybody.

He followed this with four mind-blowing choruses of improvisation. Following a Phil Woods solo would not be easy, but I made good use of the low register of the piano, a range not visited by alto players. It would be important in the next chorus that my ideas swung and I would have to play with enough technical brilliance to ensure the intensity of the music did not fall in a hole. There was no doubt that Alan and Derrick responded with equal eagerness. It seemed that from the very first song, not only would the rhythm section make it with this great American Jazz notable, but also contribute ideas to enhance what turned out to be an on-the-spot jam session that allowed all the musicians a chance to contribute.

To play with musicians who are masters of their instrument, whose ideas come easily, whose sound is sure and strong, whose range is not a problem, and whose creative juices are flowing, takes the accompanying players to a higher level. Everyone knew this was happening, and that they were attending a night they would not forget for some time.

As for Phil, he preferred to let his musicianship speak for him, not spending too much time talking to the audience, or announcing the programme. It was as if he expected his audience to know what was happening and appreciate the calibre of musicianship. He obviously enjoyed playing with us.

If I played a solo he approved of, he would cruise up to the piano and whisper in my ear, "You need more Vegemite!"

"And you need more wind," was my reply.

The next morning, I was shown an article in which a journalist had been brave enough to ask the question, "What did you think about the pianist Bob Sedergreen?"

I was moved to tears as I read the reply stating that I was the most exiting player he had encountered in some time.

This was a time in Australia when Phil was on the airwaves, mainly due to a big hit by a recording artist, Billy Joel, who would become a pop idol. The tune was called 'Just The Way You Are.'

In the middle of the tune there is a cameo spot, undoubtedly Phil Woods, who plays a gem of an alto solo. Wanting to get our conversation off to a good start I said, "I just love your solo on that Billy Joel track," hoping to get a beautiful warm response. Instead his face and posture sort of slumped.

He said, "That's something I'd rather not discuss."

A normal person with tact would have let it go, but I thought, that's a great solo, why doesn't he want to discuss it?

"Are you ashamed of it?" I asked innocently, and he softened and said, "I'm going to tell you why I don't want to discuss it. You see it's a very bad memory for me. There was this person I thought was a good friend, and he rang me and said 'Hey Phil I need a bit of a favour. There's a new young guy who wants to do a demo. We just want you to come and pop a solo in the middle."

I agreed and said "Sure, is there a fee?"

My friend convinced me that as this was not a high-profile recording I should do it for my minimum fee. When I got to the studio, the cat that was doing the demo wasn't there. I didn't want to be part of something that wasn't real, but they insisted that it could all be over-dubbed. Like a fool, I warmed up and played a short solo over the backing track. It was quite a nice tune and I forgot to ask who had written it. Anyway I took the cash payment (a few hundred dollars) and proceeded to forget all about it. After all it was only a demo. A few weeks later I was in New York in a taxicab, the radio was on and all of sudden I could hear myself on the radio.

I said: "What in the heck is that?"

He said, "That's Billy Joel, it's a big hit."

I said, "Turn to another station."

And sure enough they were playing the same thing.

It seems my friend wasn't a friend after all. It seemed that Billy Joel wasn't an unknown and here he was doing a million dollar hit; collecting big dollars for writing the song and what's worse, no mention of my name. Had I known it was going to be something commercial, I would have asked for a share in the partnership vor a big fee. I'd been tricked, so that's why I didn't want to talk about it."

I was so glad he had opened up to me. The truth with great Jazz musicians is that they can detect when you are being genuine rather than polite.

BAGS GROOVE

O NE CAN'T IMAGINE my delight upon discovering that my next big international gig would be with the brilliant vibes player, Milt Jackson.

Milt continually won *Downbeat Polls* for being the worlds best. I began to recall the Atlantic album, *The Ballad Artistry of Milt Jackson* as being one of the first jazz albums I acquired and could not help being struck by his beautiful playing on the track, 'Alone Together,' a track I had virtually worn out by playing over and over again.

Milt was also a member of the *MJQ* and I remembered how intently I had listened to their album of blues, recorded at Carnegie Hall. Of course 'Django,' one of the group's greatest hits was a piece I had recorded with Brian Brown on the album *Upward* and also played many times with Alan Lee who adored and worshipped the work of Milt Jackson. The only change in the mix of the band was that Gary Costello, a keen and fast fingered young bassist, had been booked to replace the more experienced Derrick Capewell. This was to be Gary's first international gig. The two concerts were to be held in Mackillop Street in the city, in the basement of *Discurio's* record store.

The rehearsal got off to a bad start because Bags (which was Milt's nickname) was doing the American thing of establishing his authority as band leader over us, the subservient musicians. Like so many other Americans he assumed we were being well paid to do the job. But Australian promoters were notorious at never telling them or anyone else, how little they had paid us. At one stage, Bags pointed to a section of the chart asking Gary to play the note A on his bass when the chord Ab was indicated. A gentle and concerned Gary made the mistake of enquiring why this was so, which sent Bags into command mode. Bags wasn't the sort of guy who screamed at you but was excellent at remonstrating with his fingers. Wanting to calm the situation down I interjected with a foolish flippancy. Bags got so annoyed he led me to the grand piano and proceeded to demonstrate the sort of chord voicings I should play. That was the moment I spat the dummy and without him picking up on my sarcasm I asked him to demonstrate further and when he had finished I said with much conviction;

"There's only one problem with that Bags, and the problem is you don't swing on piano."

Bags stared at me in total disbelief. If we'd been in America, my little display of temper would have earned me the sack, but the rehearsal was in Melbourne and just two hours prior to the concert, too late to get a replacement.

Pretty soon the first set had started; I called it the punishment set.

"Do you know 'Lover Man'?" asked Bags (unbeknown to him this was a feature for bassist Barry Buckley, a song I knew perfectly well).

And then he showed me five fingers.

"Do you want it in five four time?" I enquired.

"Nah" whispered Bags triumphantly, "five flats"

My stomach began churning with the fear that I could not cope with this difficult key. To make it worse, Gary was staring across at me with the look that told me: Bobby we're in deep shit and will need divine help right now. That divine help came in a realization that if one knew the progression of a piece of music perfectly it could be played in all twelve keys. I don't know how I did the mathematical calculation in such a hurry, but in seconds I hit the sharp five transpositions I needed to start the piece and floundered my way through it. Of course Bags solo shined and he delighted in watching me awkwardly plough through the changes. After we had finished this tune Bags turned to me and asked:

"Do you know the tune 'Good Bait?'

"Not really," I replied.

"Well you'll enjoy learning it with me, it's in an easier key." Bags smiled ruefully, knowing I would have to sit quietly and figure out the machinations of this tricky number.

Oh yes, the first set had Gary and I deep in thought and

perspiration without one second to relax. Fortunately Onaje (Allan Browne), played straight ahead tight time, in the spirit of the MJQ's drummer, Connie Kay.

Then came the break through. During the interval Milt, acting like a father with his family, invited us to join him for supper. He specifically wanted chicken and gave strict instructions of how it was to be cooked and served. I'd heard of Duck a la Orange but a dish I can only call Chicken a la Orange was bought upstairs to the table. He turned around to us and said;

"Do you mind if I smoke?"rolling a narrow log of marijuana, so powerful it sent him into instant nirvana.

He then offered it around the table. Our bassist Gary accepting the joint unaware of its power was sent silently spinning into another world. In later years Gary told me that grass like this was unavailable in Australia.

A different vibe now existed, allowing me to ask Bags about his upbringing. He was now out of command mode and very shyly told us he was a Sugar Hill boy. The relevance of this information became apparent to me in later years when I visited that section of Harlem in New York. Seeing that we were eager and genuinely wanting to know more, he continued:

"Being a Sugar Hill boy meant not going to school. We had to learn everything on the streets."

"Well, if you didn't go to school how did you learn to play vibes like that?"

"Well," replied Milt, "All the kids in our neighborhood would head downtown to wherever Bird was playing. Too poor to enter we'd have to listen to what was happening at the entrance. The next day if you didn't have down what Bird was playing, you weren't any body."

It was only in later years talking to my friend Gil Askey, a resident musician working in Harlem at that time, that I would realise just how difficult it must have been for a solo black Jazz artist to confront a bunch of white dudes like us, who would have been in his mind, well educated. But at that time my perception of Bags was tied to the image of the MJQ; cool, well dressed, articulate, a natural musician and intellectual giant.

After supper, Bags became the sweetest man on planet earth.

"Go out there and play something you really know well to open the second set."

After which he appeared and said, "What would you like to play?" and he obligingly romped through my favourite play list including 'Alone Together,' 'Django,' 'Bags Groove,' 'The Cylinder' and the best version of 'Wave' I have ever heard.

I had been absolutely restrained in the first set but left free to blow my arse off in the second. At one stage Milt had to spell me and let me cool down as he played a solo piece for the audience. For many members of the audience, this was a defining moment where a visiting American great, without saying a word acknowledged a local Jazz musician.

There were two concerts, with the second night being identical to the first. Set one being a punishment set, more Chicken a la Orange, more joints, and another relaxed second set. So relaxed was Bags at the end that he insisted that I take him and his two blonde Aussie girl friends dressed in white home. I had bought the CTI album *Detour* for him to sign for me and although I treasure it to this day I feel tender every time I read the childlike writing with its erroneous spelling.

SCANDINAVIAN DISCOVERIES

S TAYING WITH THE folks in Sydney was something I always looked forward to. The idyllic Palm Beach lifestyle with its scented gardens, surf beach and salt sea air provided the tranquility one needed to escape the stresses of city life. Very rarely were telegrams delivered, but one day I opened the door to have a telegram (no not an email, but a typed message on a sheet) thrust in my face by a postman). Strangely enough it was addressed to me and worded as follows:

'Report to (I forget the number) Miller Street, North Sydney this afternoon at 2 pm.'

It was unsigned. Was this a mistake? A joke? Or sent in error?

I arrived on time to a typical North Sydney address. When I entered the designated room on the second floor, I was surprised to see Ted, Barry and Brian. Champagne corks were popping and Ian Neil walked up to me with a glass of Jack Daniels.

"You may need this," he said as he walked up to the rostrum and announced that The Quartet had been invited to the prestigious Scandinavian Jazz Festivals of Pori, Finland; Konsberg, Norway and Kristianstaad, Sweden.

We would be the first Australian Jazz ensemble to visit this part of the world. It was not only surprising but especially exciting that the Scandinavians had invited us, a band from Melbourne. Normally if Australian musicians were travelling overseas, they were Sydney players and the organisations representing them had lobbied hard to get them there

A few weeks later we were flown up to Sydney for a briefing session. Despite over a century of collective playing experience in the band, none of us had ever been to such a high-profile event. When Ian, the Chairman of the panel, called for questions from the band we were all stunned. So I asked, "What's the position

138

with electronic keyboards and synthesizers?"

Ian looked back at me, with a look as if I was some sort of child in kindergarten who had asked the dumbest question.

"Bob, this is a truly international festival. You can ask for what you like and we give you the personal name and number of Scandinavia's largest music organisation, Brodie Jorgensen. They'll provide you with whatever you need."

It seemed too good to be true. Ted was next cab-off-the rank, but to our surprise his question was not about drums or drumming but about airlines. "What airline are we flying with?"

When the answer Singapore Airlines was offered, Ted quipped to the band members, "You know what that means. Free grog all the way, and not to mention those Singapore girl hostesses in their sarongs."

"How many suit cases are we allowed to take?" asked Ted.

"I asked for intelligent questions" quipped Ian. "Why, are you thinking of taking some special equipment?"

"No," answered Ted "I was thinking more in the line of clothes."

Ted's missus, Helen, told me years later that he had taken months to carefully choose the two suit cases he would bring from three wardrobes full of clothes.

Brian, on the other hand, saw this as a negotiating session. He firmly believed that in order to give our best performance everybody in the band (except me) needed to be playing the instruments we played at home and were familiar with. He therefore insisted that the band's equipment, Ted's complete drum kit, his saxophones, flutes, wooden stands, synthesizers and a huge gong as well as Barry's precious acoustic bass be packed very carefully into an airline steel freight case and dispatched to the festivals.Apparently the Yanks borrowed instruments from friends and associates rather than go through the drag of bringing stuff from home. Some eyebrows were raised at this expense but research was done and someone came up with the idea of advance freight. We would have to send our instruments overseas months prior to the performance.

Our band had actually become a quintet; Roger Chapman, a young fan who attended all our gigs at The Commune, attached himself to us, and soon became our roadie, setting up our gear, just like a Rock'n' Roll roadie. We named him 'Roger Roadie.'

Roger looked and dressed like one of Christ's disciples but whar was most important was his big beaming smile. When Roger smiled we all knew the band was kicking arse. So Brian insisted he come along with us despite the expense, and none of us was about to argue.

I was elected treasurer and sole signatory to the band's advanced funds. We arrived ahead of the impressive list of American Jazz greats that we were to play along side. Names like Freddie Hubbard, Woody Shaw, Ted Curzon, Buddy Rich, Max Roach, Elvin Jones, Ornette Coleman, Frank Foster, Carla Bley and Betty Carter. Art Blakey should have been there too but cancelled when his Russian trumpet player, Valerie Pomenerov, had been refused a visa. Pretty soon we would be in Jazz heaven, but first we had two more obstacles to overcome.

Qantas had sent our gear to Paris by mistake. The reader may be unaware that saxophonists must keep their lisp in shape. Being unable to blow his horn sent Brian into fits of depression. But there was an even bigger problem. The iron! Ted had called a special band meeting. He too was depressed.

"I've just got my first lot of clothing back from the cleaners and guess what, here in Scandinavia, they don't press them."

So began an excursion to find a shop that sold irons. Bulk stores would be a thing of the future. When we saw the prices, we nearly died, irons were about seven times the cost back home. But we bought Ted his iron. It was funny watching this iconic Australian Jazz great treasure it as though it were a diamond. Ted was staying in a room next to mine from whence came a whistling sound. Some time later the door to my room burst open. It was Ted in his clothes, displaying copy book creases.

"Da, dah" he sang as was his custom, announcing the fact that he was ready. And then asked, "would you like anything ironed?"

I gave him a heap of stuff to keep him happy.

It turned out that Konsberg was a small mining village in the mountains that doubled as a ski village. The venues for the festival turned out to be a series of old wooden halls similar to the Patch Hall in the Dandenongs and seating about two hundred people. We played in a hall next to the river; Woody Shaw's band were playing in the hall next door. Being a well-established festival, there were people everywhere. At one stage I waked around the side of our hall to find three huge Laplanders attached to the window sill by their hands, so keen were they to hear Jazz. We played our set with the determination and ferocity of Don Bradman's invincibles. We were the only band using a barrage of electronic instruments, leaving the audience in stunned silence. "Had we been a failure?"

Brian gently spoke to the Norwegian audience.

"In Australia we have little wild flowers in our mountains just as you have here," and we proceeded to play Brian's waltz 'Wildflowers' with its enchanting medieval folk melody. After a few minutes, a loud noise erupted from the floor. It was the sound of 400 boots stomping on wood and along with the stomping came the clapping of hands and the chanting of voices in perfect English, "Bry-an Brown, Bry-an Brown. It went on for ages, growing in intensity and then a whole lot of the audience started throwing wild flowers at the band. It was the most overwhelming encounter with an audience that I would experience during my life time.

From then on, 'wild flowers' meant something special.

After a while on the road, friendships began to form. After all, we breakfasted, lunched, wined and dined together. The thrill had gone from telling other band members of meeting Jazz stars, as they were now our friends. Brian seemed to enjoy hanging out with the trail-blazing Europeans; people like Jan Garbarick, Pali Danielson, Jon Christiansen and the like. I enjoyed rapping with Frank Foster because he was into astrology and we could talk about Bill Basie's band. Ted was over the moon because he had breakfasted with his idol Elvin Jones. Little did we know that Elvin's first concert (which we were all about to attend) would be the catalyst that would spell the end of one of Australia's greatest Jazz groups. It happened like this: Barry and I took up a position in the middle of the hall, leaving Ted closer to the front. We did this just in case Elvin disappointed us. Elvin got off to a bad start; his time and fills were all over the place and for twenty minutes, nothing worked musically. Then magically he began producing a polyrhythmic turmoil and counterpoint that projected the band into an a la Coltrane mode. Ted looked at us and smiled. In the interim, Brian had arrived with his European mates. They were discussing the music and in a quiet moment Brian could be heard to say, "It's just a duplication of what has gone on before. This band has nothing new to say."

Brian had booked a cab to take us home but Ted refused to go. Before Barry and I could make up our minds, Brian had disappeared. For the next two days I sought out Ted and Brian, trying to be the peace maker. We played a great set in Kristianstaad, so much so that the Americans would tease us. As we walked within ear shot, we could hear them talking,

"Have you heard the Aussie band?"

Their mate would answer, "Yeh, man, that bass player is something else and the pianist, he's a mother fucker and that drummer, he's a bitch."

I looked around to confront a great Jazz drummer I really admired, Charlie Persip. I approached him saying, "You guys wouldn't be shucking and jiving with us would you?"

"Hell, no man. We really meant it. You guys can play."

Sitting next to me on the plane to Pori was trumpeter, Ted Curzon, who had played with giants like Mingus and Eric Dolphy. Ted was very popular in Finland, so he was invited back each year to head a large ensemble, Storband, which consistedof Scandinavian players. As the plane landed Ted said, "We're sinking into the sands of Pori."

I had no idea what that meant but Ted was right. Pori was a village stuck in the sands of time. In the centre was a cobblestone market square where ladies in thick coats and scarves sold small portions of onions, potatoes, carrots and other produce. Old habits and customs died hard here. I remember hopping on a bus that carried most of the able-bodied men in the village, each armed with axes. They were on their way to work, chopping timber for the Finnish paper industry. The first problem was communication. The Finnish language, having elements of Turkish, Iranian and Russian, meant a lot of shrugging of the shoulders. I remember having severe stomach cramps and visiting the chemist. I only recognised it as a chemist by the display in the window. I walked in and told the pharmacist,

"I've a crook gut." He just shrugged his shoulders. This will take some great acting I thought as I rubbed my tummy in a circular motion slightly bending over and moaning. The pharmacist directed me to a familiar package, a roll of Kodak film.

One part of the official programme read 'International Jam Session.' It was meant to feature local musicians. Being Australians, we were sympathetic to the local musicians, knowing first hand that empty feeling of rejection as soon as musicians (some of them not such great players) from another country arrived in town, especially if they are black and American because they tended to be mobbed and adored. As soon as they left, it seemed people were ready to settle for the second best. This situation happens to me all the time. The Festival Directors approached Brian, suggesting the Australians be in charge of this night. A band meeting was called where Brian said, "You all know I hate jam sessions; they're a thing of the past and totally useless. You three go and represent me."

We arrived at a large hall with an elevated stage and we had bought a plentiful supply of bourbon. In a gesture of friendliness, I approached a Finnish pianist to commence the session. Pretty soon there were a whole lot of Scandinavian musicians having a ball up on stage. But slowly, one by one, the Yanks were entering the room; some were there to be seen, some felt it was their duty and some came out of curiosity. In a jam session, etiquette demands that as you exit the scene you call up a replacement. In a gesture of international goodwill, somebody called up an American. You've heard of the expression 'pushy Yanks'. One by one, the Scandinavians were dispossessed from the stage. To me, it was an act of sheer ruthlessness. That was it! Seething with anger and emboldened with the sting of bourbon, I lurched up to the bandstand. Not waiting for them to finish their song I snarled,

"It's the Australians turn to play." I then beckoned to Ted and Barry at the back of the hall, but they were in no condition to understand or help me. The band was led by Ted Curzon and a whole host of young, black dudes, some Mingus alumni. Taking pity on me Ted said, "What would you like to play?"

"Anything you name," I snarled.

Unperturbed super cool Ted wanting to be friendly, suggested 'Night in Tunisia,' I waited for his solo and instead of the usual harmony, provided Ted with groups of nasty harmonic clusters. It worked. Unsettled, he turned around to confront me but as our eyes made contact I quickly changed to the correct chord sequence. I repeated this process several times, depriving him of any hope of musical enjoyment and then I looked around and recognised the baritone player, Bill Saxton's unfriendly eyes letting me know that I was for it. Ted in the meantime, decided to let me have my head and solo, and my solo commenced with jagged lines and polyrhythmic punctuations. In the midst of this, an old unknown alto player called CI Williams came up and sweetly whispered in my ear, "Hey son, it's a contribution we're looking for, not a competition."

It was another one of life's defining moments. CI had cut me down to size. Jazz isn't about being a smart-arse like so many Jazz musicians one sees. It was about team work on the stand and being a member of a musical community. From now on I would begin to judge musicians by the contribution they made. I would never forget that CI had told me "it wasn't a competition."

When I looked up the hall was empty; everybody had gone home and I was surrounded by a band of hostile American musicians. As I tried to leave the hall they formed a circle around me. I knew that Mingus could be violent but would they be? A few minutes of uneasy silence passed, after which one of them said to me,

"Where did you learn to play like that?"

"In Melbourne, Australia" I answered.

I might as well have said the moon, because they were bent over in fits of laughter.

"And where's Melbourne?" asked another.

"It's on the Yarra River" I said.

That really did the trick; everyone was falling over in ridiculous laughter. Realising I had released the tension, I then pinned an eighteen-carat gold kangaroo badge (given to us from Qantas to use for special people only) on Bill Sextan, who suggested my punishment would be to carry the baritone home. The walk home was well over a mile. To this day, baritone players get my sympathy, having to carry such a heavy horn around.

On our return home it was though we had never been there or achieved anything. Nobody wanted to know about our success and nobody even cared. I felt sick to the stomach, thinking had we been sportsmen we would have been idolized.

There is no glamour in Jazz. My wife, Rae, took pity on us and contacted a former student of hers, a journalist at *The Age*, who arranged a photo and welcome home story on us. As a result of all that had happened, our band would disband.

MEETING MICKEY T

IT WAS WEIRD. Here we were, the only four Australians at Kristianstad in the middle of Sweden in a packed hall of bodies jostling to get a good view of Frank Foster's band, The Loud Minority. All of a sudden, a female voice accosted us. It was unmistakably Australian. Feeling a tinge of home sickness we stopped, "Where are you from?" we asked.

"Melbourne" said the lady.

"We're from Melbourne too."

"What part of Melbourne?" we enquired.

"St Kilda" said the lady.

"And what's your name?" asked Barry Buckley.

"Sheila" said the lady.

We all knew about sheilas from St Kilda and burst out laughing.

"What brings you to this festival?" I asked in a tone laced with sarcasm.

"Well it's actually my husband; he's up on stage now playing piano."

"Uh, oh" we thought, she should be a sheila from Kew (mental institution) not St Kilda.

Sometime later at an official function, there she was, Sheila Tucker sitting next to her husband Mickey Tucker, the pianist in Frank Fosters band. Mickey was a Jazz heavyweight who had worked with the likes of George Coleman, Reggie Workman and Art Blakey. This led to the formation of friendships between our two bands. So naturally, when we were in New York, we looked Mickey up. Mickey turned out to be a most genial host and my first New York dining experience was by his side.

"I'll call you Seeds and you call me T-bone" he quipped. "Now order anything you like and don't hold back."

Oh how I enjoyed ordering the meal American-style and having it promptly delivered.

Oh, yes Tucker knew about tucker. Just when I thought I couldn't eat another morsel, Mickey turned around and said, "Seeds, do you like blueberry pie?"

Before I could refuse he beckoned a waiter with the instruction, "Bring my friend here a quarter blueberry pie."

My eyes rolled in disbelief at the size of the portion. But Mickey had a mischievous sense of humour. Recalling the waiter he said curtly, "You call this a quarter of pie? It looks more like an eighth to me!"

The waiter returned promptly with a serving of pie that I can only call semi-circular and defiantly placed it under my nose. Mickey beamed at me. Here was a friend worth having.

Sometime later we were able to return the favour and have Sheila and Mickey dine with us at home in Glen Waverley. This was an exploratory visit before Mickey settled permanently here in Melbourne. I don't know if it was the bouquet of the wine or Rae's apple crumble, (which Mickey promptly called Brown Betty), or the warm summer night air that drifted through the mock Spanish windows, but the atmosphere was definitely relaxed. Here was my chance to hear first-hand about the problems faced by black American musicians. As Mickey hailed from Durham, (North Carolina) in the South, conditions there must be different from places like New York, Boston and Philadelphia. Mickey began the harrowing tale about a quintet of musicians packing their gear into a most reliable car and heading off to do a gig out of town, in another city seventy four miles away.

"About twenty miles out of town, on the outskirts of Durham's city limits, the police pulled us up. 'What's your story?' asks the thick-set white cop, glaring at us with a look of contempt. 'We weren't breaking the law where we?' says our driver. 'We're just musicians on our way to a gig.'

'Musicians? You boys look more like drug dealers to me. The stuff's probably in them instruments. OK if you're musicians, get out and give us a concert.'

"What could we do Seeds?" said Mickey. "We get out of the car and assemble our instruments as fast as we can and proceed to play a tune. 'OK, I'm sorry' says the policeman in mock sympathy. 'You guys are musicians, now get back on the road and stay out of trouble.'

"Now Seeds," said Mickey "try and comprehend that for them this is fun and imagine that same police officer radioing to his colleague further on up the road."

"I've delayed them darkies, now it's your turn."

"Now Seeds, remember in the States, if you don't turn up to a gig on time that's really bad, but if you don't turn up at all you'll never work in that area again and the cops know this. The rest of the drive is fairly uneventful until we get close to the gig. All of a sudden a police motor bike pulls us over.

"All right guys, step out of the vehicle. This is a safety check." "He then slowly begins examining the motor, brakes and stuff like that, all the while glancing at his watch, looking at us triumphantly."

"You guys ain't in a hurry are you?"

"He finishes, leaving us just enough time to get to the gig. Having had his fun he then radios a third colleague who positions himself about a hundred yards from the doorway of the gig. By now some of us are panicking and someone says to the driver, 'We got nothing to lose now, so step on it.' The arresting officer has stopped us inches from the gig and is now taking delight in slowly writing out a speeding ticket. He knows we can probably see some of the organisers looking out for us but we are just too far away to be heard."

There are times when you know you are being told something that is neither embellished nor imagined. Spoon, Red Holloway and Brother Nat had told me similar stories. I was deeply hurt that musicians I admired so much were treated like dirt.

THE MAX ROACH STORY

T HE RANTASSIPI HOTEL with its metal and glass facade, nestled alongside the beach on the Gulf of Bosnia and shimmered in the sunlight like some weird building block from a space station. It provided a stark contrast to the simple timber Summer homes, each with its own sauna, the Fins built into the surrounding forest.

The Festival and the national television stations had decided to broadcast live Jazz from this venue. Tonight's broadcast would feature two quartets: the Max Roach Quartet and the Brian Brown Quartet. This Summer holiday area was 15 miles from Pori and as we climbed into the transport van, I deliberately sat in the middle of the American band. As the van procccdcd on its journey there was a stiff silence amongst musicians, perhaps because we had not been formally introduced. The other problem was that even though I owned and listened to a serious collection of Jazz albums, I had never bothered to study any of the photos that adorned each album, so even though I knew the names and reputations of the musicians alongside me, I could not match faces with names. This prevented me from opening up a conversation, which I was dying to start. In desperation I made my way across to our side of the van and asked Ted who I was sitting next to.

"That's Max Roach" Ted replied and then proceeded to tell me how stiff and mechanical he thought his drumming was. Not waiting to hear anymore of Ted's commentary, I proudly sat right back next to Max, who looked like an accountant. He wore a hat, business shirt, tie, jacket and gabardine overcoat and wedged between his legs was a smart leather businessman's briefcase. Max knew that I was itching to talk with him, but waited, offering no hint of conversation, until I couldn't stand it any more. At the very instant I was about to say something, Roach turned to me and said, "Have you killed any Aborigines lately?"

This surprising remark was like being punched in the mouth by someone I admired. I could not let it go unanswered, so I replied, "As a matter fact each morning before breakfast I get out my shotgun to make sure I get a good quota; it's satisfying to see them splattered across the footpath."

Another period of icy silence followed. Max then sensing my discomfort said, "You have to forgive me man; it's just that I grew up in the south with Charlie Parker."

Turning towards him and making eye contact I said, "I don't care who you are, or who you were bought up with, you should feel ashamed that you treated a fellow human being like you did, let alone somebody who loves your music."

The next 15 minutes continued in silence, allowing privacy of thought. As we left the van Max said nothing but he turned to me, his features breaking into a smile, as if he were saying: I really got to you kid, now forget it and be friends.

That night the Brian Brown Quartet played a stunning first set, which was broadcast live to air throughout Scandinavia. As usual we received phone calls from friends and contacts letting us know we had been on prime-time TV, and had come over as being one hell of a band.

Excited at the thought of our band confronting Max Roach's group in concert as programmed by the Festival for the following night, I spent the morning wandering around the shopping mall adjoining the hotel.

There in the middle of the mall stood Max, wearing a pair of headphones. I moved in close to discover that he was listening to the master tape of last night's performance. But the sound engineer had started the tape with the recognisable sound of our band. I could not resist the temptation of coming up from behind and poking him in the ribs. Startled, he turned around and as he removed the headphones, I said loudly into his ear, "Great band eh!"

He repositioned his headphones, listened to just a fraction of our music, then faced me with a grin and as quick as a wink retorted, "Great balance!"

I waited until he had finished listening to his band and invited him to join me for coffee. Unfortunately we only spent 20 minutes together, but in that time he told me a personal story about Charlie Parker and himself.

"You know Max" I said, "there is some debate in Australia as to whether Charlie Parker was a genius or just a very gifted player, spurred on by drugs and stimulants."

"Don't worry" said Max, "He was a genius."

"How do you know that?"

"Well," said Max, "I've devoted my life to drumming, percussion and the rudiments of rhythm. I would like to think that I've developed skills in this area. Anyway I was on this gig with Bird and as you know he never turns up early. But on this night he was there before me, sitting at my drum kit with his sax strapped across his body."

"Hey Tojo!' Bird called me Tojo."

"Why was that?"

"Probably because of the shape of my face and the little round circular glasses I used to wear that reminded him of the emperor of Japan."

"Can you do this?" Bird asked. He picked up a pair of sticks lying on the bass drum and proceeded to play a rhythm so complex, I didn't even know what time it was in. "Let me hear it again Bird" I said, and he repeated the phrase two or three times. Bird looked up at me smiling and handed me the sticks. I got on the kit and couldn't even approximate what he'd laid down. Only a genius could've come up with something like that," said Max sincerely.

One thing I knew for sure after Max's story was that Bird was very special, a musician apart and one that Max truly admired.

"Before you go can you tell me anything at about Duke Ellington?" I asked.

"What do you want to know?"

"Well there's just so many people in the world that rate him up there with Bird," I said.

"What did he have going for him?"

"Well" said Max, "I remember one night getting a phone call to fill in for Sam. It was a television gig and some silly producer had decided the drums would be on a riser two levels above the band. I assumed Duke had booked me because of my ability to read music fluently. Anyway as I climbed past the saxophone, trumpet and brass section and finally got to the top of the rise I saw my music stand was empty. Cameras were getting in a position to roll and so I panicked and pushed my way back down to the studio floor and grabbed Duke by the elbow and said,

"Mr. Ellington, Mr. Ellington there's no music on my stand."

Unruffled, Duke just smiled at me and said,

"Don't worry Max, I know every note my band plays and I know the arrangements and how to conduct. Now there will be certain things you'll be required to do. Just watch me carefully and I'll cue you seconds before each fill."

I walked back up to the kit scratching my head, but true to his word it was as though he knew every part by heart, even mine, and he was such a great conductor I got through the gig just fine."

"Before you go I just want to let you know how moved I was by the *Freedom Now Suite* that you and Abbey (Lincoln) recorded."

On leaving he quipped, "I wasn't sure that you weren't a honkey? but I found out didn't I?"

BETTY CARTER & JOHN HICKS

I REMEMBER WHEN there weren't as many Jazz singers around as there are now.

Back in '78 when we were touring Scandinavia, the only singer on tour was Betty Carter, a mystical and underground figure emerging from a cocoon of relative inactivity. But we all knew she had jammed with the best: Mingus, Roach, Bud Powell and even Bird. She liked being on her own and spent a lot of time with her make-up case, looking in the mirror.

Like so many singers of that time, she was not a beauty queen but was well aware of creating a strong image for the gig. Magical sounds emanated from Betty's voice but once Betty took the stage, her movement, gesticulation and facial distortions were disturbing to watch. True Jazz is often not glamorous. Betty didn't spend her time hanging out with most of the guys, preferring to be a loner.

Her band was just as strange, certainly not an all-star band. In fact Betty was famous for discovering unknown, young musicians and nurturing them to prominence, a fact she was proud of. This is why none of us had ever heard of the musicians she chose to accompany her. I can't even recall the drummer's name, but the bass player was Ratso Harris. Nobody knew where he'd come from or who he played with. Her pianist at the time was a young dude, John Hicks.

The incident happened outside the Hotel Kna in Oslo, Norway, in an old brick and stone hotel on a wide cobble-stoned street.

Three buses pulled up to pick up the entourage of touring Jazz musicians; some of the world's greatest Jazz instrumentalists, but just one singer. We got into the third bus and found a position near the front. Then Betty Carter hopped onto the bus. She made sure she found a seat on her own in the back. The bus had little glass panels above the windows that could be opened. At the back of the bus were some really bad dudes, who were smoking, singing and carrying on. Suddenly the mood changed as the first two buses departed for Konsberg, the first of the Jazz festivals we were all to play at. Then one of the Americans made an enquiry,

"Hey, why isn't the bus leaving?"

The word came back that we were waiting for a musician. People started asking who it was we were waiting for, then someone said, "I think it's John Hicks."

After an embarrassing half an hour or so, we still hadn't left. All of a sudden Betty pulled open the little aperture above her window and in a voice that could break glass, bricks and just about anything else yelled out ferociously, "John Hicks, you lazy mother-fucker get on this bus this instant. You hear!"

Amplified by the stone wall of the hotel, it was the loudest public broadcast one could imagine. Then Hicks arrived, looking like he'd just fallen out of bed, his head and eyes were bent down in the posture of one who realises he's entirely to blame for the hold up. When he got on the bus, all the dudes up the back decided to humiliate him by giving him Bronx cheers and mock applause.

"Sure glad you could make it man," said one.

After all, being late on tour is not only unhip, it's unprofessional and furthermore should you miss a connecting ferry, bus or flight, you'll miss the festival and you may never work again.

John didn't think it was funny. Meanwhile Betty was burning like a bushfire, not wanting him anywhere near her.

The next time I saw John was in Sweden at the Kristinstadd Jazz Festival. I was in the hospitality tent, where musicians, critics, promoters and the like congregate. It was regularly frequented by Aussies because there was free grog. In those days my favourite drink was scotch and water. Joe Zawinul had written a piece called 'Scotch and Water' so I thought it was really groovy to drink this combination.

At the time I was being interviewed by a Scandinavian Jazz critic, who came in, approached me and said, "Which piano players do you like?"

The first piano player that came to mind was Chick Corea and I convinced him that this was somebody I really admired.

To my dismay I read his article the next day, which said as far as he was concerned, I was just an imitator of Chick Corea. So much for the investigative quality of that Jazz journalist.

John Hicks walked in right next to me and proceeded to order a scotch and water. I think deep down he was looking for some sympathy. Three rounds later, we were talking freely.

"You know the other day when Betty roared you up? I don't think that was really fair, do you?" I said.

"Man, not only was it not fair, it's totally unforgivable" he said, "But you were late!"

"Yeh, but to ball me out in front of everyone else, I've hardly been able to play."

"But what can you do about it? She's really famous and you're just starting."

"I've made a decision. This is the first, last and only time I'm gunna work with her."

I thought to myself he's being brave because he's drinking scotch whisky. And I was right, John continued as Betty's pianist for a couple of years and went on to become the pin-up glamour boy of the New York hard Jazz set working alongside luminaries like Arthur Blythe and Pharaoh Saunders.

Many years later John, now New York's most prominent pianist, came to Melbourne to perform at the final Montsalvat Festival. I could hardly wait to confront him in the dimly-lit lower reaches of Melbourne's Forum theatre. I spotted him lurking back stage and as he was coming out, I yelled,

"John Hicks, you lazy mother-fucker get over here at once!"

It had been a long time since the incident so it took a while for his face to register who was talking to him. Then I looked down to see a glass of scotch and water in his hand.

"You haven't changed your habits one iota. Have you seen Betty lately?" I said.

"Not for sometime." he replied with a knowing smile.

155

JAZZ GOES TO LADIES COLLEGE

A LTHOUGH OUR SCANDINAVIAN tour followed by our trip to New York had been a musical success, one needed to apply the formula that so often exists for Australian Jazz musicians. Touring plus expenses equals loss of money in ones bank account. Let's face it, I had to pay in order to play, so in a way I was happy to return to the normal lifestyle offered by my employers, the Waverley offset publishing group

Here I was leaving work at the printery at 3.00pm, and heading off to Croydon to coach a Jazz-Rock group at the Yarra Valley Anglican School For Boys. It must have been gentle persuasion. Apparently not much had changed since I had been at school: sports and discipline, discipline and sports, more sports, study, discipline and prayers. As for music, the syllabus was so far behind the times it hadn't caught up with Jazz. The fact that I was teaching Jazz and Rock was considered trail-blazing as most music schools took a different direction. I was there at the instigation of one of the most revolutionary music teachers in the State, Ros McMillan. In the past, Yarra Valley Speech nights had been dull affairs of prayer and prizes. I remember my first Speech night at Yarra Valley, leading the Jazz Rock group on trumpet, in a hard-driving version of Cannonball's hit 'Mercy, Mercy, Mercy'. Happiness radiated throughout the hall. A simple dose of Black Gospel music had changed the most sombre atmosphere. Everyone was grateful, from the headmaster down. Oh yes! The Jazz-Rock group was here to stay.

Shortly afterwards, Ros contacted me and suggested I teach contemporary piano at PLC. My first exposure to the school was as a deputy for the lead trumpet player who was sick. It was a rehearsal that involved the whole school. Here I was, a fully grown middle-aged male sitting next to a group of twenty or so teenage girls and if that wasn't scary enough, we were surrounded by a sea of hundreds of women of all ages. The thought of being in the midst of such a gathering was actually terrifying, but not as terrifying as the stares of disapproval that were coming from a very attractive young, second-level trumpet player each time I misread my notes. I realised at once that women were different. As James Brown had sung 'This is a man's world' and at that time it was. So I was determined to find an approach female students would respect. My first duty was to take the stage band. I assembled all the girls and explained how a big band was just like a family and that every member of the band should learn to love the person next to them, help them and encourage them. I remember using the word love a lot, knowing love was a buzzword of the times. I also explained that *cooperation* not competition was the key to making our band unique. I must have been convincing as some of the girls put these views into operation.

"We're taught just the opposite Mr. Sedergreen. We're taught to compete, but this love thing has changed our lives."

Some months later a whole lot of girls approached me and excitedly said:

"Mr. Sedergreen, Mr. Sedegreen, you've made *Patchwork*."

"C'mon girls, guys don't do that sort of work."

"No! No! It's the school magazine."

They showed me an article they had written about the value of loving your fellow musicians and how this had led them to the joy of making music together.

One day, the headmistress, Joan Montgomery, took Ros Macmillan aside saying,

"I have to attend a concert by that Sedergreen fellow. How should I conduct myself?"

Ros knew I was so engrossed in the music that even if my fly was undone (sometimes it actually was) or my shirt was hanging out (which it often was) I refused to be 'disturbed' by anybody once the music started. The other disturbing thing was I treated the girls just like my mates onstage, yelling out loudly, "Gas! — Yeh!" and smiling at them knowingly in a way that might be misinterpreted. Realising this, Ros said to Joan, "Why don't you keep your head lowered as in prayer for the performance and then politely acknowledge at the end."

Joan loved the experience and secretly became one of my fans.

Life has strange twists; I was suddenly introduced to two young ladies; one Helen Cox and the other one, Janet McLeish.

"You're not the first Cox I've ever met," I said to Helen. "We had a teacher at school called 'Boards' Cox, he taught Geography and Christ was he was bloody boring."

"That's my father," said Helen smiling sweetly at me.

"Don't worry I promise not to take revenge on you for your dad's misdeeds." I said jokingly.

The same happened with saxophonist, Janet McLeish.

"My father Dougal" she confessed "taught at Haileybury."

I remember the slender figure of Dougal as being the teacher who had tried in vain to save me from the clutches of bully 'zombie' Andrew.

The other subject I taught was contemporary piano. PLC allowed me to employ Allan Browne and Gary Costello (of Onaje fame) to come and play bass and drums with the girls, thereby giving them a taste of what it felt like to play Jazz, and at the same time building their confidence.

The pianist Monique Di Mattina, who today is an integral part of Melbourne's Jazz scene, was one such student. Also the vibist Carline Schwekolt, who I later taught at the VCA and whose sound I used in a Jazz television programme called 'Jazz Is Now' which I coordinated. Alicia Lilley, a young country girl from Gippsland who now runs Soul Theatre, which promotes and presents plays on contemporary issues has remained my friend to this day.

At PLC, I was on the ground floor of a wave of enthusiasm that encompassed the idea that women could achieve their dreams, and if this meant playing jazz music, so be it. I knew in future more and more women would infiltrate the Jazz world.

INSTITUTIONALISED

M Y SISTER MILLIE once told me: "Robert! If you want to get to the top you know you've got learn to crawl. Some people suck their way to the top."

"I prefer kicking arse," I replied.

"In that case you'll probably kick your way to the bottom."

And so I did. I had spent a dozen years in the printing, publishing and paper industry without once being rewarded with a worthwhile pay increase or a promotion up the ladder. I guess I was backward in coming forward. I never cared what people said about me and I did not hang around and socialize after work, like so many others. The radical and unconventional methods I used sometimes with brilliant results were viewed as sabotage by company executives, determined to maintain rigid rules on their working colony of industrial ants.

Funny how ones confidence can be restored by those who show confidence in you. Brian Brown supported by Ros Macmillan (my old boss at Presbyterian Ladies College) was confident enough to appoint me as a lecturer in Jazz at Melbourne's most prestigious new centre for the Arts, The VCA. High hopes were held that this institution would herald in a new age of spectacular young internationally recognized artists. I was over the moon at getting the job but worried about how I could succeed in this world of academia without qualifications. My suspicions were confirmed further when I was denied a full time position. However I fought back my fears, keen to be on the ground floor of what promised to be an exciting new venture.

I remember Brian calling me into his office.

"Bob I want you to give them your spirit and teach them about the Blues and how you play it, tell them how you approach playing, and how you build solos."

Now that Brian was head of the course, I knew he would pursue his dream for an Australian approach to jazz. Compositions entitled 'Hilltop,' 'Diggers Rest,' 'Shiraz,' 'Carlton Streets,' 'Coonardoo' and 'The Old Stock Rider' were his own precursors of an Australian approach to composition. I knew he would pass his passion for new directions in improvisation to the incoming wave of Jazz musicians.

Whilst full of admiration for this daring and trail blazing approach and keen to experience new music, I was also worried that the spectrum of styles ranging from New Orleans to bebop and beyond might easily be overlooked. After all, my other colleague Tony Gould kept raving about Bartok, Shostakovich, Mahler, Ravel and the wonderment of this body of incredible classical music. I used to tease him,

"How come you never mention Jimi Hendrix?"

Gould just smiled back at me.

"Not in my classes mate."

Gould's diatribes often reminded me of Derryn Hinch with the focus of his attacks directed at radio and television Rock'n Roll guru, Molly Meldrum. Molly was touted as public enemy number one, destroying the chance for students to ever see or hear any quality music. Even at this early stage I realised that Brian, Tony and I would be a formidable team, capable of inspiring students in a three dimensional way. With this in mind I convinced Brian to let me have my own class. Brian said,

"OK, I think we'll call it The Elective, and although I taught other subjects, to me it became the most important and one of the most popular classes at the VCA. Brian called me into his office because it was the first major class of each week.

"Bob it is essential that as well as the things you have in mind to teach them, you cover the drama of the music and because in the past Jazz has been taught as a river boat cruise up the Mississippi River, I suggest you start with drama first and then work your way back."

As I left the office I thought, he hasn't told me how to teach drama. There are no text books on how to teach drama in Jazz and in fact the only piece I knew that vaguely represented drama was 'The train and the river' played by the Jimmy Guiffre Trio and documented in the film *Jazz on a Summers Day*.

"Shit, they'll get tired of playing that" I thought, "what will I do?'

The only thing I could think of was that drama told a story. I took the very first class of the Jazz course at the VCA and in it I spoke about a pirate ship that had spotted a mysterious island with strange flora and fauna. On the shore of the island was a group of attractive mermaids singing in a strange, alluring language compelling the crew to come ashore. One can't imagine the look of disappointment on the students' faces. They thought they would be jamming. But somehow I cajoled and directed them to play on their instruments the ebb and flow of the waves, the sounds of wind in the sails, the beating of the oars in the long boat, the sea shanties sung by the crew, the sensuality and smoothness of the mermaids voices, the dynamic crescendo of ones heart beat as one approached the island. With each ensuing week we perfected and developed the concept. The students realised they needed to visualize and act out the situation in order to arrive at the appropriate musical interpretation. At the end of the month I called Brian down to hear what was going on. He was so impressed, we played the piece in front of the whole college and even the most doubting of students were beginning to realise that it was possible to tell a story using music.

It was about this time that infamous British train robber Ronald Biggs pulled off one of the most daring train robberies in history and so for the next class I chose a scenario of a chase across the Nullabour, involving the Indian Pacific, intercepted by police helicopters ending up in a road chase. I couldn't believe it when one of the trombone players was able to consistently duplicate the police helicopter on his instrument or how much the rhythm section enjoyed playing the tempo of the train. And the variety of honks and squeaks from the horns representing police sirens and the cars skidding across the road. Oh yes, the drama of music had suddenly become cool!

Brian gave me complete freedom to set the rest of the curriculum. I became a man on a mission, determined not to turn out clones. A good example of my teaching method related to so called music stands and so called music. As the Elective was compulsory for all students, I would wait for 25 or 30 to assemble. I would let two minutes go past in total silence to increase their expectation and concentration and then I would go to a so-called music stand and toss it up into my right hand holding it like a rifle in the present arms position. Then I would look down at the class making eye contact with every pupil:

"Which one of you thinks this is a music stand?" I would ask. In hindsight I pity the poor bastard who answered:

'I do"

"Do you now?" I would shout voicing great anger.

"Then stand up."

When the student had risen, I would bring the flat part of the stand as close as possible to their ear and shaking it from left to right I would say:

"Can you hear anything? I can't."

Then I would address the class;

"Can any of you hear anything? Do you want to come up and have a listen?"

I would then violently chuck the music stand onto the floor as if it was a piece of junk.

"Any idiot who thinks this is a music stand is mistaken. It's just a clump of metal painted black."

I would then pick up one of the student's Fake Books.

"How many of you think this is music?" I would ask

Once again there would always be someone to answer yes. I would repeat the process, shaking it in their ear and asking:

'Can you hear anything, except the flapping of the pages? This isn't music, it's a dead tree covered in toxic ink."

The word got around that Sedergreen was as subtle as a sledge hammer.

Notoriety didn't come quickly. One day the Dean, John Hopkins, called Brian into his office and said:

"Who's that fat bloke who keeps handing out cigarettes to

all your students?"

"Oh that's Bob Sedergreen," said Brian. It had only taken three years for the Dean to notice me. But pretty soon I would become scrutinized, thanks to a young student from The Peninsula Grammar, named Lachlan Davidson (now a member of The Australian Art Orchestra and guru music teacher at PLC). Lachlan had scored a work for alto sax and symphony orchestra. One of the movements was called 'Blues For Bob,' inspired by me as his teacher. And so it was we were ushered into the largest room to witness its performance. The Dean and all Heads of Departments sat behind a table following the large vertical score for each orchestral section. The etiquette demanded that it be passed backward and forward amongst the staff, who would then point to a section of the score they found worthwhile. Horror of horrors, Barry Quinn the Head of Percussion passed the score to me. In my fright I panicked and placed my finger randomly, near the bottom of the score.

A few days later Barry Quinn called me into his office and said:

"Do you realise that the other day that of all things possible in the orchestra you pointed at the part for the Turkish Finger Cymbal?

The Dean wants to know why." I entered the Deans office and he said:

"Isn't it a bid odd that you would be fascinated with such a small part of the music?"

"Not really" I said nonchalantly. "I just find the sounds of Turkish Finger Cymbals absolutely exquisite."

This matter must have been passed onto the new staff member, who had just arrived from England, Richard Haymes, a composer and specialist in contemporary classical music. Richard regarded Jazz as rather predictable. He had already bothered the hell out of Brian Brown by writing a composition for the soprano saxophone that defied and exceeded the limits of its range. It was called Zorna.

"When do you think I can hear it Brian?" Richard would nag on a daily basis, which sent Brian into a frenzy.

At the same time, Richard would call me into his office on a daily basis and ask:

"When are we going to see some of your work?"

How could I tell him that I had not written any major work or didn't have much of a clue how to. I realised that sooner or later I would be found out. This was probably the reason why Richard kept on repeating his request. A week or two later Richard asked;

"By the way what sort of ensemble do you write for?

"Well actually I love cello, oboes, French horn and trombone as well as the standard Jazz set up."

I said this in mocking tones as a kind of confession.

"Well we're all dying to see some of your work, please make it soon."

And so it was I had to learn how to compose, notate, transpose and arrange music for my imaginary ensemble. I handed the manuscript to Richard some weeks later. This seemed to satisfy everybody and I even took the liberty of recording the piece with young classical students at the VCA. This was later released on my album Bobbing and Weaving on Larrikin records.

My African methods must have been working because one day the impossible had happened, the Melbourne Conservatorium wanted to interview me about lecturing in Jazz. Surely they must know that I detested the snobbery, foppery, pretentiousness and elitist attitudes practiced by so many followers of this music. Certain members of Melbourne's musical establishment would superciliously address Jazz musicians in a manner that left no doubt they thought us inferior, oafish and incapable of producing anything of substance and worth. Whoever at the Con had recommended me must be crazy.

I remembered to walk tall as I entered the white stone façade of Dame Nellie Melba's domain. Everything smelt musty and old and I was ushered into a dark wooden office to confront the then head of the faculty, Professor Michael Brimer. My stereotype of a professor vanished as I beheld Michael, a youngish looking man sporting a smart black leather vest atop a black skivvy. Wanting to impress him, I began raving about the qualities of Duke Ellington as a seminal figure in Jazz. Michael did not interrupt until I came to a halt, realizing he had heard all this before. Now I have a question for you he said:

"Have you heard of the pianist Dollar Brand?"

"Wow, he's trying to trick me," I thought. Most Jazz musicians at that time would be unaware of who this was. But I had been a devotee of the man's music for many years.

"Do you think he is a clever composer who makes reference to his African tradition or does his work rely on an intimate knowledge of the folk music of Southern Africa?"

I was stunned by the intelligence and depth of such a question and somehow I knew Brimer knew the answer and was waiting for me to fail, and so I took a guess and chose the latter.

Brimer's face beamed: "You've got the job."

"How come?" I answered smiling.

To which Brimer responded:

"Dollar or Abdullah as he now likes to call himself and I both graduated in the same year from Capetown University. He chose Jazz and I chose Classical. So naturally I would have to know a little about his music."

The Melbourne Conservatorium is a relatively small institution and they had moved heaven and hell to give me the famous Melba Hall to run my Jazz Elective in. My class consisted of attractive, intelligent and beautiful young women and sensitive new age young guys. Nobody had taught them anything at all about Jazz and the great legacy of Black American contemporary music. These poor kids thought Gershwin's 'Rhapsody in Blue' was really groovy. My every word and command became their deed.

One night they invited me to a barbeque. Much to my surprise they were acting like jazz musicians, swearing and drinking beer.

"I didn't think you Classical people acted like this" I teased.

"We're only human" said one of the horn players.

It was at this precise moment I realised that many of my preconceptions of Classical musicians had been totally wrong and this new breed of future players would know about jazz. We all agreed that the note A was the same whether it was played by a Classical or Jazz musician, it was the execution that counted.

Ronald Farren-Price was another head of faculty who totally supported my efforts. One night we were both booked to play at a wedding, one after the other. As I got up from the stool, Ronald took my place saying in a jocular fashion:

'I hope you've left a little bit of A minor for me to play." It turned out we had both chosen the same key for our feature numbers. As we passed through the hallowed passages of the Con., Ron would say in a most affected tone:

"Splendid work, Bob,"

But I was soon to encounter a new type of person infiltrating the academic world, whose sole purpose was to ensure that these institutions of learning would run like a business. Concerned more with money than music, many of them had never seen the hard end of a performance, preferring economic rationalism and cut backs to curriculum and staff. As a result, I was unceremoniously dumped from the Con. by the first of this new breed.

I returned to the VCA in a state of disenchantment, that after some fifteen years of being upheld as an inspirational and popular teacher I still had not been given a proper fulltime position. The world had also changed in that a younger generation had arisen. Ambitious, ruthless and prepared to compete with each other, with the result that drama students sang and played, while dancers acted. Nobody at the top seemed concerned or distressed that music students were being overlooked at official college functions. The dream was fading fast. Pretty soon ambitious hearts that yesterday were friends and students would ensure my departure and build their careers on the foundations I had laid.

FUN & GAMES AT THE
SYDNEY CLINIC

I N 1980, TWO extraordinary gentlemen bought the Mel Lewis
Big Band to Sydney. As well as performing, the band was to
conduct Jazz clinics for local students.

Barry Ward was a typical working-class Aussie battler. He had
been a bookmaker, a man who knew about greyhounds and had
kept book at most tracks. Barry loved talking slang, especially
when it came to printed money, using terms like 'Strawberry' to
describe five dollars and 'Brick' to describe twenty. His partner
Peter Brindle was Swiss and worked as an accountant. Not only
were they bringing out the Mel Lewis Band, but also the singer
Mark Murphy, who at that time, was recognised as the new male
direction in Jazz vocals.

In order to make the clinic even more credible, David Baker,
America's most respected clinician and head of the faculty at
Bloomington, Indiana, was to be in charge.

Another recognised teacher from the USA was pianist Jim
McNeely and his mate Denis Irwin on bass who taught Jazz at
America's famous Julliard School of Music.

All this, with of course, American guitarist Jack Wilkins and
the German bassist Eberhard Weber. The locals were the three
principal lecturers at the Victorian College of the Arts, namely me,
Tony Gould and Brian Brown. As Don Burrows was overseas in
Egypt during this time, Sydney icons John Sangster, Alan Turnbull
and singer Ricky May were engaged as instructors.

I had flown up on the afternoon prior to the start of the clinic
and reported to John Sangster in the lobby of Sydney's flash
Regent Hotel.

"Gees, this is alright," I said.

"No Snodders," said Sangster (that being his nickname for me)
"this place is for the likes of our American visitors. You, I and Judy

(Bailey) are staying at The Coogee Bay."

"Is it a good hotel?"

"Oh, yes" said Sangster smiling, happy in the knowledge that I would be unaware this was Sydney's most raging hotel, famous for its brawls. If you were looking for trouble, the Coogee Bay was perfect.

"But before we get there, you and I need to do some serious drinking."

I was aware of Sangster's reputation. The invitation had been issued in the form of a challenge, which meant should I survive the night intact it would be something I could brag about to my fellow musicians.

Soon my head was spinning as a result of severe intoxication. Sangster pushed me into a cab bound for The Musicians Club, in Chalmers Street Redfern. At least here there was a bar that could prop me up for a while.

"Have you met Spidor?" he said, his eyes beaming with delight at the frailness of my condition.

"Spidor" I repeated incoherently.

Pretty soon the iconoclastic figure of Jazz pianist Judy Bailey was at close quarters. Sharing a drink or two, I was keen to let her know how much I enjoyed her own band at El Rocco and with Don Burrow's On Camera band. Sangster, still unsatisfied with my response to his Spidor comment, interjected, "You see Snodders, I call her Spidor because she entered this country through the spy door of Auckland, New Zealand. Get it?"

That's when I passed out. I awoke in a strange bed, in a small room. Where was I? My suitcase was at the foot of the bed. How had this got there? Maybe Sangster and Bailey brought me home. I rushed out to reception enquiring, "Do you have a Sangster booked in here?"

"No sir, no one by that name appears on the register."

"Try Bailey" I said.

"No."

"What about Sedergreen?"

"Yes, Room 18. Can I help you sir?"

Realising the time, I said, "Get me a cab to go to the Sydney Con."

As I burst through the doors, a reception party howling with laughter greeted me.

"We had to put you to bed like a good little boy Snodders."

I did not know if it was Sydney or Sangster, but this was a different mentality than I had ever encountered.

The Americans had called a faculty meeting to discuss the running of the clinic. But it seemed that Tony Gould was busy with Mark Murphy, Brian Brown was still in transit from a tour of Germany, John Sangster was missing, Ricky May felt useless at such events and rumours were circulating that Alan Turnbull was unlikely to leave the comfort of the basement where he had been enjoying an abundance of the fashionable weed.

It was frustrating that I should be the only person representing Australian participants at that meeting. To make things more embarrassing, every American turned up whether they were here to teach or not. For the first 40 minutes, not one thing was said about the Australian staff or students who had paid good money to attend the clinic. Seeing that I was getting agitated, David Baker said, "Have you anything to say Bob?" This was not a good question to ask me at the time.

"Plenty," I said.

"Firstly, these young dudes behind me might be great trumpet players in a big band situation but they don't look like teachers to me. So I'm expecting that the teachers among you will brief them on how to deal with our students and make sure they are in class on time. Also I was shocked at how Jack Wilkins, brilliant guitarist he may be, thought he was still in New York when grading students. He was so fast, they felt threatened and hassled; I mean one young musician said to him, 'I'm from Queensland, remember it's opposite down here; our deep South is like your North and Queensland is in our North, which of course is like your deep South. So I think you Americans should realise things are different here and make allowances."

Mel Lewis who was an exact look-alike of Melbourne drummer Ron Sandilands, was staring at me with that rare ugly look normally reserved for dangerous criminals. But this story is about

Eberhard Weber. I had an album of Eberhard Weber playing bass with Monty Alexander (*Love and Sunshine*), so I was looking forward to working with him and Sydney's masterful drummer Alan Turnbull.

Unfortunately for me, I had been appointed to head the rhythm section class. Much to my frustration, on the first day, neither Eberhard nor Allan turned up to class. So I spent the day with a roomful of pianists, bassists and drummers and ended up demonstrating everything myself.

Although the kids liked what was going on, they were kind of disappointed as they were hoping to see Eberhard and Allan. I made some enquiries, firstly about Turnbull. It seemed everyone knew he wouldn't be turning up to class because he was spending his time in the deep dark basement of the Conservatorium smoking stuff and he would be absolutely useless anyway.

As for Eberhard Weber – when I came out into Martin Place, there he was, tall, blond, Teutonic, wearing an incredibly shiny, silvery jacket with metallic threads. One would have thought he was taking part in a jousting tournament; he looked totally out of place in contemporary Sydney. Interviewing him was a beautiful Australian girl, also blonde, and he was lapping up the adulation. With each question you could see him breathing in proudly and answering questions about his music and how people called it 'toothpaste music.'

I waited patiently and at the end of the interview approached, saying, "Listen Eberhard, I don't know what you were doing today but you missed class, that's really bad man. You know the kids were expecting to see you there; you shouldn't do that."

Eberhard didn't like the fact he was being lectured by someone he didn't know and who may not be important in the scheme of things. He sort of muttered, "Yah, mmm, yah."

He walked away completely unfazed.

"Fuck this" I thought. He and Turnbull deserve to be dobbed in; they were being paid good money, while I was carrying the class.

David Baker was the head of the faculty, so into his office I went.

"What's happening man?" said David.

"Hey close the door. Let's have a blow together."

"But I came in to talk about the classes."

"No, no" he said, as he drew out a cello and we had an impromptu musical ideas swapping session after which he laughed and said, "Now how can I help you?"

"It's about Eberhard Weber and Allan Turnbull, one of our guys."

"What's happening?" he said.

"They're not coming to class, I had to do everything myself."

To which David replied, "Who's in charge? Didn't I put you in charge of this section? You're the pianist aren't you? It's up to you, Bob, go and assert some authority."

David Baker was an inspirational music teacher who would walk into class, dressed in the regalia of a basketball player.

He would then commence snapping his fingers and clapping his hands on beats two and four till everybody in the room could feel the tempo he wanted. He would then start to sing, hum and whistle the melody, so nobody could doubt which notes to play and how these notes were to be interpreted. He would repeat this procedure until everybody in that room was just busting to play. Then he would give the order to commence, clapping his hands and stomping his feet should the tempo drag. He would yell out encouragement when those improvising made something happen. It was like being part of a gospel service, with David the minister in charge – his energy and enthusiasm in class was always maintained at the highest level.

Strangely enough, he would be very peaceful and in some sort of meditative state when alone in his office. David had insisted that I call in every lunch break but instead of discussing what was happening at the clinic, he would invite me to sit at the small upright piano in his office, saying "Let's jam, man!"

Unsure of what his intentions were, I would commence improvising freely without form, or harmonic progression. He would smile approvingly and commence playing bowed passages on his cello that to me bore no resemblance to anything I was doing. What he did made me listen to his playing, trying to find the right harmonies to play behind him, but every time I tried that approach, he would once again find atonal areas escaping from my very friendly musical suggestions. After 20 minutes of frustration I would throw my hands up in defeat.

"Wow that was great, thank you for the work out," said David, "I sure needed that."

"That's strange I said, I didn't understand a thing we played."

"Neither should you," said David, "if we had recorded today's session, you would have found that I played each response to your ideas a semitone above where you played them." Then in a genuine tone said, "We will play together each day. See you at the same time tomorrow."

The clinic was run over three days, so on the second day I assumed that Turnbull and Weber would turn up. But when I walked into class, no Allan Turnbull and no Eberhard Weber. I was furious. After a while the students started to complain, one of the bass players said, "We were hoping to get some advice from a bass player" and a drummer, "We would like to see how a rhythm section works."

I knew everyone was pretty disappointed so I promised them Turner and Weber would be in class the next day, even if it meant dragging their carcasses across Sydney.

I was in such a fit of internal rage that I couldn't go on with the class and knocked off early.

Being from Melbourne, I didn't know my way around the Sydney Con, so I got a student to accompany me to the basement where I spotted Allan Turnbull. I could have killed him there and then. He looked up at me smiling saying, "You've been looking for me?"

"Yeah you mother fucker, what in the fuck are you doing here? I need you up there because the kids want to see you, and this German bass player hasn't turned up. Just be there tomorrow and we'll play together."

Turnbull apologised, promising to definitely make class on the third day.

The next person on my list to seek was Eberhard. I had worked myself into a state where my temper and mouth were totally uncontrollable. He was in the café hanging out with the 'more important musicians.' I went straight up to him and grabbed him by the collar.

"Hey you! You weren't in class today, that's the second day in a row. That's a disgrace. Do you think you could give up a little bit of your precious time? Tomorrow I'm going to have Dave Baker there with me and you and Allan Turnbull can explain to everyone why you've missed two thirds of the clinic."

He was very embarrassed and went, "Yah, yah, yah I will be there tomorrow."

I didn't care that I had humiliated him in front of his friends. I remember walking around The Rocks area of Sydney just to cool down.

The next morning's class was the scene of great happiness for the sixty students enrolled in my class; all three instructors were there. Happily I introduced both Allan and Eberhard, glowing in my praise at their contributions.

"Now we're going to play as a trio. Drummers, you'll notice the placement of the high hat on beats two and four."

Allan promptly demonstrated this, the class nodding in assent.

Wanting to get back at me, Eberhard said, "That isn't necessarily so" — his first words to the class a total contradiction to what I had just taught.

"What do you mean?" I said.

"Not in every music does it have to be, only in certain music. Sometimes the high hat isn't played anywhere, sometimes it can be splashed or make sounds, like in creative music."

"But we're talking about swing" I said, trying to emphasise the point. "Do you mean in the bands you play with swing doesn't come down on two and four?"

"It may or it may not." Eberhard took delight in leaving the class in total confusion.

Wanting to establish a basic concept about time I interjected, "Now we're going to play a tune where Eberhard swings just like he did with Monty Alexander, on one of my favourite albums."

But Eberhard decided not to support me. Instead of playing

lines, jerky dinks and donks emanated from the bass. There was no groove, just a cacophony of bullshit.

Our war of words continued, even at the concluding dinner, where Eberhard presented me with his beautifully engraved business card and asked me for mine.

"You may need one I said, but if you visit Melbourne just mention my name to any player and they'll lead you to me" I said triumphantly.

Fortunately for me, Barry Ward and Peter Brindle had somehow heard of Eberhard's exploits and had devised some procedure to punish him financially. We never saw him again.

The clinic consisted of a series of concerts starring the individual tutors; they were very well attended with a young enthusiastic audience of students and their friends. Normally I do not take too much notice of the audience until I'm up on stage performing. But I could not help noticing how gorgeous the women looked. Perhaps it was the Sydney sun, the easygoing lifestyle, or the warmer climate dress code.

I was sitting up the back pondering these things, when a stunning brunette with curves in all the right places approached me saying, "Can I sit on your lap love?"

Before I had time to reply she collapsed there, wriggling her gorgeous frame in a proximity that left me both delighted and uncomfortable. This had never happened to me before – ever. Part of me wanted her to leave, part of me didn't.

"Are you here for the Jazz?" I enquired naively.

She hesitated, replying "Jazz?"

"Who do you like?"

"I'm here for the Americans" she replied.

"Do they play any better than us?" I asked.

She just giggled, introducing me to four of her friends – all young, well-endowed and extremely attractive. I remain to this day, Australia's most naive Jazz musician.

"Are you girls all from Sydney?" I asked innocently.

"We are, but we've been working in Bangkok lately."

They must be air hostesses I thought.

Then they promptly left for The Regent Hotel, (perhaps they

wished to encounter their favourite musicians, I thought).

As the Regent seemed to be unofficial headquarters for the clinic, I decided to investigate. As I breezed through the entrance, Barry Ward was sitting in a comfortable lounge in the lobby, summoning me for a drink.

"Do you know why you're here?" he said.

"Do tell" I replied in a mocking voice.

"I was in New York in this famous Jazz club, the headliner being Richie Cole. I approached him, told him about my plans and asked him whom should I get. To my surprise, of all people he said you. I'd never heard of you before. Welcome mate."

He seemed so genuine I softened and said, "I feel sorry for you spending so much money and extravagance on the Yanks. I mean, putting them up here must be costing you a fortune."

One of the beautiful hostesses floated across the room to us.

"How's it going, love?" Barry said to her.

"Very well," she replied, as she passed.

"Do you know her?" I said.

"Know her?" Barry laughed "Shit mate, it's true I spent a fortune on the Yanks but these girls are getting a lot of it back for me," he replied.

"You slimly little bastard," I said trying to suppress a laugh..

It was then I recognised the well-rounded figure of Ricky May. (I had heard Ricky May singing at a bar in St Kilda in the 60s.)

"Where are you staying?" I asked casually.

"Here at the Regent," he said. "But Bob you've got to help me, I'm in deep shit."

"What is it?"

"I can't talk about it here. Let's go up to my room."

Upon entering the room, Ricky proceeded to unashamedly undress himself in front of me putting on an immaculate tuxedo shirt and bow tie. As he checked himself in the mirror, he said, "Bob do you realise what day this is?"

"No."

"Mate! This is the most important day of my life. Shortly I'm going to be singing in front of a capacity crowd, with one of the world's greatest big bands, and you know Mark Murphy sang with them last night? Do you realise how important this is to me?"

"I'm sure it is, but what has this got to do with me?"

"Shit Bob, when I saw you down in the lobby I knew straight away that you'd be able to help me with my problem. Over near the dressing table lies the big band arrangement that Ned Sutherland (a notorious Sydney based arranger) has done for me. Bob, he just rang me to let me know that there's an extra bar of 5/4 somewhere in that chart and he hasn't time to come here and erase it. So be a good friend and find it for me would you?"

Not many people in the world are as gullible as I was for Rick's tomfoolery. He must have died laughing as I flicked through the many pages of the arrangement looking for the missing bar of 5/4.

"Hey look Ricky" I said in frustration, "I just can't find it."

"Hey Bob" said Ricky feigning disbelief, "they told me you're one of the country's greatest players."

"I'm sorry mate, I'm not a big band person, I'm a bit out of my depth."

Ricky's acting skills were immaculate. He suddenly turned angry. "Well you better get on the phone and sort it out with Ned, we haven't much time."

"You want ME to ring a person I've never met, about a chart I can't find a missing bar in?"

By this time Ricky had assumed a raging temper. "Just do it," he said curtly.

I found myself picking up the phone, and ringing Ned Sutherland, who was obviously hip to the joke. "Hey Ned, Bob Sedergreen here. I'm in Ricky May's room at The Regent, and I've looked everywhere in your chart for the missing bar of 5/4, but I can't find it."

"Oh well Bob, tell Ricky if the band collapses as a whole, he'll just have to recover."

I could not hear the laughter on the other side of the phone, but I'm sure I was the butt of some fantastic joke.

Ricky, who was making final adjustments to his bow tie said, "You and Ned have been no use. You'd better go, I'll be on soon."

Sitting in the audience some twenty-five minutes later, I witnessed Ricky and the band's flawless execution of Ned's chart.

Realising there had been no missing bar at all, I was determined to try and even up the score. I broke into Ricky's club date that night, accosted him in the dressing room saying, "Is this Sydney or just you?"

"I'm sorry," said Ricky apologetically, "I didn't realise you were that sensitive. Please mate, do me the honour of playing a tune with me in the next set."

"Is this another one of your tricks?"

"Oh no" said Ricky. "Something like 'Bye Bye Blackbird' in F?"

When it was my turn to come up, Ricky got on the mike gushing compliments about my ability. It was an easy song at an easy tempo, but at the end of the first chorus Ricky started playing with the time and delivering his own version of George Russell's twelve-tone concepts. It caught the bass and drums by surprise. They halted immediately leaving me to try and find Ricky, like a slippery eel in a pond. About a minute passed and Ricky deliberately stopped allowing me to play on my own. I looked up in disbelief as he sang knowingly to the audience, "Trust me, Bob Sedergreen took the song to its coda."

I had encountered two unforgettable tricksters — John Sangster and Ricky May.

THE COMMUNE

WITH DAVID TOLLEY no longer in the band, Ted knew he must somehow persuade Barry Buckley, his most dependable friend to join.

Barry was the original bassist in the earlier Brian Brown groups, the much-talked about quintet of 58, with Stewie Speers on drums and the quartet of the 60s with Tony Gould on piano. Once given the call Barry, being such a beautiful dude, dutifully re-joined the group. The new Brian Brown Quartet would be playing at a new spot, called The Commune. This little shop located in St George's Road, Fitzroy, would become a cult mecca for the next generation of aspiring young Jazz buffs.

The group played on Sunday nights, and we played for no money. It was not that we wanted to be unprofessional we all just had full-time day jobs, Ted in advertising, Barry in dentistry, myself in printing, Brian at channel 9. It was just a matter of wanting to play whatever took our fancy. We would take up a collection and pass that money on to Colin and his mates who ran The Commune.

It was an incredibly small room, so tiny the people could smell us. The audience sat on benches, along the walls right next to us and Colin would provide them with coffee, soup or biscuits. We cultivated a small and discerning new young audience who were able to listen and watch us at close range. Each night was given over to wild experimentation and daring improvisation. No one was afraid of establishing bold, new ideas.

If one of us was absent, the others would continue on anyway. One good thing about this new band was that Brian was definitely band leader. We just enjoyed being street musicians with great hearing and a fierce desire to play.

Brian led us by example, so strong was his influence, that we followed him without question. In this new band, Brian would have time to find more of his true self. Ted, Barry and I had proved we were a solid rhythm section, who all shared the love of grooving. Brian called it 'grooveroony.' Barry was unrelenting and tireless, favouring long, growling, chromatic lines. His talent also included playing freely or rock-solid time feels. Barry would dig in deeper and harder every time a line was repeated and would often set up the direction our groove was to take.

Brian also gave me space to explore the limits of my Korg synthesizer. He played less synthesizer in those days, preferring his saxophones, gong and flute — an instrument that had come back into fashion. Brian would ride above the rhythm section with a series of long phrases and short interjections. In no way did we try to copy Coltrane's famous quartet, however I remember one night we played the song 'Nature Boy.' Having played the melody, our improvisations lasted for one hour. Quite often we would start playing with no fixed ideas and develop a piece of music on the spot that would intensify over a period of at least one hour.

Free from the dictates of promoters, club owners and others who regard success as 'bums on seats', The Commune was a liberating experience and my spirit felt free to express its soul.

No wonder I was devastated when Ted walked in and told us he was leaving town to start a new life. You see, he had fallen in love, a love which would lead him interstate, and finally to marriage in sunny Queensland. Even more disturbing was that without Ted, Barry bowed out of future music-making, leaving Brian and I to our own devices.

"What will we do?" I asked Brian.

"Perhaps we could use Allan and Gary (my colleagues from Onaje)."

Brian persuaded me that music was moving on and so should we.

"I've booked a couple of kids that will take us to new places in the music."

It sounded grandiose but who were these kids? David Jones and Jeremy Alsop. I'd never heard of them and to make matters worse they were in their teens. The old man's gone crazy, I thought.

My first encounter with David Jones was on a cold winter's night at The Commune, circa 1980. He was warming himself besides the fireplace, just itching to play and smiling a mischievous, knowing and perhaps too-confident smile. Wanting to unsettle him a trifle, I stood over him and said menacingly,

"Listen kid, you're going into the fire."

Within an instant a quiet voice said,

"No! No! You're going into the fire."

To add insult to injury, his demeanor remained unaltered.

"OK" said I, and started to lift him off the floor as one would pick up a bride.

"You're going into the fire."

His response was to look down at me and laugh as though he had been picked up and taken for a ride by a friendly bear, (which of course I was).

Just before we began playing he pointed a drumstick at me and said,

"You're going into the fire."

It was as exhaustive a first set as I have ever played, with explosions emanating from the drum kit like fireworks bursting into flight on some gala occasion.

I nicknamed him 'Bullets' Jones, his paradiddles being faster than a machine gun. David had some other endearing features; great hearing, an ability to respond and change direction, an obsession with sound that rivalled David Tolley's and a passion for free improvisation. It would be David who would continue to champion a free approach to Jazz as pioneered by Brian Brown, Ted Vining and David Tolley.

David was also possessed by the creative spirit and one night having extracted just about everything possible from his kit in a spontaneous act of desperation, he left his drum stool and began walking around his kit, playing each appendage from the front. After he successfully circled his kit, he sat down at the stool again and completed an amazing solo. This incident became famous and David expanded the concept. So imagine my horror when I saw James Morrison instruct his brother John to duplicate it, time and again much to the approval of the audience.

Another reason David and I got on so well was attitude. We were like two naughty little boys in love with life and prepared to challenge any musicians that came our way. This would lead to a lifelong friendship. We became part of a new spiritual movement, playing in a trio led by David and featuring the virtuosic bass wizardry of Evripedes Evripidu.

Jeremy, on the other hand, was a tall and gentle boy from Blackburn High, who could burst into fits of laughter like a wheezing bull. His notes on the electric bass were loud, clear and confident. It was on that same wet night that I offered to give Jeremy a lift home.

As we ploughed up a watery Brunswick Street in the early hours of the morning, we noticed a lady standing in the middle of the road, seemingly on a suicide mission, as cars swerved at the last moment to avoid her. Overwhelmed by the experience, young Jeremy wrote a piece called 'Lady in the Street' that outlined deep melodic feelings.

Brian was right into bands like Weather Report, Chick Corea, Mahavishnu and Miles. They were playing a new brand of Jazz (some called it fusion) and so many special guests would visit The Commune, to expand their bands' horizons. Musicians like violinist Steve Mc Taggart, a young Congo player, (just arrived from Chile), Alex Pertout and trumpeters Bob Venier (nicknamed 'The Godfather') and a trumpeter who really understood space, Keith Hounslow.

Brian and I had written songs as a tribute to our long-standing relationship; mine was called 'December Dance,' an astrological reference and Brian's was called 'Blue', a reference to the Blues. Both were recorded on the album *Bells Make Me Sing*.

I re-recorded this piece on a CD bearing my own name *Bobbing and Weaving* on Larrikin Records.

Unfortunately our time together was short. David and Jeremy had to leave. They had aspired to being part of a world where musicians were treated as professionals and paid accordingly, an impossible feat at The Commune.

MAL WALDRON

G OING TO SYDNEY was something I was very much looking forward to. Our band Onaje which included Allan Browne, Richard Miller and Gary Costello, were to play the warm up for the great pianist Mal Waldron. We got the gig because Mal was prepared to use Allan and Gary as his rhythm section, which meant Mal and I would share the night on piano. I was particularly looking forward to meeting Mal not only because he had worked with Charles Mingus and Eric Dolphy and been accompanist to the great singer Billie Holliday, but also because rumour had it that he was a disciple of Thelonious Monk and I was very keen to solve the riddle of Spoon equating my spirit to that of Monk. Spoon had told Australian journalists that I was Australia's Monk.

Tall, dark, thin and dressed demurely in a black skivvy with a matching reefer jacket, Mal cut quite a figure, especially as he smoked long thin black cigarettes; I remember the brand, it was called 'More.'

I had played a pretty hot set and as Mal came over to greet me, he said in a gentle tone, "I see you've kept the seat warm, thanks for that."

Before I had time to decide if this was a compliment or a reprimand, Mal commenced his set, starting with George Gershwin's 'Summertime' and although his right hand held the melody, his left hand began a series of wandering chromatacisms that bore no resemblance to the chord changes whatsoever. I could see the strain on Gary's face as he tried to hold down the normal bass tonic roll, which Waldren insisted was cool.

No one in the room had heard anything like it before, and I thought: either he's demented or gets off on disenfranchising his audience, or, like Monk, he's a true revolutionary.

Occasionally during bass solos, his tall figure could be seen peering out from under the lid of the dark black piano blowing puffs of grey coloured smoke into the steamy atmosphere of the club. The system of left hand chromatic romps continued unabated during the set as he proceeded to enhance or destroy, depending on one's point of view, a dozen or so standards.

At the end of his set he beckoned me to the bar and over a couple of bourbons we began to talk.

"What was that all about?" I asked disbelievingly.

"Oh, you mean the music?" he answered smiling.

"Is that what you call it?" I said light-heartedly.

"I just thought I'd try something different tonight. Something people may not have heard before."

I suddenly realised I was talking to a man who totally understood the spirit of Jazz and its experimental nature.

A lot of today's musicians play to a formula, but not Mal.

I told him about Spoon and the Monk thing. He listened earnestly and said, "If you want to understand what Spoon was driving at, play the piece 'Mysterioso' everyday for at least the next three months and all will be revealed. The answer is in there somewhere."

'Thanks" I said, like someone who had just visited the dentist. "Is there anything I can do for you?"

"Do you play chess?" he looked at me.

"Oh, yes" I said reassuringly, "But I'm no good at it."

Mal looked a little disappointed, so I quickly added, "But my friend Ray Martin over there, he always beats me."

"That's ok said Mal, "You see, I'm a chess master, I'm looking for someone to give me a good game."

I realised I was dealing with a smart dude.

So back home in Melbourne I began to practice 'Mysterio'; I played it every day. And one day my left hand wandered onto a different bass note, and as I traversed up the piano chromatically I found the open voicings that I had heard so many black American gospel and Blues pianists play. I would incorporate it into my own approach forever. Thanks Mal.

PART FOUR

ON THE BOIL

BLUES ON THE BOIL

IN THE LATE '70s, I received a phone call from a Mr Bill Martin, who was Head of Muisc at the Yarra Valley Anglican Boys School. He wanted me to set up and coach a Jazz/Rock group. There were many reasons why I felt that teaching was not for me, however Bill was obviously genuine — a characteristic in people I find impossible to refuse.

This young guitarist with a great feeling for Blues and Country music had an almost perfect showbiz name as his real name; Dene Ford. One day, following an exciting class session, Dene took me aside to ask a barrage of serious questions, his young eyes scrutinising me for any signs of exaggeration or falsehood. His questions seemed stupid, like "Sir, are there other bands like ours in the real world?"

"Of course," I answered patronisingly, "Blood Sweat and Tears and Chicago are recognised as outstanding fusion bands worldwide, and then there is Nucleus in England, and groups like the Galapagos Duck here."

"Do you play in bands like that?"

"Well not exactly that style, but in all the bands I play in, I make reference to the Blues and my fellow musicians love me for that."

"Do you think I would find something like that to be part of?"

"Those who look usually find," I said.

"But where will I find the right musicians who would want to play this music?"

"You're talking as though I should form a band especially for your benefit," I said sarcastically.

"Would ya Sir?"

It was at this point that I knew he was deadly serious, and somehow I felt guilty at the thought of not helping Dene fulfil his ambition.

"Muddy Waters, Howling Wolf, Otis Rush, Buddy Guy... sounds like a pack of cowboys to me," said Ted Vining nonchalantly, revealing that here in Australia, one of the country's most outstanding jazz drummers had no knowledge of these legends of Black American music. Sadly most musicians I had worked with seemed to share Ted's point of view. Rather than being the touchstone of Afro-American music, Blues to them represented an inferior brand of music, played by unskilled musicians, people not brilliant enough to play jazz.

In order to satisfy my curiosity further, Rae and I visited the Royal Oak Hotel in Bridge Road, Richmond. The music room was aptly named the Tiger Lounge. Waiting inside were the fans: tiger-like people, women dressed in thin revealing tiger-skin blouses and very short skirts, guys dressed up like a pack of bikies. This was obviously a place where being tough was more important than being beautiful. The featured band was Southern Lightning, a quartet consisting of electric guitar, electric bass, blues harp, and drums..

Encouraged by their boyfriends and alcohol, the women began to confront the musicians with taunts like: "Can youse play something we can dance to, play something with a beat!" The band's response was immediate, but also loud and ugly. Music astonishingly lacking in everything but brutal delivery of electronic distortion and pounding backbeat. Two more shuffles featuring more of the same shameless lack of musicality followed. I realised this was what the crowd wanted; it was me who was totally out of place. I had come to listen to the Blues, but that's not what the band's followers wanted. They came here to experience something else, something exciting that might happen, driven on by the stimulus of alcohol, suggestive and explicit dancing and the intake of raw musical energy that was supposed to lead to sexual abandonment..

I would have left there and then, but all of a sudden, the crowd eased off on the band which proceeded to play a very slow Blues. I could not believe the amount of genuine musical feeling these guys were able to transmit, strong and sensual enough to have me glued to my seat. Totally devoid of affectations or slickness, these rockers had delivered the deep feelings of the Blues with such innocence and honesty; they touched my soul.

As I thought about the gig at the Tiger Lounge I realised the performance of Blues in Australia was similar to what happened in England; it had been left to either Rock musicians, or dedicated Blues aficionados to play rather than Jazz musicians, whereas all seriously written, filmed, or recorded evidence led to the conclusion that in America, Blues was the foundation stone of Jazz, the roots of Black Afro-American music. Reports of Miles Davis attending Jimi Hendrix gigs, and Dizzy Gillespie checking out B.B King were common knowledge in the USA at this time.

Well here was my chance to go out and prove that Jazz musicians could and should play the Blues with greater authority than any one. As there were no Blues bands on the Jazz scene, it would be a ground floor opportunity, to not only establish myself as a worthy bandleader, but also to make a genuine contribution to Jazz simply by widening the appreciation of musicians, audiences, and venue providers. The larger the spectrum of music, the greater its appeal and therefore its audience.

Excited at the prospect of forming my new group, and realising the controversy a Blues band would create amongst the Jazz community, it was important to make sure the personnel would be able to convincingly deliver the goods. Young Dene Ford sang and played like a natural, but there was another brilliant young guitarist at the VCA: Ian Tritt, who also played mandolin, violin and sang. Ian had experience playing in a Bush band with his father. Ian preferred the dirtier more full-on approach to Blues exhibited by artists like Clapton and Hendrix, which would form a contrasting sound and approach to the relaxed open solo style of Dene. However, neither lads were ready for the lead singer role. For this sort of music we needed someone capable of delivering Blues material over the top of a very powerful and spirited instrumental group and the only singer I had seen do this was Judy Jacques. How well I remembered hearing her unbelievable vocal delivery as she stood in front of the raging Yarra Yarra Jazz Band, singing Blues and Gospel Songs. Oh yes! Judy had a lot going for her; a natural photogenic beauty, personality and charm, experience in the commercial world of radio and television, the ability to instantly communicate with a wide audience, and the vocal power to penetrate the density of a full-on Blues band.

The next problem was finding the right drummer. Jazz drummers offer flexibility, swing time, fills and the ability to blend in to the various dynamics of the ensemble. In Blues, the drummer needs to penetrate the backbeat with force and intensity, and patiently sit on the time feel, making sure it and the ensemble remain rock steady. Perhaps these requirements were too disciplined and not inventive enough for your average jazz drummer. I immediately thought of the Dorset Gardens Hotel in Croydon, a place pulsing with live music and a huge pub lounge. Everyone from Johnny O'Keefe to Kamal had featured there, but most of all was the house band The Fendermen. Their drummer, Gordon Pendleton, anchored that band, night after night with sessions of pulsing Rock'n'Roll covers. I could not remember the few people in that lounge who did not immediately feel the urge to get on up and dance. I couldn't comprehend how a drummer stayed so solid night after night. I assumed it must have been part of growing up in Geelong.

There was only one bass player I could ask, there would be no solos, few chord changes and it could almost be deemed boring for the likes of flashy young bass players like Geoff Kluke and Gary Costello. So I turned to Barry Buckley, knowing how dependable his sense of time was and said, "Hey Barry, do you remember when we first played I used to make fun of how long your bass notes were? Well that's all I want now —long notes."

Barry was such a beautiful human being; he not only agreed to do it but also wanted to know in great depth what it was I wanted him to do.

About this time Michael Hancock was opening a new musical venue, a pub called The Limerick Arms in South Melbourne. In those days, Friday and Saturdays might work but Thursday nights seemed like a risky proposition and I convinced him he'd have nothing to lose by letting a Blues band have the residency. –Blues was getting air-play at the time and I suggested that perhaps it might be the next big thing. I also figured that a lot of Melbourne musicians had become a little precious at the time, considering themselves so special, that the old fashion idea of a 'sit in' had become impossible. After all, John Adams had let me 'sit in' at Opus '61. It really tickled my fancy to reinstate a custom that had disappeared as a result of so called originality. The first 'sit in' was a young lad called Justin Brady on harp. A passionate and earnest young man with red hair and freckles, he'd been washing dishes at Taco Bills across the road and played during his work breaks. It was after listening to his sounds that I realised how special the harp playing was in this music, how popular it was in Australia, and how important Mojo Burford was in creating Muddy Waters band sound. Justin became a regular member of the band. Proud of his Irish roots, he also played violin, which would be really beneficial in expanding our band sound.

It was also a time when FM was becoming popular, and I remember my son Malcolm making me tune in every Saturday, to radio station 3PBS's Blues Show, presenter Jake 'The Snake' Roberts who played artists like Freddy King, and telecaster master Albert Collins. It was after listening to this show —especially Muddy Waters' eight-piece blues band featuring harp and alto sax— that I realised this was the sort of sound I was hoping for. Malcolm was learning sax and flute at the time and taking a keen interest in what I was doing with the band. He kept insisting that we check out what seemed to me a Rock act, Stevie Ray Vaughn and Double Trouble. They were appearing at Melbourne's Concert Hall and as Mal and I sat in our seats looking down at the stacks of amplifiers and huge baffles in front of them I thought, 'Oh no, Rock'n'Roll in The Concert Hall. What a disaster!' My fears seemed to be confirmed when the audience walked in, young cats and chicks, looking for a hot young band. To my surprise, a trio of young white dudes walked out: Stevie Ray dressed traditionally in the clothing of a Texas Blues man and much to the disgust of the young audience, most of whom had left by interval, played an eclectic program of slow Blues and shuffles.

"See I told you dad," said Mal, who seemed to have his finger on the pulse of new directions in music, and it was then that I decided to include him in the band, named Blues On The Boil, after his temperament and playing.

They say fortune favours the brave, and pretty soon there were bums on seats at the Limerick on Thursday nights. This was a new development in music. In the fifties and sixties, musicians were regarded as professionals who were paid a fee for their services like any other professionals. But the eighties signalled a new development — the door deal. Now musicians had to prove to management that they could put bums on seats in order to be paid, or face expulsion. The quality and standard didn't seem to matter. No bums on seats meant 'no band playing here'.

At one stage, Thursday nights were more popular than any other night. About this time the ABC rang me about recording the band. Just like my idol Cannonball Adderley, I believed that live recordings were a better representation of a band's work. This meant the ABC had to establish a landline to the pub and bring an Outside Broadcast van, virtually a studio in a van. The supervisor Paul Petran and the engineer Mal Stanley went on to become ABC music presenters. It was a good feeling to have pioneered this move.

The rumours were flying around town that I formed the band because I couldn't play Jazz any more, lost the ability to swing, sold out on being creative, to name just a few. I thrived on rumours like this and invited Blues-men Dutch Tilders and Martin Cooper to guest on the album. I was one of the first Australian band leaders to employ an American singer. Although Little Larry Weems hailed from Cincinnati, Ohio, he was of African-American descent and a handful of trouble. Larry could turn up drunk or stoned or both and he had been seen frequenting some of the more dubious gay bars around town. He would never turn up on time and suddenly appeared on stage like a star saying, "Hey Bob, what set is this and what am I singing?"

The band members would always smile as I burst into fits of rage abusing him for his misdemeanours, but once he opened his mouth, he sang in the spirit of Don Hathaway (one of my favourite soul singers) and exuded brashness, confidence and high energy. I was also lucky enough to have recruited the new kid on the block, Doug De Vries, a brilliant guitarist then musical director for Vince Jones. Doug really knew plenty about the blues but was so gifted he would soon spread his wings internationally.

The album started getting airplay around Australia. Without knowing it, we were riding a worldwide wave of Blues, spear headed by Albert Collins and Stevie Ray Vaughan, with emerging artists like George Thorougood, Robert Cray and Robben Ford. This led to tours to Sydney's famous Basement; the band, at one stage, eclipsing Vince Jones attendance record. A snowball effect was an invitation to appearances at The Festival of Sydney, with concerts in Hyde Park and the Victoria Barracks. A lot of people came to check the band out, everyone from Paul Grabowsky to Pat Metheny. One of the by-products of the 'sit in' policy was the appearance of Australian poet laureate Eric Beech. I don't know of any other Blues band who regularly performed with a poet, but Eric's mood and poem 'Got to have a Blood Test Blues', really hit home with the HIV/AIDS controversy raging at the time, and gave the band a true Aussie flavour. Let me make it clear: people like Steve French and Eric Beech were friends to us and achieved fame much later.

My first stint as bandleader was proving both enjoyable and taxing; enjoyable because of the controversy the band created, and taxing because there is nothing harder than playing nothing but the Blues day in and day out. As a bandleader, I had myself to blame as my instruction to each guitarist was, "I want you guys to cream all over me."

Most guitarists would look disbelievingly at me. You see, most guitarists have a healthy respect for the piano as an instrument in defining melody and rhythm, but no piano player in Blues had really 'done it' for me.

Things got so hectic that Barry Buckley couldn't continue. Once again a bass player with the right attitude was critical. I remembered a young man, Scott Dunbabin, turning up with a real book and a music stand to his first gig with us and the fun the whole band had teasing him about it. Scotty Scorps as we called him, became Barry's replacement.

The 'sit in' policy was fraught with danger because some players really wanted to do it but just didn't have the necessary equipment to drag the feeling of the Blues from deep within their souls. I entrusted Justin Brady with the job of screening the ever-increasing number of guests wanting to sit in. Justin, who had a winning smile, came up one night flashing it and said, "You've got to let this young girl sing with the band. She sings Blues just like an angel."

As the lady in question sauntered up to the bandstand, a young, pale, blue-eyed blonde who was certainly not unattractive, I thought, 'Oh Oh, perhaps Justin's judgment has been impaired by the lady's obvious charms. '

"What's your name?" I asked politely.

"Jacki."

"What would you like to sing?"

"What about 'Stormy Monday' she said smiling at me.

"OK," I whispered to myself thinking 'you poor young thing, you're about to be mutilated by a very hard rocking band'.

What followed was an exercise in soul singing that rivalled the approach taken by Australia's Renee Geyer. Gus had been right, her silky and husky vocal qualities gave the band a new, wonderfully smooth approach and Jacki's stage manners and presentation were always cool and classy. When she told me her surname was Gaudion, I said,

"You're not related to Peter Gaudion, are you?"

"Well sort of," she replied with a smile.

When the band was asked to appear on television, I was grateful Jacki was our lead singer. It was Jacki's first television experience and we both laughed as she said, "I thought it was their job to make me look beautiful, not concentrate on all my blotches."

A singer of a totally different ilk was Rebecca Spalding. She called herself Big Mama Spalding after her idol Big Mama Thornton. Rebecca had her own Blues program on 3PBS radio. She sang in the Blues scene with the band Rocket 88. I remember being a guest on their recording and the guys being very suspicious of my motives for playing Blues. I think Rebecca had asked them not to punch my head in and convinced them it might be a good thing for the band. The other thing I discovered about these Blues dudes was how committed they had to be to the band. Yes, their last fifteen gigs had been put aside to pay for this expensive recording session. I remember ringing Rebecca in desperation to do a gig at Sydney's Basement. She had never met me nor heard of my playing, but gladly agreed to help out with strong, powerful and convincing mannerisms, sort of reminiscent of a female B.B. King. That was another thing I enjoyed about singers— that their instruments could be so different, with each voice having its own magic colour.

Helen Jennings was a lady attracted to the music scene and musicians in general. Her placid blue eyes and long flaxen hair reminded me of Mary from Peter, Paul and Mary.

Like Rebecca, she also had a Blues program on 3PBS and crossover friendships with Blues and Jazz musicians. She and Rae had been talking about the idea of having a Blues Festival. After all, if Jazz musicians could have a Jazz festival why couldn't Blues musicians have their own festival? Helen loved the work of Aussie Blues-Man Dutch Tilders, who she managed, and she knew all the local Blues players. So they both launched Melbourne's Own Home Grown Blues Festival. If this concept worked, it would mean that people would start recognising something I had known from the beginning; if Australia's sports people could beat the world's best, and our actors could be the toast of Hollywood, then surely it must follow that our best musicians would be in a similar class. Not only could Rae and Helen not afford to bring in US Blues-men, but also we made it a policy not do so.

There's something about the bottom end of Swan Street in Richmond, near the station: the factories, sweatshops, knock shops, workers store like Dimmeys. It's an old hard and tough part of Melbourne, with the most prominent hotel in the area being the Corner Hotel. Not so flash and run down in the eighties, one could walk into its dark interior and smell the remnants of rotten beer and vomit that couldn't be removed from the carpets. The timbered bands stand was a haven for termites, rats, and cockroaches; the old PA system a remnant of the golden days of Rock'n'Roll twenty years earlier. – It was the perfect home for our Blues Festival. Seeing the publican was no slouch himself, and was known to play Blues guitar, we started the festival there with his blessing.

In our minds, a festival was a celebration of Blues music and would include Folk and Delta Blues that were performed by solos and duos in the quieter surroundings of the upstairs lounge, while Texas, Chicago and New Orleans styles were played downstairs in the lounge. Of course Blues on the Boil, Dutch Tilders, Rocket 88, The Paramount Trio, Chequer Board Lounge were just some of the many bands that rocked the joint for twelve hours on the Sunday before Cup Day. The festival grew each year with internationally-accepted artists like Fiona Boyce, Geoff Achison, Carl Panuzzo who today regularly tour and perform in the USA and Europe. But they cut their teeth and honed their performance skills at our festival, which grew alongside the world resurgence of Blues for nearly a decade. Towards the end, the venue had to shift to The Palace in St Kilda because thousands of interested fans couldn't fit into the Corner.

The other interesting thing was that the bands invited to play from Sydney like The Bondi Cigars and The Mighty Reapers of Vengeance, played the music no differently than us. They were hot. Strange because in the Jazz world, Melbourne musicians favoured a more avant-garde and modal approach with the emphasis on experimentation; they seemed like different animals than their Sydney counterparts who preferred the smoother sounds of big band swing or early Be bop. What is really interesting is that Blues as a style of music is a leveller for musicians who play it, no matter where they are from, while Jazz is a much more individual form of expression.

Blues on the Boil had introduced Blues to a Jazz audience, and vice versa, thereby influencing a whole lot of new players. No band has since emerged from the Melbourne Jazz scene prepared to play solely the Blues and nothing but the Blues. But we had made the point made by John Hammond earlier in the USA, that Blues like Jazz was an African-American experience and that no self-respecting festival event could be complete without having a Blues component.

MAGNIFICENT MONTREAL
& ITS FESTIVAL DE JAZZ

T HERE'S SOMETHING FRENCH about Jazz and it's not just Sidney Bechet.

Even the word itself is supposedly derived from the French. New Orleans was really Nouvelle Orlean, a French outpost, and the Arcadians who migrated there did so from Quebec in Canada. The cities of Quebec and Montreal proudly fly the fleur de lys, not the maple leaf.

I was in Belmont, Geelong when the news filtered through that the Melbourne Group, Onaje were booked to play at the Montréal Jazz Festival,1990. To me Canada was part of the British Empire: the maple leaf and the Royal Mounties and stuff like that. As one of the sponsors were Canadienne Airlines, we spent 28 hours in the back of a DC10 and it seemed odd that the pilots continually broke into French and the word 'sortie' was marked across the exit. When we arrived everyone was in jubilant spirits, it was Summer and reason to be celebrating because of the long and harsh Winters people had to endure. So severe was their Winter that retail and commercial activity was forced underground, safe from the covering of ice and snow.

OK, what's different about French Canada? I wondered as I headed to a pub for a counter lunch. I was soon to find out when the cutlery was dropped rudely at my side after I ordered my meal in English. Then I noticed that everything was in French, from the local beer, Labatt Bleu, (a major sponsor of the festival) to the shop names. I dropped into one called La Salles and pretty soon one of the sales girls explained,

"You're now in French Canada and it's considered courteous to say something, anything at all, in French."

So I practiced the word 'certainment'. It worked wonders. I called into the same pub to be served by the same girl the next day and was treated like King Louis himself. Montreal was to be a steep learning curve for me. It was a city no bigger than Melbourne but boy did the festival have things under control. The first thing I noticed was that they were keeping tabs on all the bands. Even in the small motel where we were staying, a lady was radioing into headquarters the fact that we, Onaje had arrived. The other thing I noticed was the support for the festival. Not only was the brewery involved but also the airlines and Alcan, the national manufacturer of aluminum. It seemed every business in town, large or small, was somehow hooked up with the festival. The organising committee had the power to block off streets and to requisition venues at will: cathedrals, theatres, school halls, art centres, clubs and restaurants or any place they needed. Every business seemed keen to play ball for fear of being excluded from the festivals activities that drew enormous crowds of locals and tourists.

The programme was a veritable who's who of the Jazz world and the organisers told me that the plan for every concert was to achieve a sellout. Performers were placed in venues that suited their drawing power. People who didn't book early would miss the concert, which created an eagerness to book in advance and pay top dollar. The musicians, of course, were very happy playing to full houses.

The programming was imaginative, pairing the most unlikely people. The city was buzzing with talk of a forthcoming concert featuring Cuban singer Celia Cruz and David 'Fathead' Newman. I remember the Festival Director, David Jobim telling us that we were virtually an unknown band and the greatest service the festival could do for us was to give us 'exposure'. Good to his word we found ourselves playing on a large stage in the main street of town, closed off to traffic and packed with people 400 metres in each direction. Behind us a series of large screens depicted the wheat harvest in Australia. The lighting and sound equipment were top quality and operated by sophisticated engineers. Towards the end of the set, Jobim arrived with body guards carrying a silver case.

"It seems you had a good effect on the audience," he told Allan and promptly paid us in cash. This had never happened at home. Our other gigs were in large shopping centres, which ensured that we retained a large audience, with all our gigs free to the public. The other big public stage was a huge metallic Blues stage in another main street with Blues bands from all nations playing for free.

I had come as a performer musician. Little did I know that I would return three years later as the Artistic Director of the Montsalvat Jazz Festival.

ART ATTACK

I T ALL STARTED one night at the *Concert Hall*. Perhaps it was the tension that builds up the longer artists are kept waiting to go on, or perhaps a touch too much wine — people often react sharply just before a performance.

Brian Brown turned around on such an occasion and said to me: "Hey Bob, when are you going to make a serious artistic contribution to our music?"

"YEAH," echoed Judy Jacques, "we're waiting to see what your contribution will be."

Even though these words may have been spoken in jest, they prompted the realisation that despite the efforts I had put into Brian's quartet *Onaje*, *Ted's Trio* and my own band *Blues on the Boil*, it could still be argued that as yet, I had not come up with anything conceptually brilliant.

Australia's bicentennial was to provide the necessary stimulus. The media was going into frenzy about all things Australian. A replica of James Cook's yacht, the *Endeavour* was sailing to Sydney, which of course would be the hub for the celebrations. I was fortunate enough to be staying at Sydney Harbour that very night. Bicentennial funding had been used to glamorise what had always been one of the world's most beautiful cities. Roads had been widened, footpaths lined with sandstone pavers, docklands cleared, exposing new buildings, hotels, gardens and aquatic wonders and fairy lights lovingly adorned trees. In fact, the city was ready for what Prime Minister Bob Hawke described as one show we would never forget. Here I was at Kirribilli sitting on the roof of the Mount Street floating ferry terminal, on the Harbour watching that show.

At the time, Sydney had never seen a fireworks display of that magnitude. With each new explosion, you could hear the people gasp in awe as it crowned the natural beauty of the Harbour. Then as promised, three F111 jet fighters flew overhead, their afterburners aglow with streaks of brilliant orange flame, creating the sensation of sunlight across the night sky. One could feel the excitement building up from the thousands of spectators surrounding us. Crowds of people were watching, hanging out of windows, congregating in parks and gardens and perched in trees.

As I looked up at the faces of the spectators, I realised many dramatic changes had taken place in the cultural makeup of the Australian public. I saw Greeks, Turks, Indians, Chinese, Japanese, Aboriginals, British, Europeans — the many and varied faces of man. Yes! Australia had turned into a multicultural society. Shortly after this, I began to dream.

I had not had visual dreams since my childhood. Yet these dreams were very real, almost on the threshold of consciousness, despite the fact that the medication I took each night ensured deep sleep. I would awaken every few hours, excited, exasperated and intensely aware of what the dream was about.

In the first stage of the dream, I was transported to New Orleans. At that time, I had never been to the real New Orleans, but this felt right. I found myself sitting in a bar surrounded by multicultural faces — there were Africans, American Indians like Cajun, Navajo and Sioux, British, French, Hispanic and South Americans. My best mate was a big fat Creole gentleman, who looked remarkably like Fats Domino. He enjoyed telling me that Australia would never be the home of Jazz, because Jazz was born in New Orleans and the whole world knew that Jazz came from New Orleans. In fact, Jazz was a result of the cultural mix that existed in New Orleans around the turn of the century.

In the second part of the dream, I would argue my point of view that despite jazz being an American art form, it was totally unfair that Australian musicians, some of whom could play Jazz as well as anyone else in the world, received little or no recognition for their efforts and made far less money than their American counterparts. "Okay, okay," replied my Creole friend, "but remember Jazz will always be the music that came from New Orleans and if you Aussies want to have a music that is intrinsically Australian, go back home, look at your people and their histories and examine the cultures that exist there."

The dream would climax just before dawn and I would settle down to sleep for the third time, to witness James Cook's *Endeavour* sailing into Botany Bay. Up the front of the vessel, two pipers were piping the vessel into port; I could hear the familiar strains of the tune Bonnie Dundee, played exactly as on the *SS Cameronia* each time it made port. While this was happening, across the water at Le Sands, a group of Aborigines complete with didgeridoo, clap sticks and boomerangs, were chanting their response.

In my dream, I had heard the sound of bagpipes and didgeridoos. The next day, in order to make it a reality, I purchased recordings of Scottish reels and marches by the Gordon Highlanders, as well as music from Aboriginal tribes from *Kununnura* in Western Australia. I would play each one side-by-side for 15 minutes at a time. A new intrinsically Australian sound was filling my ears; both bagpipes and didgeridoos were instruments that droned so well together. After this discovery, my dreaming stopped, leaving me the puzzle of solving how this exciting new music would develop.

A few days later, I was watching a television show about Melbourne's Greek community. Most Australians associated Greeks with the local fruit shops or fish and chip shops. Con the Greek fruiter was a television comedy icon, and the show *Wogs out of Work*, had sell-out crowds. The most incredible statistic that came from this show was the fact that Melbourne boasted a Greek community almost as large as that of Athens. It rightfully followed, according to the rules of my dream, that Greek music must be part of this new music.

Next day, I walked into a music shop to be shown the traditional instruments of Greece (the bouzouki) and Turkey (the baglamah). Yes, the legend of *Anzac* was about the battle with the Turks at *Gallipoli*. There was no doubt that Greeks and Turks played an important part in Australian history and culture and that their music was modal and droned away in a single scale or key. I decided to call this new music *Joz*, meaning the jazz from Oz — a trendy word substitute for Australia.

Some time later, I was listening to Brazilian singer Milton Nascimento, singing in unison with my favourite soprano sax player Wayne Shorter, whose pure tone and flawless pitch added such a unique dimension to their sound. Their music possessed a mystical quality that I found not only irresistible, but also totally engrossing.

Why not apply this approach to the Australian jazz band I had dreamt about? The voice would provide the melody, with soprano sax in unison. The didgeridoo would provide the bass line, the bouzouki would play fills, and the bagpipes would improvise. This led to the drumming which of course must be exciting. Firstly the tight syncopation of Scottish military drumming, blended together with the percussion of Irish dance music and superimposed on top of today's funk beat. Now, for mission impossible — finding the people and putting together a band that could actually play *Joz* Music.

The first person I asked was drummer Michael Jordan. After all, we were playing alongside each other in Brian's new band *Winged Messenger*.

Brian had pronounced him to be the most exquisite drummer in town. I remember when I had been invited to his wedding. Back then he was one of our students at the Victorian College of the Arts (VCA). On that night, Jordan told me that he was indeed Irish and had played Irish folk music in his father's band. Jordan loved Jazz, especially bop, he played with taste and a lightness of cymbal time, his fills were melodic and he also sang like a choirboy.

Michael's wedding was an emotional affair especially at the end when he and his dad performed the stirring, 'Victoria Gardens.' I would just have to wait for the right moment to ask him.

That moment came when I offered to drive him home from work, and after a few whiskies, I told him that I needed an Irish percussionist who wouldn't mind dressing up like an Irish potato farmer. "It's crazy," said Michael, "but I'll do it if it happens."

I've never been a fatalist, but in the space of a month, two things happened that were inexplicable. Firstly, whilst playing a gig at *Jazz after Dark* for the Victorian Arts Centre. I couldn't concentrate all night due to interference from the didgeridoo that made up part of the band in the room next door. It was so strong, the walls shook; animal sounds and explosions of air emanated from that didgeridoo. When I went next-door I asked, "Who is responsible for that didgeridoo playing?"

"That's Joe Geia. He's famous, he sings, plays guitar, writes his own songs and plays incredible didgeridoo. He's worked with people like Stevie Wonder, Archie Roach and a whole bunch of big names."

Naturally I was keen to hang around and listen to Joe's music; it was contemporary, funky, and catchy with lyrics that spoke of his love for Australia, its land, wildlife and indigenous people. There was one song called "Yil-Lull" - this was as good as any composition I had heard. So I approached Joe Geia, looked him straight in the eye and said, "My names Bob Sedergreen. I come from the Jazz side of things and I really need someone like you to play didgeridoo and clap sticks in my band and do a bit of singing for me. This band will be special. Your music and culture will be included and we will not care about the colour of people's skin. In fact, we will stand against that sort of narrow-mindedness."

We hugged and Joe said "Looks like someone's done a good thing for the Aboriginal people - I'm your man."

Later I found out that Joe was a nephew of the famous Alby Geia, the first Aborigine who refused to be re-settled at Palm Island— a correction establishment for Aboriginal people established by the government of Queensland. I now saw Joe as the Aboriginal prince in my band.

I had my Aboriginal prince and my Irish potato farmer, what could I possibly want next? A Maori Princess?

About a month later, I got a call from singer Bridgette Allen. We had never worked together before, but on this night her pianist Peter Jones couldn't make it, so she asked me to come and do the gig with her. It was at a restaurant in Carlton called *Original Sins*.

To describe Bridgette as stunning, beautiful and all-woman would be an understatement. She had a voice like a songbird and swung in the spirit of Carmen McRae. Her dances and gesticulations during performance told the story of the songwriter's intentions. One would have thought that all my Christmases had come at once, especially as we did not pay for drinks. But on the night, I just couldn't find the place she was phrasing from. It did not seem to matter where I placed the accompaniment, or how hard I tried to anticipate her phrasing. Yes we were both swinging, but in different directions. At the end of the night, I apologised and promised to get it right next time. As I was walking out of the place, I spotted her car. On the back window was a sticker, displaying something about New Zealand. I read it again, thinking: *Yes... New Zealand...I thought she looked Maori and she's very beautiful... wow, I wonder if she's a Maori Princess?*

I ran back inside the restaurant and said, "Hey Bridgette, are you a Maori princess?"

She smiled at me and said, "Yes I am."

"Oh-boy!" I said, "You're just what I've been looking for."

She allowed me to explain about the band and how she would complete the regional end of things. After all, Australia and New Zealand were the two British dominions in the region and Aboriginal and Maori were the two indigenous peoples.

I added with a smile, "You don't sing too bad either...."

Things were taking shape nicely, but where was my Piper?

One afternoon I switched on the car radio to hear the unmistakable voice of Johnny Farnham singing his latest hit, 'You're the Voice.' I had always liked Farnham's vocal texture and quality, but this song really caught my imagination. Perhaps it was the Celtic feel, but in the background I heard bagpipes playing brilliantly, as though the Piper was improvising. If only I could track down who was playing them. This would have to be the person I required.

My frustration increased, as it seemed that no self-respecting Scottish bandmaster wanted to discuss John Farnham, or his number one hit. I tried every pipe band in Melbourne without success, and then remembered the young keyboardist David Hirshfelder, the kid from Ballarat who played piano with David Jones and Jeremy Alsop; he had even played on sound checks for me.

At that time he was Farnham's musical director; he must know who played bagpipes for him on that session. He did. It was in fact the pipe tutor at Scotch College.

I rang him at school only to be told that the success of Farnham's hit single was due to the work of a young student of his, Colin Dodds, who played piano, guitar and flute. Colin was a champion piper, who could transpose from bagpipes to concert and write the parts accordingly. It was Dodd's talents that had made 'You're the Voice' possible.

I pondered how a teenager in Year 12 at one of Melbourne's most prestigious schools would react to being asked to join this strange band, by a person he had never met. Still, I made the call to set up an appointment to discuss my proposal.

I arrived at his house, a double-storey brick residence in the heart of Camberwell, to be greeted by his parents. Yes, this was a solid no-nonsense professional family. Even so, I detected an inner warmth the Dodds family shared.

Colin was ushered in; he was an absolute young gentleman, with impeccable manners, serious aspirations about bagpipes, a genuine love of music and the motivation to succeed. Apparently his room was full of trophies, for his outstanding piping. He was the kind of guy who would never tell you this. It was great to be invited back to that house to hear Colin play at his mate's 21st birthday and even greater to be told, "Yes I'll join the band, providing you don't compromise the sound of the pipes."

How does one define best friend? I guess this is someone you share your inner most thoughts and feelings with.

John Halliday and I had hit it off from the very first gig we played together at the Fitzroy Town Hall. John loved surprises and apparently was most impressed at the way I had turned a corny evening three step, 'The Tennessee Waltz,' into an up-tempo gospel groove. John could not disguise his delight in finding a pianist who chose such unusual material and performed it in a most daring and unconventional manner. He never stopped smiling all night.

John loved my lateral approach to Jazz and I admired his unwavering steady sense of cymbal time, together with the thick round tones he produced from his kit. Roy Hayne's drumming style would influence John for the rest of his life.

John was what we called a vinyl junkie, not only for his unbelievably huge collection of albums, but due to the fact that he could not pass a record shop without buying at least four albums. This process continued during his lifetime, with the result that John had heard more Jazz music than anybody I knew. Historic figures like Louis Armstrong, Billie Holliday, Charlie Parker, as well as the esoteric Roland Kirk and controversial Ornette Coleman fascinated him. John's vision and taste covered the whole gamut of Jazz music. He was of Scottish/Irish descent and it was easy to remember the times I had visited the family home.

You see I had started my career working as a clerk at the Spotswood terminal of Esso Oil. John was studying to be an engineer at nearby Footscray Technical College, so we would always arrange to arrive at John's house just in time for dinner. It was a joy to dine in this Western suburbs working-class home. Mrs. Halliday in her broad Scottish brogue never failed to ask me, "Bob, would you like a wee bit more pie?" And as she served me a third generous helping, looked around with a smile at the others and said with a wink, "He looks as though he could use it."

I loved her pie and her generosity. During dinner Mr. Halliday talked to me as though I was an equal and despite the differences in age, he seemed up-to-date with current trends and events, most importantly he seemed genuinely interested in what I was doing. So you see, it was easy for me to give my best friend John the role of playing with the pipes. He may not like the idea, but he would understand and perhaps give in if I insisted.

At the time I approached John, he was Managing Director of a well-respected Engineering group. After explaining the concept of the band, he just smiled, and said, "You're probably looking for a Greek bouzouki player. You won't believe this but one of the engineers who works for me has his own band. In fact they play at most cultural gig events in the northern suburbs. His name is Takis Dimitru. Stranger still his specialty is Greek and Turkish music. Would you like me to set up a meeting?"

This sounded too good to be true. The thought of our bouzouki player working as an engineer alongside his boss, who just happened to be our highland drummer, was stretching a series of coincidences to an unbelievable level.

Takis turned up at my place complete with a range of Greek and Turkish instruments. He played each one for me, demonstrating traditional sounds and melodies. He also played a tape of contemporary world music that featured Greek instruments and showed how traditional style could be fused with jazz-rock. Takis came from a normal Greek family: his mama dressed in black, complete with black shawl, a dark-haired sister, nieces and nephews and a tall, dark younger brother named Tsarsis made up the rest of his family.

Before leaving my house, Takis told me the story of his migration to Australia. Upon arrival, he had applied for a job at General Motors Holden and when the foreman asked him his name, he answered "Takis."

"No that will never do," said the foreman, "from now on your name's Jim, Jim the Greek."

B*lues on the Boil* had been an excellent training ground for my son Malcolm. We had toured nationally, appeared on television and performed across a wide range of venues.

Malcolm had started his career on soprano saxophone, and then switched to Alto and finally Tenor sax. I felt he would be challenged by playing in unison with the vocalist and could be counted on to contribute exciting and energetic Jazz improvisations. As for myself, I could provide bass lines on one synthesizer and breathy melodies, or improvisations on the other. I would look for sounds that no self-respecting keyboardist would dream of using, thereby give uniqueness to the band.

There were plenty of funky young drummers in town, but none captured my imagination as much as Sonja Horbelt.

Sonja was so keen on drumming, she had joined the jazz ensemble that I taught at the Melbourne Con, as well as keeping up her full-time Arts studies. Sonja had many qualities, including incredible patience, motivation to succeed, guts and determination and a competitive nature I knew would eventually bring her success. She was the perfect choice for this new band, possessing young feminine innocence, which contrasted with the mean funk grooves she produced from her kit. Being of German background, she would add yet another nationality to the group's cultural diversity.

One night we were watching a television programme depicting unusual new techniques used by young American painters. One guy called his work "Art Attack." A disc jockey would commence by playing a classic Jimi Hendrix track. At the same time, the young artist would hastily splash various paint colours across an un-marked wall. While the recording reached a halfway point, one could tell the massive amounts of paint drops spread across the wall must have a meaning, and then as if by magic, the artist proceeded to complete a very realistic portrait of Hendrix, which only became apparent at the time the track finished. The concept was the music, and the musician became the inspiration for the portrait, which had to be completed at the finish of the musical performance.

Never before had I seen anything this hip and obviously I had been telegraphed a name for this special band I had recruited. From then on, we would be called *Art Attack*.

DON LIEW KNEW

IMAGINE ACHIEVING THE pinnacle of your lifetime's work. You have conceptualised a new hybrid sound, a new style of world music and a completely new musical instrumentation. You have recruited a unique band — one that could play Jazz, Blues and Funk, whilst adopting a totally Australian approach, a group of people who had crossed the boundaries of colour, race, religion, gender and cultural differences, people who were prepared to openly show love and respect for each other, as well as for the music they play.

Imagine being lucky enough to have that group appear on national television, to be interviewed during the programme and be a part of something visually stimulating, politically controversial and musically exciting. I felt like a CSIRO scientist who has just made a significant discovery that not only added knowledge to a specific area, but also resulted in a direct benefit for the community at-large. Surely somebody must pick up on what I knew to be my greatest contribution to Jazz music in Australia.

Happiness soon gave way to despair. One would think that this was special enough to at least promote conversation. Not one word of encouragement was I to receive from my fellow musicians, not one word appeared in the newspapers, not one word from any organisation involved with music. All this led me to believe there must be a conspiracy of silence, led by those who realised that Art Attack represented a threat to the status quo, or to those unprepared to accept its moral or musical implications.

As a person who had given his soul to all styles of Jazz, Blues and contemporary music, I found it totally demoralising that Melbourne's musical community and the Arts community in general would be incompetent enough to so easily reject, what to me was, and is, my greatest achievement, whilst at the same time praising work that in my mind represented a much smaller musical achievement. Nobody could have guessed that another set of coincidences, already in progress, would propel Art Attack overseas.

Don Liew ran the most successful Jazz club in Malaysia, located in the heart of Kuala Lumpur. It was called the Barn Thai, because of its shape and thatched roof, and because it actually resembled a typical Thai barn. Many famous internationals had played there; even Uncle Don Burrows and the boys from Sydney had visited the club. Don Liew had persuaded a group of major sponsors (including American Express, Hilton Hotels, Malaysian Airways and Heineken) together with a committee of influential politicians and wealthy business tycoons, that a prestigious Jazz festival should be held in Malaysia. This festival should feature bands not only from the USA, but also from neighbouring countries such as India, Hong Kong, the Philippines, Indonesia and Australia, as well as Sweden, Holland, Iceland and Singapore. A festival like this would boost Malaysia's image, create a local market for Jazz and cater for the many American and Canadian tourists and residents there.

Don visited Australia regularly. He enjoyed mixing business with pleasure, choosing to stay with his Australian friends as a guest and actively participating in the holiday lifestyle. As a well-travelled business executive, he could also monitor developments in the Australian building and investment industries. Running his Jazz club, the Barn Thai, was an outlet that allowed him to express his love for Jazz music, as well as enabled him to book musicians he particularly admired.

The first Malaysian Jazz Festival was to be held in September '93. As a result, Don visited Sydney at the beginning of the year with the intent of booking an Australian group. He checked out the Basement and Soup Plus, two of Sydney's best-known Jazz clubs, but found nothing exciting. Don then called in at the office of the national Jazz co-ordinator, whose suggestions of James Morrison, Don Burrows, Bernie McGann and the usual bunch of Sydney musicians that tour the world, failed to capture Don's imagination. It seemed the Australian Jazz taste was centred in the bop and post bop eras and fusion Jazz, which he dearly loved, was a dirty word here. He had gone through all the correct channels, but had almost given up on the idea of booking an Australian band for his festival.

Before heading home Don called in at the Victorian Rock Foundation in Port Melbourne. Instead of meeting his normal contact, he was introduced to Jacki Geia. That's right, the wife of our didgeridoo player. Jacki had been head of the Student Representative Council at Latrobe University. She was totally familiar with the Melbourne music scene and had many times booked my band Blues on the Boil. Don must have mentioned to Jacki how disappointed he was at not having an Australian band at the festival, when Jacki said,

"My husband Joe has just joined a group that is experimenting with a fusion of Jazz including Celtic and Aboriginal elements."

"I'd love to see that," said Don, whereupon Jacki played him the videotape of our ABC television show.

To say Don was highly excited about Art Attack would be an understatement. In fact he went wild, "There's nothing like this anywhere in the world, I must have this group headline my festival."

And we did.

REMNANTS OF THE JAZZBIRDS

J OHN 'MCCABE' BUCKLEY was a trombonist in Brian Brown's Jazzbird Orchestra who had played along side me at the live concert with Dizzy in the halcyon days of Moomba and during the famous recording of the album *Carlton Streets*.

John had a broad smile, an easy going manner, fuzzy hair, dark skin and yet spoke in the heavy brogue of a Scotsman.

Actually John was from Leith. I never made it my business to enquire about other peoples' backgrounds. I didn't care where people were from, as long as they could play. John had formed a band named after himself, he called it *McCabe's Bones*. The band consisted of five trombones and the gifted alto saxophonist Peter Martin; all pros. Pros were musicians who could read fly shit going up a wall or anything else for that matter. Pros prided themselves on being employed and remunerated award wages. Their hours spent in radio, television, studios and recording studios or in an orchestra pit, effortlessly playing the written parts of the shows. Pros liked being in special big bands booked to back up singers like Frank Sinatra, Mel Torme, Judy Garland and the like. Pros didn't have much praise for Jazz musicians; perhaps because many were prepared to play for peanuts in what to them must have seemed music that was unrehearsed and uncontrollable. In those days the word 'Jazz' could be taken to mean players who could not sight read satisfactorily.

John loved the smooth sounds the five trombones made and he chose easy to play charts. Did I say easy to play? I can still see the pros sniggering as I failed to get my piano introductions right.

"Don't worry about that" said John. "Your job is to do what you do. Do you know what I mean? And the same goes for Gary (Costello) and the governor over there (Peter Martin)."

John had been right, playing with the pros, including drummer

213

Ron Sandiland, was like riding a sure footed horse. Nothing went wrong, so all I had to do was provide some intensity and excitement. How could I not with tunes entitled 'Pork Fat and Black Eyed Peas' and 'Standing up in a Hammock'. We played mainly in pubs, being a band in the too hard basket for jazz purists. We even did a stint on Channel Nine. It was the smoothest outfit I had ever played in.

As my new Valiant hemi, 245 Pacer, hurtled down Glenhuntly Road I perceived the familiar thin and callow figure of Jazzbird orchestra trumpeter Ian Hellings making a beeline for the bonnet of my car. A very deft swing to the left and brilliant braking saved Ian. I rushed out of the car to confront a man who didn't know who he was or where he was. Rae and I managed to secure him into the back seat, waiting for him to dehallucinate before taking him home. I'd always admired Ian's pure tone, use of space and brooding trumpet sounds reminiscent at that time of Miles Davis.

Some twenty years later a healthier Ian rang me and said: "By the way I've formed this band; it's called The Australian Radio Rhythm Orchestra. We play music of the twenties, thirties and forties. I've acquired a lot of original charts, so what we play is the real thing."

I recoiled in horror, knowing full well the next question I'd be asked... and it was asked.

"Come on Ian," I protested "I'd be really useless in a big band."

"Oh, I thought you'd appreciate being asked," said Ian in a tone revealing hurt rather than desperation.

"Well, Ian if you really want me, I'll be there."

And so it was that I entered into a theatre of music as foreign to me as the Great Wall of China.

Big bands attract a certain type of musician, musicians who enjoy reading the parts and getting it right. Musicians prepared to attend endless rehearsals be they sectional or the whole band. Musicians happy to wear dinner suits, white shirts and bow ties. Musicians with romantic notions about the sound and style of a big band. Musicians who instantaneously obey instructions both those written on the chart or given verbally by the band leader.

There was no doubt about it, Ian's ability and leadership drew great respect from every member of the band.

For me things got off to a shaky start, even the best ear and the most wonderful intuition is no guarantee that you're going to play the part right. Fortunately I was to find a personal trainer in the form of young guitarist Myles White. Every time we played I could see the perplexed look on his face, he was probably told I was some sort of star. Here I was making very obvious musical mistakes.

Myles had played in the band long before I arrived and he was gracious enough to point out all the things I was missing and to support my efforts from the guitar chair. Pretty soon I began to feel like Count Basie and my confidence soared.

Eventually the band gained a residency at a place called Aunty Sues, a long hall running along the lane adjacent to the Victorian Arts Centre. Aunty Sues was known as a multi purpose venue, it was a restaurant, it was a dance hall and it was also a pub lounge with games and pool tables. Fortunately for me our tenure there was only to last for two years which was as much big band as I could possibly cope with.

I'll never forget the culture of a big band, it was so different to anything I had experienced. The shortness of the solos, the few members of the band who could really get it on, the section players who were happy just to turn up and the multitude of large and heavy briefcases full of charts, the largest and most heavy one of all being marked 'piano,' with some four hundred parts in it. The parts were numbered starting at one and progressing through to somewhere near five hundred and although they were presented in numerical order many numbers were missing for no apparent reason. At the end of the night we'd all sit there for hours putting every chart in consecutive order for the next gig.

It was a custom I'll never forget. It was just one custom of many I'd never get used to.

MONTSALVAT MEMORIES

PERCHED ON TOP of a hill in Eltham's leafy glades, lies the property Montsalvat, home to painters, sculptors, and craftsmen. I can never forget the darkness of its grey exterior, complete with gargoyles, arches and mud brick buildings. Dark and brooding oil paintings of its founder, Justus Jorgensen, seemed to be everywhere.

My first gig there was a farewell concert for the Brian Brown Quartet prior to our Scandinavian adventure. Everything seemed old and dingy, a totally unsuitable environment for Jazz, that is, until I saw the cover of a Bill Evans album depicting the castle at Montreux. If it's good enough to have a festival over there, then it's good enough to have our festival here I quipped to Montsalvat controller Sigmund Jorgensen. Sigmund was a man after my own heart: large, broad-shouldered and often dressed as if he was on a hunting trip. His passions included: art, fine wine, good food, hearty companionship and quality music.

I remember entering the property during the early days of the Jazz festival to be confronted by the plinkity plunk of banjos, the thimble tapping rasps from washboards and the belching of bass blurting from tubas. Oh yes! The unmistakable stomp of traditional Jazz, not surprising as the festival's musical director, drummer Allan Leake, led The Storyville Jazz band and was a devotee of this style. However the festival fulfilled a useful role by giving musicians a chance to drink and catch up. Not since the halcyon days of the Musicians Union had they been able to do so. This was the magic of Montsalvat, where musicians once again remembered they were part of a community and where partying long and hard was acceptable.

Another great feature of the festival was that all events took place within the grounds of the property, so you couldn't help bumping into musicians along the way. Even today I'm confronted by people bemoaning the loss of the Jazz festival that created this special atmosphere.

One of my favourite Montsalvat memories is of Brian Brown and a new large Jazzbird Orchestra assembling on the flat concrete toilet roof outside the Great Hall and giving a concert to the crowds on the lawns below. I certainly enjoyed playing in many memorable performances with the Ted Vining Trio, Onaje, The Brian Brown Quartet and my own band, Blues on the Boil. But perhaps the biggest personal highlight was in 1989 when Sigmund announced I had been inducted to the Montsalvat Roll of Honour. I was quite touched, as never before had the name 'Sedergreen' been displayed in gold letters on a polished wooden board. Shortly after, I was co-opted to help direct the festival and for three years I was able to put my stamp on it and assist in its growth. Under my stewardship, attendances exceeded ten thousand, all enjoying a feast of Jazz over the Australia Day long weekend.

My proudest moments came when the group Mistaken Identity, co-led by my two sons Stephen and Mal, took to the stage. Mistaken Identity had created something new, a stylish and sophisticated fusion of Blues, Hard Bop, Funk and Salsa grooves delivered at the highest level of intensity. However, the greatest thrill of all came courtesy of the Wangaratta and Bangalow Jazz Festivals, where I was privileged to watch my sons perform convincing sets of hard-core Jazz with my mentors, Ted Vining and Barry Buckley.

I was also very pleased to have the Nat Adderley Quintet appear at the festival and also to match American trumpeter Eddie Henderson with Sydney tenor man Dale Barlow.

However, all good things come to an end and when the Festival's car park was reclaimed by the Eltham Cemetery trust, Sigmund called me into his office with the idea that we expand the festival into the city.

"Who would you book for the Melbourne Concert Hall?" At the time my favourite pianist was McCoy Tyner, who specialised in concert hall gigs around the world, regularly filling halls in London and other European Capitals. As I was planning a holiday to North America, I propositioned Sigmund,

"You pay my expenses in Montreal and I'll book a headliner you'll never forget."

So it was that I was able to visit Montreal for a second time, this time as Artistic Director of the Montsalvat Jazz Festival, which meant I could head for that special room where the festival's artists fraternised with press and other agents. I began negotiations with Ron Carter, Elvin Jones and McCoy Tyner. While I enjoyed hanging out with these giants I would have much preferred playing with them. McCoy Tyner appeared at The Melbourne Concert Hall to a near sell-out crowd of over 1800. I remember teasing him about his recent recordings with Carlos Santana;

"You know you could be accused of selling out," I chided.

"Things have changed so much these days that to stay in the business even Jazz musicians have to reach a wider audience or perish" he replied.

"But you must like the man's music, otherwise why would you write a piece called 'Senor Carlos'"

McCoy just chuckled.

"OK" I said," I'll only make one demand: that every time you play a concert here you play 'Senor Carlos' for me.

McCoy remained true to his word.

PART FIVE

FAITH REAFFIRMED

COUNTRY PREACHER

HAVING BEEN UNCEREMONIOUSLY dumped by the Victorian College of the Arts, it was imperative that I find work. Joe Geia had spoken about an agency called Nexus Arts that placed artists into schools. The proprietors, Sue and Rob Russell, were glad to have me on board as a working artist. Thanks to their endeavors I found myself visiting a whole host of great Melbourne schools including Tintern, the head of music there was my dear friend Ronald 'Zoot' Trigg. There was also Wesley College whose head of music was John 'fatty' Lee. I visited my old school Haileybury and St Kevins, as well as reaching out into Melton's Mowbray College and Belmont High in Geelong.

It was great fun spending a week at a school and blending into its daily routine and activities. I met lots of dedicated teachers and some very special pupils. Nobody was walking around with their noses in the air as some of my colleagues at institutions were prone to do. My visit to Belmont received rave reviews in the State education magazine. Since I handled Geelong, Sue and Rob saw no reason not to send me to Colac.

The key to my success in Colac was guesting with the town's notorious favourite Blues band, The Recliner Rockers. This gave me immediate acceptance by everyone in town. A master musician coming into a small country town can make a huge impact. I was treated like an American star might be treated in Melbourne, but managed to convince the locals that all I wanted was to be accepted as an ordinary member of their community. My wish was granted and I was invited out for a game of golf after school. The next day the buzz went around the whole of Colac, "He maybe an amazing musician but his golf game's very ordinary."

Perhaps because I had not only survived the rigours of staying in the old and decrepit hotel, but actually enjoyed being part of the town, Rob and Sue suggested I tackle the Western District to visit towns like Dimboola, Nhill, Kaniva, Rainbow, Yapeet, Yanak, Marnoo, Minyap and Murtoa. There would be no back-up and no comfortable accommodation; I would either have to be billeted on a farm or do it tough, living in the stockman's quarters of the old and run-down country pubs.

I knew that no other musician in their right mind would accept this offer, but I relished the thought of getting away from the hurt and pain of the city. The project would also offer me an opportunity to experience first-hand country culture and communities.

It was a heavenly feeling taking off down the Western Highway, heading for the farm operated by Rodney and Dawn Coutts, whose property lay between Nhill and Kaniva, encroaching on the Little Desert. As I drove up to the house, I could see the large figure of Rodney, reclining on the couch watching the footy on telly. Neither Rob, Sue or myself had met any of the people I was about to visit. They had taken me, an unknown quantity, on trust and I had no idea of whom or what I would encounter. Not wanting to disturb, I gently knocked on the open door.

"You must be the Jazzman from Melbourne" said Rod, "Come in, and close the door. Now mate, let's see what you've got."

I was in a state of shock. Did he want me to undress? The thought terrified me. Then Rodney proceeded to open a cupboard which contained an old tenor saxophone.

"Hey Dawny!" Rodney yelled, "The piano man's here."

Dawn's mum was a pianist and she just loved the piano.

By this time, Dawn was leaning up against the piano, her smile a welcome sight. After a short jam session we sat down to tea with Rod proclaiming,

"What do you reckon Dawny? This Jazz man's sure got something."

It was Rod's suggestion we go camping in the Little Desert, the three of us under the stars drinking Billy tea laced with brandy and eucalypt leaves, enjoying the home-made tucker that Dawny had prepared and swapping stories until the break of day. For a city boy like me this was very special.

The next morning, I called into the local bank. The girl behind the counter commented on my after shave.

"It's nice to see a guy who likes to smell good. The boys around here are always working and often don't bother to smell nice for us."

As I arrived at the local Lutheran school I could hear the excited yelling of a multitude of young kids.

"Here he comes. Here he comes. Here he comes, the Jazzman" they said excitedly.

I was ushered into a class where pupils and teachers had all assembled to witness their first taste of this stranger from the city. I would slowly undo my trumpet case, holding up my golden trumpet to the approval and astonishment of all. I would slowly insert the mouth-piece and in the style of Dizzy, blow a whole lot of stuff. I would start up high and slowly descend, the valves of my horn pumping fast, much to the amazement and astonishment of kids, teachers and a few onlookers who had come to see the 'show.' I would then say,

"I'm a Jazzman and we Jazzmen like to change things" as I proceeded to insert a series of mutes into the bell to demonstrate new sounds. Sounds that none of them would have heard.

"Which one of you kids would like a go at my trumpet?" I would say, as every kid in the school clamoured for a turn. There would be howls of laughter when candidate after candidate could not get a sound from it. I would then set up my keyboard, selecting a different pre-set sound for each student wanting to play it.

"The first thing you're going to notice is that we're all different individuals," I would say.

Successive kids would play their own burst of improvisation, some aggressive, some careful, some creative. The looks of genuine enjoyment on their faces as they heard the sounds they were making went over big time.

Teachers and towns people couldn't stop thanking me for what I'd done for their children. In my mind I hadn't done very much, but I had stumbled onto a successful formula that I would now use in every town.

News travels fast in the country, so my exploits would be telegraphed ahead to the next town I would visit. A town I fell in love with was Rainbow, on the edge of the Whipperfield National Park. As I walked past the Post Office I could hear the familiar strains of a Bach Prelude being played on a Grand piano. I couldn't believe my ears or eyes, but nothing was wasted in the country; neither buildings nor people's talents. I looked inside and to my surprise there was a music lesson in progress. Country kids were as crazy about football as my son Stephen was. Their local team, the Saints, was the pride of the town. It didn't take me long to figure out that the very tall kid who played drums in the school band was probably part of the team.

"You must be a ruckman with the Saints."

The fact that I got this right gained me the utmost respect. Then something magic happened. I played Abdullah Ibrahim's 'The Wedding' for them.

"Now we're going to play a game to see how well you listened to the piece. You can ask any questions you like and I'll just say hot, hotter or cold."

First question I heard was, "Is it a ceremony?"

"Hot," I answered.

"Is it romantic?" was the next question.

"Hotter" I answered.

"Is it a wedding?" was the third question put to me by a nine-year old girl.

I jumped up in absolute astonishment. Here we were in the middle of nowhere, where no one knew about Jazz, let alone Dollar Brand. My best students at the Con or the VCA would not have been able to correctly answer such a question.

It was a moment where I learned that if one plays with honesty and genuine feeling for the composer and their musical intentions, a child raised in the still peacefulness of an environment free of city prejudice could comprehend the meaning of the music far better than the most hardened or corrupted devotee.

THE WINGED MESSENGER

N O ONE IN Australia had done more to broaden the boundaries of improvisation than Brian Brown, whether it be playing tenor, soprano, alto flute, flute or synthesizers.

The music we were making was propelling us into outer space. We had explored the world of electronics and now we had returned to further reinvent ourselves acoustically. Brian acquired a wonderfully liquid-sounding European pan pipe. I began further exploring the insides of the grand piano. One day I picked up a drumstick left lying on the floor and began using it to rebound off the taut steel strings of the grand piano. The sound was zither-like and most exotic. The beating of the steel strings contrasting with the liquid sounds of the pan pipe had created a totally new sound that Brian and I expanded on. Neither of us cared what the Jazz world thought. Life was a series of musical adventures.

Judy Jacques had a voice that could go any where; it could be powerful or soft, screaming in the higher registers or smooth and silky in the lower registers. Sick and tired of singing Blues, Gospel and traditional Jazz, the adventure Brian was offering was the challenge she had been looking for. The band was called The Winged Messenger, comprising myself, Geoff Kluke on bass, both colleagues at the VCA and a young student, Michael Jordan, whose work at the drum kit displayed delicate touch and finesse, so much so that Brian proclaimed him 'exquisite.' Judy provided the perfect linchpin for a new type of music Brian was writing. The lyrics were highly romantic, with titles like 'Wild Roses,' 'On This Night,' and 'Woman in the Mirror.' Brian also encouraged Judy to use her voice as an instrument for free improvisation, and she became so good at this that the purists labelled it 'vocal gymnastics.' The natural outcome of all this was to be a Jazz opera.

"Wow" I thought, remembering how much I had enjoyed the

American Jazz adaptation of Bizet's 'Carmen' in the musical 'Carmen Jones.' Nobody in Australia had even thought about writing a Jazz opera before.

Intrigued by the concept I wanted to know more.

"What's it about Brian?" I asked.

"Well actually it's set here in Australia, in the convict settlement of Port Arthur. A love story, where the spirit of the 'winged messenger,' triumphs over the harsh and desperate separation of two lovers: a convict and the daughter of a sheep station owner." The actual opera opened the 1994 Montsalvat Jazz Festival, with expanded orchestra and some sensational young singers including Nina Ferro and Katrina Seiffert and the well-known actor, Allan Hopgood as the narrator. The music was by far the most demanding I had ever had to play and thanks to the keyboard wizardry of my protégé, Sue Johnson, (a member of Melbourne's famous a capella group Coco's Lunch) who created an aura of magic with her spiralling appegiations.

In my mind the event had pioneered something very new and unique. At last Australia had a Jazz opera it could call its own. But my excitement soon turned to dismay and just like the apathy that had greeted the incredible achievements of Art Attack, the Winged Messenger was to suffer the same fate. Like Art Attack, it was totally representative of Australia; it was composed and conceptualised from an Australian point of view and fulfilled the dreams that so many had for the arts in Australia. Once again the notion of Australian artistic achievement had been rejected in favour of a few musicians known to and supported by the hierarchy of bodies supposedly set up to foster such events. Farewell to the dream of an original Australian Jazz approach. Only musicians with enough influence to secure funding would be showcased and heralded.

RAMBLING WITH BROTHER NAT

MY IDOL, THE man I admired most of all in Jazz, a prolific conversationalist with whom I shared the most incredible times, was brother Nat Adderly.

I remember our first meeting. Nat was lying on the bed of the hotel room with Melbourne promoter Martin Jackson sitting at a table. I burst in ignoring Nat and said to Martin, "Well did you tell him?"

"Tell him what?" asked Nat.

"He told me that you are a reliable young guy who's touring Australia with me, but do you know anything about me or anything about my music?"

I commenced a tirade that included a concise history of Nat's career with exerpts of Nat's favourite recordings and my favourite solos. It must have been overwhelming because Nat smiled, turned around to Martin and said, "This guy knows more about my music than Larry Willis."

"You can bet your balls on that" I said as I walked out.

The next morning I called into Nat's hotel, The Sheraton, in Spring Street. It was the first day of our Australian tour. I picked up the phone in the lobby and Nat said, "Hey Bobby, you can come up to my room, but realise I've got a whole lot of show girls up here."

"What?" I thought to myself," Nat Adderley, a secret sex fiend!"

As I entered the room it appeared empty.

"Alright then, where are the show girls?" I asked.

Nat took me to a table on which lay an open can of sardines.

"These are my show girls" said Nat, pointing out the curves of the sardines and pouring lemon on them.

Nat could have ordered any fancy breakfast he wanted but

preferred this simple and humble lifestyle.

Our first gig was at the Southern Cross club in Canberra. After the gig a young, black American dude appeared.

"Bob, meet Lucky Peterson. Lucky employs me to play brass on his recordings back home."

Lucky Peterson looked me n the eye and said, "Man I wish I could play blues like you."

Both Nat and Lucky could see I was embarrassed by the compliment and we retired to the small band room where a West Indian percussionist was bothering the hell out of Nat. After a minute or so, a voice from the roof speaking in a thick Jamaican accent said mockingly, "Yeh man, I know man."

This happened a few times, interrupting the percussionist in the middle of every sentence. He freaked out and left. It turned out that Nat was a skilled ventriloquist and had pulled this stunt for fun.

"But where did you get that Jamaican accent?" I asked.

"C'mon Bob, think of the names, Julian and Nathaniel, and try and see a picture of a father holding his two son's hands saying 'Julian and Nathanial let's go and learn the language of the gods.'"

Our next gig was in Sydney where we were to be joined by Sydney saxophonist, Andrew Speight, son of John Speight who ran the Manly Jazz Festival.

A message came through from the ABC in Sydney.

"Could Mr. Adderley come for an interview and bring some of his albums with him?"

Like me, Nat loved making fun of sacred institutions.

"I've been on this earth a few years now and made a lot of albums. You would think that your national broadcaster might just have one or two of them." I suddenly had a brain wave.

"OK Andrew, you're from Sydney, go home and get all the Adderley albums you have (he should have at least one I thought), and come back here and take Nat. Andrew returned some twenty five minutes later in a Holden and on the back seat was a sprawling sea of Adderley albums.

Nat was delighted, "Hey young Andrew I didn't know there

was this many albums in Australia. There's one here that I forgot I made."

"Really! Would you sign it for me?"

"Sure" said Nat.

From then on Nat referred to him as 'Mr. Spite,' in a mock Aussie accent.

That night after the gig, Nat sought my counsel on 'Mr. Spite.'

"I thought he did a great job and played a lot of the same harmonies Cannonball did."

He had made a good impression on both of us. Thanks to Nat, Andrew Speight would head to the States where his career would blossom. To this day he remains one of America's top educators.

During the tour, I had the chance to learn the answers to questions I'd been dying to find out. The reason that we clicked so well together from the start was because Nat realised that I wasn't bullshitting about him being my idol and loving him as much as Cannonball and loving the band as much as them both. Recognising this as the truth, he opened up to me and treated me as a friend, not just a musician who was playing with him.

One of the first questions I wanted to ask was about Nancy Wilson.

"I read somewhere that Cannonball discovered Nancy Wilson. Is that true Nat?"

At the mention of the name Nancy Wilson, Nat's eyes softened, he went somewhere else. "Yeah the babysitter."

"The babysitter?" I said

"'Yeah the babysitter, that's how we came across Nancy" replied Nat in his normal gravelly tones.

"In fact it was my idea" said Nat.

"What happened? I asked.

"I don't know about you and Rae, but when we were starting to get known, and the band began going on tours, the girls (Ann and Olga), would get mighty upset. We guys were going on these tours and having a great time. We would come home and tell the girls just how great the tour was and how much fun we'd had and all the new things we'd seen. The girls were home, stuck with the babies and weren't travelling anywhere. And then it dawned on me that the solution to this was a babysitter. If we could find a babysitter, then we could take the girls on a trip with the band. Of course we'd make sure we'd take them on a tour not too far away, somewhere like New Mexico, making sure we were only going to be away for a few days. So when that tour came up I looked up the Yellow Pages under Babysitting services teed up to have a babysitter for my son, Nat Junior. Well Ann and I were busy packing and getting ready to go when the door bell rings. Now I know you've got a similar house to mine Bobby, and you have a fly-wire door on your house and we have the same in Florida. Anyway I run to the door, open the door and through the fly wire I see this apparition and I mean apparition, young, beautiful, innocent, the whole thing. Why she was so beautiful I didn't know what to do, my knees were shaking. I said how could I help you Miss?"

She said, "I'm the babysitter. My name's Nancy Wilson."

"Aw, come on inside."

So we invited young Nancy in and Ann and I showed her what we expected her to do as part of the babysitting with Young Nat."

Then we promptly forgot about her and went on the tour.

"Well Ann had a lot of fun and so did I on that tour and when we were coming home I started to think about the babysitter and hoped that she didn't have too much trouble. So I hurried my steps along to the house and somehow I got there in front of Ann and as I walked through the door, there was Nancy with little Nat Junior in her arms and she was rocking the baby and she was singing to that baby. Not only did she look good but also she had a voice like an angel."

Nat would often end sentences like that without resolving them.

"Of course my brother Cannonball took an interest and pretty soon I got a call.

"How did that babysitter work out?"

"Just fine, just fine! Pretty soon Nancy was baby-sitting for Cannonball as well. So when you ask about Nancy's appearances at our gigs realise it wasn't going do us any harm to have the babysitter come on and sit in at our gigs and it wasn't going to do her any harm either. It was good for everybody."

"You stayed friends forever?" I said.

"As a matter of fact, Nancy sang at Cannonball's funeral. It was just a wonderful moment. She sang 'Everything must Change', which was one of the tunes she sang to baby Nat and there wasn't a dry eye in the house."

It was ironic that the song mentioned had moved singer Jacki Gaudion and myself to tears when we heard Fontella Bass sing it and we have been performing it ever since, so it was a song that meant a lot to me anyway.

Mostly our conversations would be frivolous; I'd be laughing, Nat would be cracking jokes or telling funny stories. But every now and then our conversations would be of a serious nature and because he knew that I'd spent most of my life listening to him and his band here in Australia, he was interested to know my thoughts about the band and its development. This was really very enjoyable for me because Nat was genuinely interested, not just passing time.

One day I remember saying, "One of the reasons I admire you Nat is you never played first! So many Jazz albums feature a trumpet player like Miles Davis playing first followed by John Coltrane, Hank Mobeley or whoever plays second. You hear a Dizzy album and Dizzy plays first and James Moody follows up on sax. But in Cannonball's band, Cannonball used to play first and you would have to follow him. Your brother was no slouch, why would you want to follow his amazing solos? "

Nat laughed and said, "Well, it started many years ago in New York when we were coming up at The Bohemia Café which was our regular gig there."

"What happened?" I asked.

"You told me Bob, that one of my biggest influences was Dizzy, as was yours, and then Miles."

I said, "Miles and Dizzy were big, but at the time I much preferred Dizzy; he had an open, big sound, he was bold and flew high, and Miles was sort of like an introvert with that mute in the horn."

Nat said, "Well Dizzy influenced everybody. Imagine me being a Florida boy, that would be like you coming from Darwin (one of Nat's most endearing traits was that he always seemed to know more about the countries and cultures he visited than we did about his). There was a whole lot of etiquette to be followed."

I said, "What sort of etiquette?" (remembering the rules Melbourne musicians followed regarding sit-ins)

We had check in and check out people. There'd be a check-in counter at the front of the club. Normally there was a pretty girl checking in the guests, and you'd check in your coats and hats, because it could be pretty cold. If a musician was visiting they'd check in their horn; that was considered polite. But if you were there to have a play, you'd bring your horn into the room and leave it in a place where the musicians on the stand could plainly see it. I was going great guns till one night Dizzy walked into the room. I had a touch of nerves because I knew who Dizzy was and how good he could play. In a way I'd patterned myself on him."

"Yeah," I said, "it would have been nerve wracking."

"I was totally nervous and what's worse Dizzy bought his horn into the room and left it right on top of the table so we could make no mistake he wanted to play. I panicked a bit so I grabbed my brother Cannonball's sleeve and began to tug it up and down, saying Hey, Cannonball! Cannonball! Dizzy's in the room!'"

Cannonball was a bit cool and said,

"Yeah, I know."

"Yeah but he's in the room and he's got his horn and he wants to play. What'll I do?"

Cannonball looked down at me and said, "I don't know the answer yet, but I'm going to figure it out before we ask him up."

About fifteen minutes later Cannonball looked down at me, smiled and said "Don't you worry."

"So he asked Dizzy up to play, placing Dizzy on his left hand side and placing me on his right side, so he stood in between Dizzy and me. We proceeded with a number Dizzy wanted to play. Dizzy played a marvellous solo that went on for quite a while; the sort of solo that says 'here I am and I'm establishing what's happening.' Fortunately for me, Cannonball had the right idea and played a long solo. It must have gone for every bit of twenty minutes. It felt like it was hours. Then he turned around and said, "Keep yours short brother."

Then I proceeded to play a little bit after Cannonball, then we wrapped it up. You see my brother had figured out a way around the problem, so we made it a habit that I would play after Cannonball. We discussed the idea of the band being a little bit different in that way."

On one plane flight, Nat asked me who my favourite rhythm section in the band was.

"That's easy," I said, "Vic Gaskin, Joe Zawinul and Roy McCurdy."

"Do you mean to tell me that you think Vic Gaskin is the best bass player in our band?"

"Listen Nat" I replied, "if it's just about the bass players, then I would have said Sam Jones."

There was only one moment of bad blood between Nat and me. Nat thought I'd lost the form of Sam's tune in 'Unit 7.'

I said, "Don't be bloody stupid Nat, I wouldn't do that."

Nat grabbed me and shook me by the collar.

"If I thought you were fucking with Sam's music I'd kill you." He really meant it.

The rest of the time we were a mutual-admiration society that grew with every gig.

"Well my favourite bass player is Walter Booker."

"How can you say that," I chided, "Walter's got a big sound but he never lays anything down, not like Sam."

"Let me explain" said Nat. "We were at a gig one night where the people didn't like me, my brother or the band. They kept making nasty faces and jiving remarks. It was so bad that I wanted to punch their lights out. But Cannonball said, 'Cool it Brother, let's be professional and not blow the gig.' I waited till after the gig and rushed out and began punching their lights out. And it happened that Walter, who was loading his bass into the car, noticed what was happening and in a moment ironed out those motherfuckers. Now that's a good bass player"

I thought about what Nat had said for sometime. He had chosen loyalty in preference to performing ability. One day I couldn't resist asking who was the best blues player in the band, after all, no other modern Jazz band played Blues as often and as comprehensively as the Adderley's. Nat's reply was soft and serious.

"Yussef." he said, "Yussef played blues so well he could reduce people to tears."

"Wow, and to think we in Australia used think he was 'useless'; we even used the name 'Useless Latrine.' "

"Well check it out, you'll find Yussef was the best at the Blues."

Once again I got to thinking about how listening to recordings alone would never provide all the answers.

We decided to discuss the piano players that had been seminal figures in Cannonball's bands.

"Firstly Bobby Timmons, Victor Feldman and thirdly Joe Zawinul."

"It's funny that in your band, the piano players wrote a lot of your hits, Joe Zawinul with 'Mercy Mercy,' '74 Miles Away' and stuff like that. Victor Feldman with 'The Chant and one for Daddyo' and Bobby Timmons with 'Dis Here and That There.' those sort of tunes. What can you tell me about Victor Feldman and how did he come to be in the band?"

"Well," said Nat "When we rehearsed, any one could bring tunes and ideas that could be put into the band democratically. So I might write a tune, Cannonball could contribute one, Sam Jones would have something and Bobby Timmons. If you check out our albums you'll see it's true.

So when Bobby Timmons left the band we were really distressed, after all we were a tight little unit and we were really used to working together.

My brother Cannonball wasn't stupid and he knew our mother sure could cook. Every musician who came to our house used to await the joys of mum's cooking. Any way one night Cannonball instructed mum to prepare a real feast of all the things we like to eat: corn bread, potatoes, grits, all the things that southern Americans like to eat. As a result, everyone was having a great time, when Cannonball out of the blue said, "What are we going to do about getting ourselves another piano player?"

There was silence; Sam didn't know what to say, Louis didn't know what to say and I didn't say anything. Finally Sam asked, "Who is available?" Nat told me Cannonball had secretly been checking out Victor Feldman, because of his incredible sense of time, prodigious technique on the vibes and incredible comping on the piano. So secretly Cannonball wanted to get Victor into the band but he had to get it passed us first and that's the reason why we'd been invited to dinner.

"Well, there's the Englishman, Victor Feldman."

With that, Sam began laughing uncontrollably. Sam had a funny laugh like the cartoon character Goofy. He laid back and said, "Hell everyone knows ain't no Englishman that can play Jazz."

"In sympathy with Sam, we all fell about the place laughing our heads off."

"Well," said Cannonball waiting for the right moment, "I happen to know that Miles Davis is in the recording studio right now with the said Englishman and he's going to be on Mile's next recording."

"Really," said Sam, who suddenly got serious "We'd better get him then." That's how Victor came to be in the band.

The final gig was in Melbourne and Nat could feel the tightness of the rhythm section and the Cannonball-tinged sounds of Ian Chaplin's alto. He could also see the band was family and told us we were the Australian version of his quintet. It was as though an angel had come down from heaven to fulfill my dreams of playing my favourite brand of Jazz. At my instigation, we were to reunite at the Montsalvat Jazz Festival of 1992.

The sportiest car I ever owned was a green RX7 rotary, two-seater sports car. Nat insisted that Rae sit in the front with me and somehow he squeezed into the back.

"Are you sure you're comfortable?"

"Oh yes," laughed Nat, "I've been in tighter squeezes than this," as we headed off for a gig at the Warnambool Arts Centre. We broke the drive at Colac for a counter-lunch at a local hotel with Ted and Barry. Everyone was having a fun time except Barry, who was restless. Unbeknown to me, Barry had become a collector of fine basses, antiques and other music instruments. It was here he committed an act that is now legendary in Australian Jazz folklore. Barry had looked through the window across the road and spotted an antique store and probably thought to himself that in a country town like this he might just pick up a great bass for a good price. Excusing himself, he headed across the road and as was his manner, asked politely of the lady at the counter,

"Do you have any basses here?"

"Oh, yes!" said the lady, "we've got a beauty but it's out the back."

It had been a quiet Sunday morning and the lady could see Barry's excitement and assumed it must be a sale.

"Don't worry mate" she said, "we're bringing the base out now, would you like a mattress with it?"

Disappointed was written all over Barry's face as he returned to lunch to tell us the story.

The next day on the way home I introduced Nat to Joe's Café, a well-known cheap eats joint in Geelong. Like so many cafes and restaurants, above the counter was the blackboard, describing the menu.

"Look up there Bobby" said Nat, "we're both on the board."

"How could we be on the board?" I retorted.

"Well, see the word 'short black'?... that's me" said Nat laughing,

"Ok where am I then?"

"Hey, Bobby you're under me, you're the flat white."

Life was never dull when brother Nat was around.

In 1994 I was in a position as Musical Director of the Montsalvat Festival to invite Nat back, this time with his working band.

In the same way I had rebelled against mum and dad's ideas about music, my daughter Tammy followed in my foot steps, and hated Jazz with a passion.

Who could blame her? Her two brothers and her dad, totally immersed in the art form with no other music ever heard in the house and with little else discussed.

But one thing Tammy and I had in common was our love of

cars. When Tammy heard that Mazda, the Major sponsor of the Montsalvat Jazz festival, had provided a fleet of brand new cars, including a sleek white MX 5 sports roadster, Tammy joined the volunteer brigade as a driver. Her first duty was to pick up Brother Nat who was headlining the festival. Nobody would have thought that a special friendship would develop between these two. The first thing Nat noticed was that Tammy always arrived on time, in fact right on time. He called this 'being on the number.' At the first pick up she enquired,

"What shall I call you?"

"You just call me Uncle Nat and I'm going to call you 'the Button.'"

"Why?" enquired Tammy.

Nat had noticed in detail every ring, bracelet and button she was wearing. No other guy in her life had ever been this thoughtful.

"OK Button" commanded Nat, "let's go."

They both enjoyed the exhilaration of putting the roadster through its paces up and down the hills on the way to Eltham.

The prospect of seeing Nat's working quintet, including drummer Jimmy Cobb and bassist Walter Booker, was something I had looked forward to. Nat insisted on the Button being driver once again. As part of the publicity, the band had its photo taken on site. Imagine my joy as I saw my favourite musicians following Tammy and hearing Nat say, "Follow the Button, the Button knows what's happening." and Walter and Jimmy responding with,

"Yeah, the Button's cool."

Sometime later Tammy and her best mate, Dyon Cahill, took off for New York. Like so many young Aussie kids, they had booked into a cheap backpacker's hostel in Lower Manhattan. Despite every story I had told them about how dangerous New York could be, the girls wouldn't budge. And so it was no surprise when I got the ring from Tammy; her voice tense in genuine fright about her surroundings. The only friend I had in America was Brother Nat so I immediately telephoned him. Nat was calm and said, "Tell those girls to get on the first flight and fly down to Orlando."

Nat drove all the way from Lakeland, picked the girls up and he and Ann looked after them. From photos in their albums, Tammy knew that Nat loved fishing and asked,

"Could we go for a cruise on your boat?"

When I asked Nat if the girls had been any trouble, he replied, "I had so much fun with them Aussie girls. You see the Button wanted to go fishing. So she and I and her friend set out on the Lake. It was mighty hot and pretty soon their pretty little hands would be dipping into the water. That's when I played the trick on them. I would knock the oar against the side of the boat.

'What's that uncle Nat?' The Button would say.

'Well I think in your country you call them crocodiles, but we call them alligators.'

"The girls' hand would come straight out the water again. But pretty soon they were back at it. I had so much fun with them."

Nat was a consummate actor who loved surprising people with tricks and games.

Our friendship went past music; we were communicating by phone as good friends should. It was then I decided that Rae and I fly to Miami, Florida, with a view to visiting Nat and Ann. We rang Ann at the house only to find Nat had had his leg amputated. I just had to see him but Ann said, "Do me a favour; ring him at the hospital before you come."

Nat's voice at the end of the phone seemed weaker. He begged us not to come. His last words to me being in jest, "As I only have one leg to stand on, so to speak."

I put the phone down and wept profusely. A few months later Nat split off planet earth.

SIX OF THE BEST

NESTLED IN A lane at the Paris end of Collins Street, was Mietta's Restaurant. A lavish, chic and fashionable place adorned with the most elegant chandeliers, lampshades, reclining sofas, oil paintings and thick and darkly-polished timber tables, Mietta's appealed to Melbourne's posh and upwardly mobile.

Of course I remembered it as the Naval and Military club, a place where sailors, soldiers and airmen chundered on the footpath after excessive bouts of mateship during the good old days of six o'clock closing. So you can imagine my surprise when Mietta O'Donnell and her partner Tony Knox requested that I visit them. Mietta was small, slim and smartly dressed, with long, dark flowing hair and eyes to match. There was an intensity about her that made me think she was a woman who knew where she wanted to go.

"You see Bob" said Tony, "we've had the very best of music here, be it chamber, classical or Jazz but nothing seems to work and we're getting to the almost desperate stage."

"Is that why you rang me?" I laughed. "I'm not god, you know."

"Well let's go downstairs and I'll show you the room and maybe you can come up with something."

I could not help feeling a little bit cheated, for a decade or so Mietta's had presented what was supposedly the cream of Melbourne's Jazz pianists without so much as a hello to me, and now in their hour of need they had called me to fix things.

But when I saw the trouble they had gone to turn what had been a drab club into a very special place, I began to sense that Mietta was a perfectionist who had devoted her life to this project and was in genuine need of help.

The room underneath the restaurant where music was

presented, with its thick wooden Venetians, its richly brown swags and curtains, its ornate wooden carvings, marble table tops and luxurious pile carpet, reminded me of a classy New Orleans bordello.

"What do you think of the room and what should we present?" enquired the softly spoken Mietta.

By now I'd learned if you were going to offer advice it had to be expressed strongly and confidently and delivered with a sense of self-belief.

"Looks to me like you've been taking the wrong advice. This is definitely a singer's room. I think you need a show where the singers match your ambience and décor. A killer show. "

"Can you come up with something?"

"I'll think of something and get back to you." was my response.

I began to think of singers and how each generation had changed or modified their approach. First of all vaudeville, then early Jazz, then the swing era, the crooners, the soul singers and so on. I visualised a show that would be elegant and that would feature women. Women who knew how to dress well, women unafraid of being glamorous and appealing. The show would consist of six singers, each one a representative of their generation's approach to singing. They must be matched with a suitable rhythm section, also preferably consisting of women. Of course Sonja Horbelt, having been a member of Art Attack, would have to be the drummer and here was my chance to work with her soul sister, Annette Yates (then Jenko). I remember watching how well they had worked with Mickey Tucker at The Montsalvat Jazz Festival. Like any normal guy, at first I was suspicious of Mickey's motive for choosing women but when I heard the music that he and the girls were putting out, I realised he was training a tight rhythm section that was ready, willing and able to match his sophisticated stylistic swing. And besides why should he have all the fun?

Only politicians kiss babies and old ladies. But my first brush with Madam Pat (Pat Thompson) was unforgettable. It was 1994 and Mal Harrop, who worked for the Montsalvat Jazz Festival, insisted I go and check her out. It was a stinking hot day and I arrived outside the venue to see an elderly lady sitting on a wooden stool.

"Oh, Bob Sedergreen, what are you doing here?" she exclaimed. Not wanting to be out foxed, I replied quickly,

"I've come to see you, Madam Pat!'

"Oh Bob, she said in a mocking tone, "I didn't think that stars like you would spare the time for a little old lady like me."

What was so special was that I was being teased and yet every word that came out of this lady's mouth seemed so genuine. For some compelling reason I found myself bending down and kissing her forehead, which was sweating profusely due to the heat. I stayed for the first number of her set. She belted out one of my favourite songs, 'Some of These Days' in a voice strong enough to crack bricks. The atmosphere she and her band created was like being at a Billy Graham crusade rather than a Jazz concert. Madam Pat's magnetic personality spread like wildfire through her audience and at the end of each song, they stood up and cheered wildly. Oh, yes, she was a killer and would be the perfect opener for my show, which I had entitled Six of the Best, remembering the six strokes of the cane I had so often received from the headmaster at school.

Who would be my big band singer? I had remembered watching Beverley Hay on television on The Cool For Cats show.

Gregarious, groovy and possessing a great sense of time, the hard-swinging Bev could be counted on to keep bodies swaying and toes tapping. What a winner!

If that wasn't enough, how about the sultry and exotic story-teller, the Maori princess, Bridgette Allen, whose movements, gesticulation and sense of dynamics are hypnotic.

These three covered the first three generations and it would be necessary to rest the audience with an interval.

After interval, it would be good to present Margie Lou Dyer; she could rightfully be introduced as Jazz royalty, being the daughter of legendary Aussie Jazz icon, trombonist Wocka Dyer and wife of Allan Brown who had reached total legendary status as a Jazz drummer. Margie Lou had approached me for piano lessons at a time when my playing relied heavily on the Blues, which meant I could take a rest while she accompanied herself playing low down dirty shuffles. Her gritty voice (somehow reminiscent of Satch) did not match her appearance. She reminded me of that vivacious blonde actress Michelle Pfeiffer.

There are people who, no matter what you present to them, will find alternative gods to worship. So now let's bring on Jacki Gaudion: tall, thin, blond, elegant, dressed in black, with a smooth soft husky voice, classy demeanor and enough soul to fill the largest void.

The idea of awarding a medal at a Jazz festival seemed preposterous to me, but the news filtered through at Montsalvat that a young teenage girl had won the Yalumba Medal. Nina Ferro was a name I'd never heard of, but when I queried her award, her hundreds of fans and the whole committee assured me that she deserved to win it because she was the most popular singer at the festival. Most popular! I thought, perfect! Let her close the show.

Now that I had dreamt up the show, what about a cherry on the top? What about Gil Askey? His Texan charm was winning over Melbourne audiences and bringing people to the places he played. I remember first seeing him at The Corner Hotel in Richmond, dancing arm-in-arm with Jimmy Witherspoon.

"Who's he and what's he here for?" I asked Spoon.

Spoon looked at me incredulously,

"He's here for me and he's here for the vibe, but one thing you gotta watch out for is he sure can chaw (talk)."

Even so, Gil had been an arranger for the famous Motown record label and had toured as Musical Director for Dianna Ross. He would be an excellent wild card for the show and the only other male.

As usual the nuts and bolts of organising these events would be turned over to Rae, who loved lining things up and making things run smoothly.

I had done this to address Mietta's problem and even though the band was really a support for the singers, in effect a brand of what I call 'cabaret', which demanded restriction and focus rather than creative release by the musicians. This lack of creative satisfaction was balanced at the end of the show, when I experienced a new satisfaction, due to the fact that every member of the audience was totally blown away by the concept. Nobody had ever seen six singers on the one platform, nor had they seen such a range of ages, voices, repertoires and Jazz genres. The audience insisted that we repeat the show, which we did for many years.

So successful was the show that the demand kept up year in year out, forcing us to change venues and cast. This allowed us to select from a pool of superb singers including: Julie O'Hara, Michelle Nicol, Kerri Simpson, Anastasia Aspeling, Anne Marie Sharry, Shonah Honeyhill Sonko, Mattilda White and Alison Wedding. The wave of interest continues to this day.

FAITH REAFFIRMED — POPPY & THE DANCING SHOES

BOB DYLAN HAD proclaimed 'The Times They are a Changing' and they surely were. Music shops were now places that sold CDs. Purveyors of dance music were DJs: non-players armed with turntables and machinery who played music for the kids to dance to. Strangely enough, the kids thought it hip not to dance to live bands. Apparently high-tech light shows and a new range of mind-blowing drugs were supposed to make up for the natural high people experienced during inspirational live music performances. Money ruled the world and only music for the masses was marketed.

Certain sections of the jazz world too, had become fickle, prepared to market and promote 'Johnny come latelies.' These new young messiahs were supposed to lift the music to new heights, but many never did. Players began competing with each other and factions formed, thus losing any chance of the feeling of 'a brotherhood' that had been such an important part of the origins of Jazz.

Jazz players had become cool, dark, brooding intellectuals playing music they had learned in institutions; music highly influenced by European styles and values. This absolutely amazed me as musicians like Miles Davis were moving in the opposite direction, returning to the roots of black music, the music of Hendrix and James Brown. Josef Zawinul had formed his syndicate of African musicians, even people outside the Jazz world like Paul Simon were returning to Africa for their musical inspiration and collaborations.

Alex Pertout and I were on a panel auditioning for drummers wanting to enter the VCA. A young hopeful entered, accompanied by a young lady, tap dancing on a white tap-board. The drummer just couldn't get it together and in a moment of humour Alex Pertout turned around to me and said,

"Hey Bobby that tap dancer has got better time than most of the drummers we've heard today. "

"Maybe so," I said "but this is a Jazz course not a tap-dancing academy."

"But Bobby, I was thinking she can come in and learn piano from you."

Her name was Shonah Hill.

"Where are you from Shonah?" I asked.

"Shepparton," she replied.

'Well Shonah from Shepparton, who is a Jazz pianist you're really fond of?"

"That's easy, Abdullah Ibrahim (Dollar Brand)" she replied.

This was at a time when I had just composed and recorded a piece, dedicated to this pianist called 'Dollars and Sense.' I remember playing her a full-on rendition of the tune and asking,

'Well what do you think of it?"

"Great." She said "I've also written a tune for him."

"Really" I said sarcastically, "let's hear it."

Shonah's tune smacked with the authenticity of the understanding that could only be influenced by African music. I had waited for fifteen years, hoping all students might have similar interests.

It was later that Shonah told me about an all-girl group she was a member of called Wazuri. I couldn't believe my eyes or ears; wild, uninhibited and primitive Senegalese dancing; full-on African percussion played on a host of hand-made drums; bells and whistles cowbells and kit drums, all coupled with songs and chanting in the African language. It turned out these Aussie girls had been to Senegal and learned first-hand from the head of a Senegalese National Dance Company.

So I envisaged a show focused on Shonah, who would sing, tap dance, play the piano and percussion. She would be aided and abetted by young and exciting horn players, students like Melissa Sydney Jinni Merange, Savannah Blount and to keep the intensity at a peak level, my son Malcolm. Once again I would choose to use two drummers to reinforce the importance of drums and drumming. There was Brazilian-born, Carlos Ferreira, for that Airto touch and the wizardry of master percussionist David Jones. I named the show 'Poppy (after all poppy was a symbol of an old soldier) and the Dancing Shoes' (after Shonah). To increase the appeal and the colour, I added the hypnotic work of singer Bridget Allen and incorporated the frenetic dance and percussion of Wazuri into the show.

These were happy times and I began meeting more and more people interested in Africa and its music. Suddenly Shonah took off for Senegal to dance and drum in the streets. It was here she met the dancer Lamine Sonko and after a while they returned to Australia and were later married. Lamine Sonko renewed the beliefs that I had held all my life. You see, Lamine knew nothing about Jazz. Coltrane, Miles or even Randy Weston meant nothing to him except for the fact that they looked like cats from home. It was at Shonah's insistence that Lamine, Malcolm and I join her in a group she named Mandaela, (named after Nelson Mandela and Mandala) with the aim of fusing the Sedergreen boys' expertise in Jazz and Blues with traditional Senegalese songs. The strangest thing was as they sang their classic 'Wulabear Jo', the melody and the time felt parallel to the modal music of John Coltrane. The next piece was called 'Fanta Sonko.' Lamine began chanting:

"Denmah, denmah Fanta Sonko denmah."

"What does it mean?" I asked Lamine.

"Fantah Sonko was my grandma and denmah means gone."

I was staggered by the fact that the lyrics exactly paralleled a Blues. But even more intriguing was that the melody was identical to a classic Muddy Waters Blues riff. And here was Lamine, with no idea of who Muddy Waters was. The group Mandaela is still working around Melbourne today, blending a mix of Jazz, Blues, African music and tap dancing, but remains on the outer limits of acceptance by an ever increasing conservative Jazz world.

REMINISCING

S OME SAY, LOOK back in anger, but I look back in joy at the incredible musical collaborations and sometimes confrontations, that I shared with some astounding players.

When remembering Red Holloway, my thoughts go to a Black-Tie Dinner at the Montsalvat Jazz Festival, where Red was left stranded in a sea of people who were too shy, star-struck or snobby to sit with him. So I grabbed him and sat him right in the middle of a friendly table of locals. Red and I were due to perform together at the festival and he suggested we have a rehearsal at the Elizabethan Motel in Box Hill. When I asked for his room number, he just smiled and said,

"Don't worry, you'll know me."

Unbeknown to me, Red had made a mental note of the registration number and colour of my car. As I drove through the gates, a motel door opened to reveal Red, dressed in a bright red sports coat, golden tenor in hand, and as I opened the window of my car I heard four bars of furiously honking tenor sax. No musician had ever welcomed me like this before (or since).

"I told you, you'd know me" he quipped.

Our rehearsal consisted of swapping Spoon stories and me talking about his Musical Director duties with Etta James. Red might not have been the greatest sax player I had worked with but he had an uncanny ability of stretching me out. It had something to do with urgency, energy and anticipation. I left the stage musically exhausted.

Plas Johnson was a warm, friendly Texan tenor man, with a tone as wide as the prairie. He confessed to being trapped by the lure of Hollywood. Henry Mancini capitalised on his big sound in the famous Pink Panther movies. We actually played this for a laugh at our gig at the Limerick Arms. Plas was so happy to be playing Jazz with a solid rhythm section instead of movie music. He just stood there and glowed.

I remember my gig with Scott Hamilton because I was dying to let him know that while I was watching cable news in New York in'78, I discovered that he was touted as an incredible young genius, the next big white hope for Jazz. Of course I was only teasing Scott but this sent him into a reflective mood.

Obviously hurt by my comments he said,

"Christ Bob, do you know I've only been on television once in my life. I'm a Jazz player after all and the stuff you heard was like media hype."

Scott's ability to swing on the saxophone was absolutely sensational as was his feeling for the melodies he chose to play.

Jerry Bergonzie was an animal of a different kind. He had a big, hard, tenor sound with notes flying everywhere. Jerry had asked me to sit in but had the attitude that I must prove myself. It started off friendly enough but each ensuing choice of song became more complex, until at last I was forced to play a piece I didn't know. Jerry handed me a piece of paper, filled with many small cryptic changes. Playing music should be a pleasure, not a test of toughness.

Lee Konitz was an alto man I never fully understood. He loved to tell the story of how Charlie Parker had thanked him for not imitating him. I had heard stories about Konitz and Lenny Tristano creating new directions in bop. At our sound check, Lee popped a piece of manuscript on the piano and said to me,

"Do you read?"

Remembering The Troika I answered carefully,

"Sort of."

"Well at least do you think you can read this?" he pointed at a chord written in the bass clef and working its way up into the treble. Take your time, don't hurry it."

When I finally played the chord Lee said, "Look again."

"What did I get wrong?" I asked.

Lee laughed prodigiously.

"Look again, there are eleven notes written and you've got only ten fingers. It's an old trick that pianist Marshall Solal taught me and a great way to relax before the gig."

My dearest friend, drummer John Halliday idolized Lee Konitz and Geoff Kluke was a most groovy and accomplished bass player. I had booked them for a session with Lee that was to be recorded by radio station 3PBS. Sometime during the evening I heard Lee say, "Get out of my way! Get out of my way! Get out of my way you mother-fucker!"

Was it the microphone stand? Or a faulty key pad?

And as I looked up Lee said, "Yes it's you."

Apparently my habit of injecting harmony up front was upsetting his thought processes.

Nobody had ever called me a 'mother-fucker' at a gig.

"I must find a way to humble him" I thought.

Fortunately the next piece was 'Stella by Starlight.'

"If you're so fucking good why don't you sing it then," I pronounced loudly to a stunned audience. And he did, in Mel Torme-type style. Just as Lee was pausing at the end, I played the most ugly Chicago Blues-style ending, ridiculing his efforts. Lee actually enjoyed what had happened.

Then there was Branford. That's right Branford Marsalis, Kenny Kirkland and Omar Hakim. All Sting's men had come to the VCA to give a workshop. I sat back in disbelief as the apparently gullible staff and students were told there was a new music sweeping in New York called Salsa. As an example they proceeded to play the well-worn standard 'What Is This Thing Called Love?'

"Wow" I thought, "How old hat! Didn't I play this tune on my nineteenth birthday?"

I had given up my Blues on The Boil night at the Hot House Restaurant to make way for the visiting Americans. Martin Jackson had booked Barry Buckley to play bass with them. Fortunately for me their pianist, Kenny Kirklands, was late and the joint was packed so Martin asked me to start the night off.

"What would you like to play?" asked Brandford.

'What Is This Thing Called Love' I said, "but definitely not Salsa."

Half-way through my solo, Branford must have realised that he had seen me earlier that day at the VCA and said meaningfully,

"I'm sorry." The actions of a man after my own heart.

There were some pretty cool dudes who used to drop into the VCA to give workshops. But one day Urbie Green walked in. Urbie was regarded as one of the world's best trombonists, as I found out after we had played our first tune together. A shy yet humble gentleman, Urbie typified the nature of most trombonists I have encountered.

Another beneficial encounter was with the leader of the New York loft scene, Dave Van Ronk. Dave was as famous as anybody, having influenced the lives of Bob Dylan and Joni Mitchell. I remember a radio announcer looking at me in disbelief when I confessed to not knowing anything about the guy.

Our gig, of all places, was at Hanging Rock, beside the race track. When Dave arrived, I couldn't believe my eyes. He looked like the sheriff of Dodge City, dressed as he was in a brown, buckskin cowboy suit with a neck tie and a big cowboy hat. He was chewing tobacco that he occasionally spat out, revealing a breath that had tasted hard liquor. I had always been suspicious of Folk music, feeling there were only two kinds of music that had nothing to do with Jazz; Country and Folk. Van Ronk however, was a surprise package. His hoarse voice and gritty guitar had played and sung Jazz, Folk and Delta Blues. I remember him cutting loose on the material of Sun House, Elmore James and 'Blind' Lemon Jefferson with so much feeling for the Delta Blues. He was one of the best I have heard. What intrigued me even more was that he was a big, broad white man.

"Don't you feel guilty when you play the Blues that good?" I asked him, "Guilty that you're white and you're playing the black man's music?"

Astounded by my brashness and yet sensing a genuine concern to know, Van Ronk pulled me towards him and said,

"I may be white but when we put our 'stamp of authority' on the music then we own it."

The term 'stamp of authority' got me thinking about the musicians I had admired all my life.

'It ain't what you do it's the way that you do it,' so the song goes, and this especially applied to my meetings with alto saxophonist, Richie Cole. A fresh-faced disciple of Phil Woods, Richie presented a show tinged with madness; alto madness. He used the term alto madness and lived on a ranch named Alto Acres in California. Blessed with a wicked sense of parody, his shows would include elements of spontaneous satire aimed at ridiculing rock super stars. I remember a segment called Punk Jazz where Allan Browne, Gary Costello and I would be issued instructions by Richie to stomp, jump, hit and kick our instruments.

"Just think of it ladies and gentleman, Kiss, (who were appearing in concert that very moment in Melbourne) is being paid millions of dollars for doing the same shit as we are." With the band and audience heaving with laughter, he would then launch into a Charlie Parker bebop classic.

"You got to sneak it up on them somehow," he said, referring to the audience. "I give them something different and then I let them have some 'Bird'."

But my favourite moment with Richie came one cold wintry night in Hobart. As we alighted from the aircraft, we were greeted by a severe stinging dose of icy Antarctic weather. The gig was at Hadley's Hotel. Unlike their Sydney cousins, Tasmanian audiences sit there in silence, a group of faceless masks revealing no emotions. It was their polite and parochial way of letting one know they are listening. It was as though Richie and I had entered a tomb. So Richie walked up to the microphone and in a pleasant voice said,

"Ladies and gentlemen, welcome to Hobart, Bossa Nova capital of the world."

That was it! The reserved Hobart audience broke into smiles and giggles. Oh Yes! Richie had the gift of the gab that audiences could not resist.

But the greatest moment of gratification came some years later when Richie appeared at Melbourne's Concert Hall with my son, Stephen Sedergreen, on piano. How remiss of me not to have mentioned Stephen earlier. Perhaps it was my fault he was a pianist; after his birth my first act was to count his fingers, ten and in perfect working order. Years later Stephen enrolled in the VCA. Worried about nepotism, I had given them permission to throw the book at him if he deserved it, which they duly did. It was hard for me to disguise my pride and admiration at his abilities as a pianist. He possessed harmonic skills that I could only dream about and an attack and improvisational flair reminiscent of Herbie Hancock. Steve was as good a pianist as anyone, but it was Richie Cole who pulled me aside after their concert together and said, "Man, Steve's so good he should be in New York. He'd really make it there, why don't you send him?"

Richie really meant it and I was forever grateful for the advice.

Another incredible character was trumpeter Jack Sheldon, looking remarkably like Barry Buckley. Jack was a handy trumpet player but an even more brilliant comedian, having appeared on numerous television shows including the Steve Allen show in the States. Jack's comedy routine was absolutely fabulous until someone reminded him of the grubby little hotel he was staying at. The humour soon disappeared, giving way to a stinging attack on the so-called hospitality.

I hate the word 'veteran' but it's the word that I think of when I recall the gig I played with Wild Bill Davidson. The cornetist (not organist) must have been at least eighty years old, yet still managed to play recognisable phrases with a broad tone reminiscent of Louis. It was a gig that brought Allan Brown to life.

Bobby Shew and Bill Reichenbach were names I had never heard of. They must obviously be white and from the West Coast I thought. How right I was. Our confrontation was at the Prince of Wales Hotel in St Kilda and these guys looked like members of the Sandringham Yacht club. I could just see both of them at the helm of their craft vying for The America's Cup. The gig was another one of life's lessons: names and reputations count for nothing until the music starts. Bobby was an articulate trumpeter and played flugelhorn with depth and feeling. Bill was a consummate and smooth trombonist with flawless facility. I could see by the looks on their faces that the rhythm section overwhelmed them. It was during the piece 'Blue Bossa Nova' that Bobby broke down, confessing to the audience that he had not expected to encounter such musicianship in Melbourne.

"I want you to know that these guys are great players." Bobby told the audience in earnest tones. What I did not know was that Bobby commanded the respect of so many trumpet players because of compositions like 'Blue' written for trumpeter Blue Mitchell and 'The Red Snapper' for Don Menza. And so it was that Freddie Hubbard was at that gig paying respect to Bobby Shew.

We had met Freddie in Scandinavia, where the media at the time had declared him the greatest, perhaps giving him an inflated idea of his own importance. As I walked off the stand at the Bobby Shew gig, Freddie came up to me and said,

"Hey man, I heard some of that shit you were putting out, you ought to be a band leader."

I knew this was a Freddie jibe and only an insult would correct his behaviour.

"You're not still hanging out with that dumb Russian agent?" I said. Freddie was impressed with my memory and suggested we adjourn to the bar.

"Hey man, is there any place I can get to see a kangaroo or koala bear?"

"Yeah" I said, "there's the Colin Mackenzie Sanctuary in Healesville. Just ask at your hotel and they'll put you on the bus."

Freddie had taken a shine to the shapely young barmaid cleaning up.

"Would she take me there?" he asked.

"Why don't you ask her yourself?"

Freddie's face fell when the barmaid rejected his offer. Realising she knew nothing about Jazz and wanting to have some fun at Freddie's expense, I said to the barmaid,

"Hey, don't you know this guy is the best trumpet player in the world?" It was a line Freddie often used about himself.

"I don't care who he is, mate." came the gruff reply. The story didn't finish there as my dear friend, Australian Jazz icon Bob Barnard, told me the next day. Disappointed with his reception in Melbourne, Freddie took off for Sydney and like many tourists, gravitated towards the Rocks area. Bob Barnard's band was playing their regular gig at a venue called The Rocks Push and attracted by the sounds of Jazz, Freddie walked in, only to sit down next to some of Bob's aunts and cousins down from Bowral. They had come for a treat and the only Jazz musician they cared about was Bob. Bob could see Freddie talking to one of his aunties but Freddie left soon afterwards, scratching his head nonchalantly.

"What happened?" Bob asked his aunt.

"Oh nothing love, it's just that bloke walked in and told me he was the greatest trumpet player in the world. But don't worry, I pointed to you and said that's Bob Barnard, he's the greatest trumpet player in the world. He didn't seem to like hearing that so he got up and left."

I could go on for hours. but one thing I know for certain is that every Jazz musician I met was as individual as the sounds that came out of their inner beings and those sounds and their playing didn't necessarily mirror their personalities.

HOW THE WHEEL TURNS

S OMEHOW, MIRACULOUSLY I had made it to the twenty first century. It seemed I was living in a different world, a consumer driven society that worshipped the new; new cars, new homes, new televisions, new technology, and rejected the old. For the first time I would hear the phrase 'yesterdays people,' referring to those above middle-age. Then along came Sonja, that's right Sonja Horbelt my drummer in Art Attack and Six of the Best.. Sonja had scored a teaching job at Ruyton Girls School in Kew and she was determined to make use of my talents. Sonja mentioned she had a group of special girls. She didn't use that word lightly, and it turned out the 'special' she was referring to didn'trelate to their ability to play their instruments but rather the chemistry that existed between them.

They decided to call the band SABA which was Swahili for seven. There were only six of them, so I was included as the seventh member of the band. The music staff at Ruyton had given me free reign to take the band in any direction I wished. I remember our first meeting in the schools' Royce Hall, their eager young faces betraying a certain sense of excitement . I stared down at these fascinated young princesses and said:
"From now on you're not girls; you're going to be Jazz musicians! And by the way from now on everything we do will be by ear."
We began by learning a selection of the music of Dizzy Gillespie and later gravitated to deeper explorations of the music of Cannonball, Zawinul, Bird and Mongo Santamaria.

The SABA girls were not only students at the same school but were the same age and part of the same teenage peer group, a group that held up matchstick thin models as the ideal.

Living on little but water by day, they would finally weaken at our after-school rehearsals. They would each bring cakes, sweets and biscuits (especially Tim Tams). At first I thought it was out of politeness that each girl offered me these delights. Let's face it, I was three times their weight and didn't need such treatment, but in actual fact it was their way of accepting me into their fold. It's a very unique and special feeling to be part of a band where each member cares about the other as a friend.

Bands share unique bonds that strengthen with each performance. And so it was with our band of seven, SABA. When we were playing it was as though nobody could touch us. I knew this because during my lifetime I had played with thousands of musicians but had only been a member of a dozen or so bands. But this was different.

Here we were, six beautiful young white teenage princesses who wanted to play Jazz and enjoyed performing the music of Billy Harper, McCoy Tyner and Dizzy Gillespie, and one old and grossly overweight pianist sharing the same musical adventures. I will never forget the girls suggesting that I should be called Roberta or being told by our drummer Elissa,

"We're going to our rooms to make ourselves beautiful; don't you want to make yourself beautiful to?"

The period prior to playing with SABA was like being in heaven. No drinking, no sledging of other musicians, no tacky dirty jokes, just silence. There was just the silent joy of expectation in the performance of young and eager hearts. Let's face it, our sound and technical facility were embryonic compared to so many of the great musicians I had played with but we made up for it in a determined commitment to give our band the very best. I had played with musicians who could lift and inspire bands but no single person carried the group. We had an old saying in the Brian Brown Quartet that each member must put in a percentage of the group total: 100% for solo, 50% for duet, 33.3% for trio, 25% for quartet, 20% for quintet and so on. No one counted the percentages after the performances but we were all well aware of them before playing. And so it was with SABA. For the girls this was not a career move but the excitement of being part of something special, like playing club dates at Dizzy's and Bennetts Lane and open air concerts at Federation Square or travelling to Canberra to workshop and jam with other young Jazz aficionados.

Sadly, I knew the end of school would spell the end of SABA, because kids today somehow know the future of live music is under threat. Some years earlier, I remember leaving Eltham College after a long hard day of teaching to find a young girl named Rebecca sitting on the lawn and sobbing.

"What is it Rebecca?" I asked, looking into her tear-laden eyes.

"Well Mr. Sedergreen" she replied,"I'm actually saying goodbye to my trombone today. You see I've loved my trombone more than anything, but a trombone doesn't bring security, status and the better things the world has to offer. So I'm saying goodbye to it now."

As for Jazz, Jimmy Rushing used to sing "There'll be some changes made." and so there have. So often I find myself in playing situations, totally lacking spontaneity. I work alongside younger musicians unaware of being trapped in the bondage of over arrangement, plagiaristic cover mentality, vague concepts, and musicians totally lacking in either personality or humour. There are few movies made about Jazz but I've just taken part in one about the band BLOW, co-led by Peter Harper and Ted Vining. I hope the movie will be released, although in today's commercial climate both the film and the band are still 'underground' because BLOW represents one of the last bastions of free, spontaneous and liberated jazz... a sound and approach foreign to most.

That's my story or as Sun Ra would say, "that's his story." A Jazz musician's life is never humdrum and there are so many beautiful, dedicated and talented people and tales that I have not told you about in this book. As the old joke goes: 'Have you heard about the Irish Jazz musician? He was only in it for the music!' That's definitely me.